Political Violence in MENA

MEI Publications

Persian Gulf 2012: India's Relations with the Region, Kindle

Persian Gulf 2013: India's Relations with the Region, New Delhi, Sage

Persian Gulf 2014: *India's Relations with the Region,* New Delhi, Sage

Persian Gulf 2015: *India's Relations with the Region,* Smashword

Persian Gulf 2016-17: India's Relations with the Region, New Delhi, IDSA and Pentagon Press

Persian Gulf 2018: India's Relations with the Region, New Delhi, Palgrave Macmillan

Persian Gulf 2019: India's Relations with the Region, New Delhi, Palgrave Macmillan

Contemporary Persian Gulf: Essays in Honour of Gulshan Dietl, Prakash C. Jain and Girijesh Pant, New Delhi, KW Publishers, 2015

Islamic Movements in the Middle East: Ideologies, Practices and Political Participation, New Delhi, KW Publishers, 2018

Political Violence in MENA

Edited by

P R Kumaraswamy
Md. Muddassir Quamar

KNOWLEDGE WORLD

KW Publishers Pvt Ltd
New Delhi

ISBN 978-93-89137-38-5 Hardback
eISBN 978-93-89137-39-2 ebook

Published in India by Kalpana Shukla

KNOWLEDGE WORLD
KW Publishers Pvt Ltd
4676/21, First Floor, Ansari Road
Daryaganj, New Delhi 110002
Phone: +91 11 23263498/43528107
Marketing: kw@kwpub.com
Editorial: production@kwpub.com
Website: www.kwpub.com

Printed and Bound in India

To

Professor Gulshan Dietl

With respect, admiration and gratitude

Contents

Acknowledgements

About MEI@ND

The *MEI@ND* has undertaken this volume towards encouraging and shaping young and budding scholars on the region. This is the second volume in the series followed by the first on Islamic Movements published in 2019. The MEI further intends to come up with volumes on political economy and democratisation in the broader Middle East. It is our fervent hope that at least some of the contributors would eventually become passionate students and continue their interest in the subject. We are grateful to all the contributors who took time out and worked on their chapters within a tight schedule.

The *MEI@ND* and the editors would like to acknowledge the support and encouragement of the trustees of the Forum for Middle Eastern Studies (FMES), namely, D Shyam Babu, G V C Naidu, Sreeradha Datta, and Atul Kumar. The support of the members of the Academic Council of *MEI@ND*, especially, its chair C Uday Bhaskar, has been significant in our academic journey. The editors also acknowledge the diligent work of KW Publishers Pvt Ltd and its team, especially of Kalpana Shukla, and Kishan Lal, and the copy editor Rehana Mishra in improving the quality of the manuscript.

The yeoman role of friends and colleagues at Jawaharlal Nehru University and Institute for Defence Studies and Analyses, especially Girijesh Pant, Jayati Srivastava, Meena Singh Roy, Rajesh Rajagopalan, Sima Baidya, Srabani Roy Choudhary, and Sameena Hameed was pivotal in enhancing the knowledge on the subject and we acknowledge their support at various stages of our academic pursuits. We would like to extend our deep gratitude, respect and admiration for Professor Gulshan Dietl, to whom we dedicate this volume, for her guidance and inspiration.

Finally, we would like to extend our thanks to our families and friends who have been pillars of support in all our academic pursuits. All the omissions are ours!

Contributors

P. R. Kumaraswamy is a professor of contemporary Middle East Studies in Jawaharlal Nehru University (JNU), New Delhi. From 1992-99, he was a Research Fellow at the Harry S. Truman Research Institute for the Advancement of Peace, Jerusalem. Since joining JNU in September 1999, he has been researching, teaching, and writing on various aspects of the contemporary Middle East. His works include *Squaring the Circle: Mahatma Gandhi and the Jewish National Home* (2018); *India's Israel Policy* (2010); and *Historical Dictionary of the Arab Israeli Conflict* (2015, second edition). Prof. Kumaraswamy has edited a number of volumes and published research articles in a number of refereed and non-refereed international journals, and regularly contributes to Indian as well as international media outlets. In February 2010, he set up the virtual Middle East Institute, New Delhi, and serves as its Honorary Director. He is the editor of *Contemporary Review of the Middle East* and the series editor of *Persian Gulf: India's Relations with the Region.*

Md. Muddassir Quamar is an Associate Fellow in the Institute for Defence Studies and Analyses (IDSA), New Delhi. He holds a Ph.D. in Middle East Studies from Jawaharlal Nehru University (JNU). His doctoral thesis examined social developments in Saudi Arabia between 1991 and 2010 within a conceptual framework of Islamic modernism. Dr. Quamar's areas of interest include politics and societies in the Gulf, Middle East strategic affairs, Indo-Gulf relations and political Islam. His research papers have appeared in leading international journals such as *Asian Affairs, Strategic Analysis, India Quarterly, Contemporary Arab Affairs, Digest of Middle East Studies, Journal of Arabian Studies* and *Journal of South Asian and Middle Eastern Studies*. He has co-edited two anthologies: *Contemporary Persian Gulf: Essays in Honour of Gulshan Dietl, Prakash Chandra Jain & Girijesh Pant* (Knowledge World, 2016) and *Islamic Movements in the Middle East: Ideologies, Practices and Political Participation* (Knowledge World, 2019) and co-authored two books: *India's Saudi Policy: Bridge to the Future* (Palgrave Macmillan, 2019) and *Persian Gulf 2018: India's Relations with the Region* (Palgrave Macmillan, 2019). Dr. Quamar was a Visiting Fellow in the King Faisal Centre for Research and Islamic Studies, Riyadh, and serves as Associate Editor of *Contemporary Review of the Middle East.*

Amna Sunmbul completed her Ph.D. from the Centre for International Politics, Organisation and Disarmament (CIPOD), Jawaharlal Nehru University (JNU), New Delhi in 2019. She specialises in security studies and diplomacy. Her publications include articles in *South Asian Survey, Indian Journal of Society and Politics, Islam and Muslim Societies: A Social Science Journal, Political Science Review* and *International Journal of Multi-disciplinary Education Research.* She has a forthcoming co-edited volume titled *Indian Foreign Policies: Identities and Issues.*

Arshad teaches political science in Zakir Hussain Delhi College, University of Delhi. He completed his Ph.D. from the Centre for West Asian Studies, School of International Studies, Jawaharlal Nehru University (JNU), New Delhi in 2019.

Hirak Jyoti Das is presently working as a Research Associate at the Vivekananda International Foundation, New Delhi, and is a doctoral candidate in the Centre for West Asian Studies, Jawaharlal Nehru University (JNU), New Delhi. His doctoral research focusses on "Israel's Security Predicaments since the Fall of the Hosni Mubarak Regime in Egypt." His research interests include India's relations with the Persian Gulf, Israel's domestic politics, security and foreign policy, and post-Arab Spring developments in Egypt, Libya, Syria and Yemen.

Jatin Kumar is a Research Analyst in the West Asia Centre at the Institute for Defence Studies and Analyses (IDSA), New Delhi.

Lakshmi Priya is a Research Analyst at the Institute for Defence Studies and Analyses (IDSA), New Delhi, and her areas of interest are politics and societies in the Middle East. She has worked on the status of women in Syria under Hafiz Al-Assad for her doctorate. She has published peer-reviewed articles on the subject in journals such as *Journal of West Asian Studies, Social Action, Women's Link* and *Journal of South Asian and Middle Eastern Studies*. She has also contributed opinion pieces for a number of Indian websites and magazines.

Parnika Praleya has a Masters in International Relations from Jawaharlal Nehru University (JNU), New Delhi, and a Masters in Economics from the Indian Statistical Institute. In 2019, she joined the graduate studies programme in the University of Chicago and is set to pursue further studies in the Committee on International Relations. She has worked as a Project Assistant to the Coordinator of the East Asia Centre at the Institute for Defence Studies and Analyses (IDSA). Her research interests include climate change and security studies issues. Her enthusiasm for travelling, reading and healthy living culminated in a blog, Maverick Feet. Travelling across India and staying with local communities has provided her with an understanding of, and sensitivity to, the people's culture and their life choices.

Paulami Sanyal is a Research Analyst in Institute for Defence Studies and Analyses, New Delhi. Earlier, she worked as a Research Assistant at the Institute for Conflict Management. She completed her Ph.D. on "Role of New Media in the Arab Spring in Egypt" from Centre for West Asian Studies, School of International Studies in Jawaharlal Nehru University (JNU), New Delhi in 2019.

Rashmi Muraleedhar is a graduate student in the University of Chicago. She has a Masters in International Relations from the School of International Studies, Jawaharlal Nehru University (JNU), New Delhi.

Yasir Ali Mirza is pursuing his Ph.D. from the Centre for West Asian Studies, School of International Studies, Jawaharlal Nehru University (JNU), New Delhi. He has a Masters in Journalism and Mass Communication from Aligarh Muslim University (AMU) and M.Phil. in West Asian Studies from Jamia Millia Islamia (JMI), New Delhi. He has presented papers in national and international seminars and visited Baghdad, Iraq, thrice for presentation of papers at the University of Mustansiriya. His articles have been published in national dailies and websites. His areas of interests are the history and politics of West Asia and

North Africa (WANA) in general and the Fertile Crescent in particular, including the domestic and foreign policies of Iran, Iraq, Turkey, Lebanon and Syria, the Arab-Israeli conflict, political Islam with special reference to Shia Islam, and India's relations with the WANA region.

1. Introduction

P R Kumaraswamy and Md. Muddassir Quamar

The post-colonial states in the Middle East and North Africa (MENA) have struggled with internal upheavals and external interferences, often accompanied by political violence. In some ways, these are a continuation of the colonial legacy that sowed the seeds of discord and disharmony during the run-up to their independence, but in other ways, they also reflect the failure of these post-colonial states, most of them Muslim-majority societies, to address the primary questions of resolving internal differences and disagreements over the nature of the state without resorting to political violence. Most of the MENA states have failed to resolve the issues of national identity, territorial claims and colonial boundaries without tension and conflicts.

In many instances, the issues of the political, social and economic exclusion of citizens based on primordial identities have conflated deep internal divisions, leading to friction. Demands for equal rights, freedom and respect are often accompanied by violence and this, in turn, evokes state violence to suppress dissent. In other words, the territorial claims of the states and the hegemonic ambitions of the leaders have caused inter-state conflicts and wars between countries, but, at the same time, the inability to recognise plurality, and exclusive approaches to nation-building and suppression of voices of dissent have fostered violence within the states. Resultantly, more than seven decades after the Second World War, many MENA countries face an uncertain future: some are on the verge of collapse while others are becoming failed states.

The continuation of political violence and its ever-expanding socio-political scope have made the MENA region fractious and vulnerable to outside interference. The post-colonial history of the region is dominated by autocratic states, authoritarian rulers, military *coup d'états*, inter-state conflicts as well as civil wars, revolutions, rebellions, mass unrest, terrorism and violent nationalist and transnational movements. At the dawn of the 21st century, many scholars, policy-makers and rulers had hoped for a new beginning whereby the MENA countries could bring about internal socio-political and economic transformations and resolve internal and external tensions without recourse to political violence. The *Arab Human Development Reports* [United Nations Development Programme (UNDP), 2003; 2004; 2005; 2006] highlighted the need for socio-political and economic changes for a conducive environment to avoid the recurring political violence. However, despite the apparent signs of the discontent and growing unrest over the direction and nature of the affairs of state, until the outbreak of the Arab Spring in December 2010 in Tunisia, none had been able to assuage the degree of the discontent and the deep-rooted malaise that had corroded the social contract between the states and the people.

In the beginning, the Arab Spring resulted in the overthrow of long-serving authoritarian rulers through peaceful mobilisation, generating hopes for democratic transitions in Tunisia, Egypt, Libya, Yemen and Syria. However, these hopes proved premature as the mass unrest devolved into civil strife in many countries, and eventually transformed into civil war in Syria, Libya and Yemen. The emergence of the Islamic State in Iraq and Syria (ISIS) further accentuated the conflict situation, redefining the potency and dangers of *jihadi* terror by not only creating a terrorist proto-state but also inspiring lone-wolf attacks in various parts of the world, including Europe and the US. The civil wars in Iraq and Syria resulted in mass migration and refugee influx which eventually reached the southern borders of Europe, causing severe challenges for policy-makers. While the Bahraini rulers were able to turn the tide against them with the use of force and military help from Arab allies, especially Saudi Arabia, Egypt's experiment with democracy ended within a year after Hosni Mubarak's overthrow, as the military intervened to remove Mohammed Morsi and restored the old political order. The only country that continued on the path of democracy in the wake of the Arab Spring was Tunisia, but it too could not remain free from political violence and terrorist attacks.

Scholars define political violence differently; while some do not consider state repression or inter-state conflicts to be political violence (Hewitt, 1993), others tend to include state perpetrated violence in political violence (Jackson, 2008). Scholars such as Edward Said (1988) and Noam Chomsky (1988) questioned the legitimacy accorded to the state's use of violence and argued that such subjective understanding of political violence is flawed. While it is difficult to arrive at a consensus on defining political violence and the academic discourse is multifaceted, there is no doubt that contemporary debates on political violence tend to include all forms of violence aimed at achieving political ends or with origins in political motives. Although the differences over defining political violence are difficult to overcome, the significance of understanding the causes and consequences is widely accepted.

Hence, for this volume, political violence is considered in its broadest and most comprehensive manifestation to refer to violence caused by both inter-state and intra-state conflicts as well as violence perpetrated by state and non-state actors. The objective of this volume is to examine some aspects of the political violence one witnesses in contemporary MENA. It is neither an exhaustive discourse to cover all aspects of political violence in the region, nor does it define a specified set of questions to be examined by individual contributors. The chapters stand on their own and examine a unique aspect of political violence in a given country or situation and hence, one finds a degree of variation in their formats and analyses.

Political Violence in MENA

The various manifestations of political violence in MENA can be divided into four broad types, namely, conflicts between states; armed rebellions or revolutions; suppression of dissent by states; and violence perpetrated by non-state actors. The first category includes conflicts or wars between countries emanating from differences over boundaries or conflicts based on ethnic, sectarian, nationalist and geopolitical pursuits. The second category comprises armed rebellions against regimes or violent revolutions to get rid of an existing political order. The third category is state-sponsored or state-induced violence against political or ideological opponents, minorities, refugees and migrants, or suppression of political movements by authoritarian rulers or autocratic states. The fourth category is political violence engaged in by non-state actors to achieve political ends either in the form of limited nationalist acts of violence or transnational acts of terrorism.

Inter-State Conflicts

Conflicts and wars between two or more states from within MENA or military interventions by external actors from outside the region have been a continuous feature of politics in the region. The longest and most complex of these has been the Arab-Israeli conflict over the Palestinian nationhood. The Arab countries and Israel fought four major wars over the issue, in 1948, 1956, 1967 and 1973. Subsequent to the 1978 Camp David Accords between Israel and Egypt, there has not been any major Arab-Israeli War but the conflict over Palestine has continued and has caused serious bouts of violence between Israel and Lebanon (1982 and 2006), the Palestinian uprising or *intifada* (1987 and 2000), terror strikes and suicide bombings inside Israel, continual political strife in the Occupied Territories over the Israeli policies, conflict among Palestinian groups (2006-07) and serious military exchanges between Israel and Hamas (2008-09, 2012 and 2014), leading to loss of life on all sides. As a complex and sensitive conflict, various international efforts for peace, and mediation have not been successful. In recent times, however, the conflict has metamorphosed from being a major regional conflict involving all the Arab states and Israel to a localised issue of resistance to the Israeli occupation and the demand for Palestinian statehood.

The Israeli-Palestinian conflict is not the only conflict afflicting the region. Other nationalist, ethnic and sectarian issues have caused conflicts and wars over the past decades. Some Arab countries have intervened in the affairs of their neighbours, leading to political upheavals such as the Egyptian and Saudi interventions in Yemen in the 1960s; the Syrian intervention in Lebanon (1976-2005); the Iraqi invasion of Kuwait in 1990; the Gulf Cooperation Council's (GCC's) military involvement in Bahrain in 2011-12; involvement of the Gulf countries and Jordan in support of Islamist and secular rebels in Syria to overthrow the Bashar al-Assad regime (2011-12); and the Saudi-led coalition's military intervention in

Yemen in 2015. Moreover, the ethno-sectarian conflict between the Arabs and Persians has caused several tensions after the Islamic revolution of 1979 in Iran, including the eight-year-long Iraq-Iran War (1980-88), the Iranian involvement in support of Hezbollah in Lebanon, and the Iranian military intervention or involvement in Iraq, Syria and Yemen after the Arab Spring. The other major ethno-sectarian conflicts include Turkey's conflict with Greece over Cyprus, the Turkish intervention in northern Cyprus in 1974 on behalf of the Turkish Cypriots and Turkey's problem with the Kurdistan Autonomous Government (KRG) in Iraq over giving refuge to the secessionist Kurdistan Workers' Party (PKK) of Turkey and the ongoing Turkish involvement in the Syrian crisis on behalf of the Islamist rebels or to prevent the emergence of a Kurdish autonomous region near its southeastern border.

In addition to conflicts and wars among the regional countries, MENA has endured a series of external military interventions, causing serious political churning and internal strife in the targeted countries and the neighbourhood. One of the costliest and longest wars was caused by the US-led invasion on Iraq in 2003. While eliminating the Iraq strongman Saddam Hussain from power, the war created a serious political vacuum in the country, causing internal strife and sectarian violence, and provided fertile ground for terrorism. Al-Qaeda gained an upper hand in Iraq in the aftermath of the US invasion and eventually resulted in the emergence of the Islamic State of Iraq, which, after the Arab Spring, metamorphosed into ISIS and caused mayhem not only in Iraq and Syria but in the whole region and beyond. After the Arab Spring, the US-led North Atlantic Treaty Organisation (NATO) intervention in Libya also precipitated into a civil war in Libya and since then, Libya has been on the verge of becoming a failed state.

On the other hand, the Russian military intervention in Syria in September 2015 changed the Syrian conflict, with the Assad regime gaining lost ground. The US has also been involved in the Syrian crisis by extending training and weapons supplies, and providing air support to the Kurdish-dominated Syrian Democratic Forces (SDF) to fight the ISIS. The US and UK have been involved in providing air support and intelligence to the Saudi-led coalition forces fighting against the Houthi rebels and on behalf of the Government of Yemen.

Historically, external powers have been involved in conflicts in the region, contributing to a serious spate of violence in various countries. The legacy of the colonial powers—the UK, France and Italy—between the two World Wars as well as the Ottoman Empire in the late 19th and early 20th centuries caused longstanding conflicts leading to continued violence. During the Cold War, the competition for influence between the US and Soviet Union caused violence in various regional theatres. The US military interventions continued even after the end of the Cold War and one of the major conflicts that in many ways changed the shape of the regional order was Operation Desert Storm—a 32-member coalition headed by the US—to repel the Iraqi invasion of Kuwait. The First Gulf War, as it came to be known later, was also responsible for causing discord within Saudi Arabia as Islamist groups opposed the stationing of "infidel" American troops in the Holy Land of Arabia. Osama bin Laden, who until then had hobnobbed with the Saudi, Pakistani and American agencies to steer the *jihad* against the Soviet occupation in Afghanistan, turned against his former benefactors over the First Gulf War and thus, started the story of *Salafi-Jihadist* terror, pioneered by Al-Qaeda, which, in 2019, has become one of the biggest challenges for security in MENA as well as the globe.

Revolutions and Rebellions

The modern history of MENA is full of revolutions and rebellions, causing political violence. Among the earliest rebellions was the Arab revolt against the Ottoman Empire spearheaded by Sharif Hussain of Mecca in 1916, actively aided and supported by the British Empire to weaken the Ottoman position amidst the First World War. The revolt caused mayhem in the whole region and eventually led to the expulsion of the Hashemite family from Hejaz in 1925 by Ibn Saud who had also secured British support for the fledgling Saudi Emirate. The Hashemites had been promised an Arab state by the British through the Hussain-McMahon correspondence which propelled Faisal, the son of Hussein, to declare the formation of the Arab Kingdom of Syria, comprising Arab areas that were under the Ottoman control. However, as the situation developed, France, which was given the mandate of Syria, expelled Faisal from Damascus, bringing to an end the dream of a unified Arab Kingdom led by the Hashemite family. Eventually, the Hashemites were appointed as the nominal rulers of Iraq and Transjordan that had come under the British mandate.

During the inter-war period, nationalist movements gained ground in the region and demands for secular republicanism emerged as one of the leading ideological tools for mass mobilisation. As the colonial powers started to retreat from the region at the end of the Second World War, they continued to influence the regional affairs through rulers or monarchies appointed or chosen by them. The growing tide of Arab nationalism and Pan-Arabism led to a series of military coups and the overthrowing of monarchies began in 1952 in Egypt when the Young Officers overthrew King Farouk. Military coups followed in Iraq (1958), Yemen (1962) and Libya (1969) and a series of *coup d'états* led to frequent political changes in Syria until the advent of Hafiz al-Assad in 1971. In addition, several failed coups were detected by the rulers in Saudi Arabia, Jordan and other monarchies, causing serious regional political divisions, tension and violence. The period saw several assassination attempts against rulers and a spate of internal rebellions were suppressed by the monarchies for their survival. Jordan had to use brute force to end the armed rebellion by Palestinian refugees in September 1970, while the Baathist Syria and Iraq were facing increasing challenges from religious groups against the authority of the rulers.

The conservative Persian Gulf monarchies had faced threats in the 1960s, but two events in 1979 changed the complexion of the region for all times to come: the Islamic revolution in Iran in February that ended the rule of the Pahlavi dynasty (1925-79), and the siege of the Kaaba in November which caused a serious challenge for the Saudi and other Gulf monarchies. The Saudi rulers had to take the help of French paratroopers to flush out the Islamist rebels led by Juhaiman al-Uthaibi who had taken over the Kaaba and the Masjid al-Haram surrounding it. On the other hand, Iran came under a revolutionary clerical regime whose early rhetoric for the export of the revolution caused panic among the neighbouring monarchs who encouraged Saddam Hussain of Iraq to militarily contain the new revolutionary regime, and this caused the prolonged Iraq-Iran War. Despite the spate of revolutions and rebellions, the region remained largely devoid of democracy, and leaders who overthrew the monarchies or governments with promises of republicanism and democracy, failed to democratise, and proved to be lifetime rulers who settled for autocracy over democracy.

The Arab Spring protests and the mass uprisings that they led to, raised some hopes for the replacement of autocratic systems and authoritarian rulers with democracy but the popular protests only created mayhem and violence. This provided an opportunity for the Islamists to stake claims over governance and they were given a chance to run the states after the democratic elections in Egypt and Tunisia; while the Egyptian experiment failed, it has not yet created significant results in Tunisia. In other places such as in Syria, the Islamists were hounded by the state for calling for regime change and were equated with the *jihadist* terrorist groups that had been gaining ground in Syria, Iraq, Libya and Yemen.

State-Sponsored Violence

One of the major problems faced in MENA is state-sponsored violence whereby political and ideological opponents, minorities, refugees, migrants, stateless groups, civil society, media and political movements face suppression at the hands of autocratic regimes and authoritarian rulers. The problem is not new and has been a major source of friction and cause for political violence in the region. It is also not confined to a few countries, but has been witnessed in the whole region, without any serious exception. Before the Arab Spring, long-time authoritarian rulers and their regimes, including Hosni Mubarak of Egypt, Zein El Abidine Ben Ali of Tunisia, Muammar Qaddafi of Libya, Bashar al-Assad of Syria (who survived the Arab Spring), Ali Abdullah Saleh of Yemen and Saddam Hussein of Iraq (who did not survive to see the Arab Spring) were infamous for their autocratic rule and ruthless suppression of any expression of dissent. Incidents such as the Hama massacre in Syria in 1982, the Halabja massacre in Iraq in 1988, and suppression of Shias by the Baathist regime in Iraq are testimony to state-sponsored violence against political and ideological opponents.

This problem is not confined to long-serving republican rulers—even monarchies and elected governments have not been free from using force and violence to suppress dissent. The AKP (Justice and Development Party) in Turkey has become one of the most authoritarian elected governments in the world after President Recep Tayyip Erdogan decided to target opposition groups, media, civil society and liberal elites who are considered a threat for the AKP government and are opposed to the political reforms brought about by Erdogan. On the other hand, the conservative monarchies in the Gulf too have not been amenable to any expression of opposition or dissent, and have not shied away from using violent means to silence opposition groups and individuals. Among the most notorious and recent cases has been the brutal murder of Saudi journalist Jamal Khashoggi in October 2018 for vocal criticism of policies pursued by the Crown Prince Mohammed bin Salman of Saudi Arabia. After the Arab Spring, some monarchies have introduced new laws to monitor and censor websites and social media and have acted against even the minutest of voices deemed critical of the policies pursued by the leadership.

Besides minorities, refugees and migrants, the Middle Eastern women too have faced structural violence in many societies and often find themselves at the receiving end of political actions for the appeasement of the majority. Political movements that have tried to mobilise public opinion against the sitting government or the ruling regime too have been targeted with state-sponsored violence in the region. One of the recent examples has been the suppression of the Green Movement in Iran in 2009 by the Islamic Republic or the targeting of the Kurdish-dominated People's Democratic Party (HDP) in Turkey on the accusation of being a front for the outlawed Kurdistan Worker's Party (PKK). The targeting of the Muslim Brotherhood in Egypt after the removal of Mohammed Morsi and the coming to power of Abdel Fattah el-Sisi is another example of state-sponsored violence against opposition groups or political movements.

Non-State Actors

Violence perpetrated by non-state actors on rival groups, religious, sectarian and ethnic minorities, and unarmed civilians, and terrorist attacks comprise another form of political violence prevalent in the region. The regional countries have been afflicted with the presence of a large variety of non-state actors who have propelled political violence in various ways and forms. Some of these non-state actors are nationalist such as Hamas and Hezbollah, while others are transnational entities such as Al-Qaeda and ISIS. There are groups which are secular such as Fatah (that renounced terrorism in 1988), Kurdish Peshmerga in Iraq and Syria, and others which are religious such as Hamas, Hezbollah and Shia militias in Iraq and Syria. There are groups such as the Muslim Brotherhood which are transnational Islamists and though they do not engage in violence, they have inspired political violence in many parts of the region due to their ideology that is at odds with secular governance. Further, there are *Salafi-Jihadist* terrorist groups such as Al-Qaeda and ISIS which have caused mayhem, sectarian strife, attacks on minorities, and targeted civilians to create terror. These groups have also been able to build transnational terrorist networks and have been major perpetrators of political violence in the region and beyond.

About the Volume

The volume, as mentioned earlier, is not exhaustive to cover all aspects of political violence in MENA. It intends to provide insights into specific instances of political violence and examine their causes and consequences within a specific time or space. In addition to this introduction, it comprises nine chapters that deal with a particular issue, instance or country. The chapter by Amna Sunmbul raises the question of political violence in Libya in the aftermath of the Arab Spring. It goes deeper into the socio-political dynamics prevailing in the country to examine the events in Libya that led up to the violent killing of President Qaddafi and highlights the role of regional and external players in worsening the civil war in the country. Lakshmi Priya examines the evolution of the Syrian crisis from a localised protest against the government policies into an international conflict with the involvement of major regional and extra-regional players. Apart from creating one of the worst humanitarian crises in recent time, the chapter highlights the Syrian crisis as a critical case of the vulnerability of the regional countries to devolve into political violence in pursuit of power.

Paulami Sanyal analyses the emergence of the Salafist Al-Nour Party in Egypt after the fall of Mubarak and the policies it has pursued since then to underline the existing political dynamics in the country. Rashmi

Muraleedhar, on the other hand, focusses on the Green Movement in Iran which challenged the existing political dynamics in the Islamic Republic and how it has faced suppression by the regime. Arshad analyses the post-Mubarak political process in Egypt and how the Muslim Brotherhood faces an existential challenge due to the oppressive policies pursued by the Sisi regime against the group. Hirak Jyoti Das examines the critical role of Hezbollah in the Syrian civil war for the survival of the Assad regime. Jatin Kumar delves deeper into the problem of terrorism in Yemen and underlines that Al-Qaeda has found fertile ground in Yemen due to the ongoing civil war and has regained the position which it had lost in the US-sponsored war on terror pursued by Saleh before his exit in the wake of the Arab Spring. Yasir Ali Mirza maps the evolution of the Sadrist Movement in Iraq while Parnika Praleya analyses the Houthi uprising in Yemen and the way it has led to normalisation of violence in the Yemeni society.

References

Chomsky, Noam (1988), "Middle East Terrorism and the American Ideological System" in Edward Said and Christopher Hitchens (eds.), *Blaming the Victims: Spurious Scholarship and the Palestinian Question* (London: Verso), pp. 97-147.

Hewitt, Christopher (1993), *Consequences of Political Violence* (Aldershot, UK: Dartmouth Publishing).

Jackson, Richard (2008), "The Ghosts of State Terror: Knowledge, Politics and Terrorism Studies," *Critical Studies on Terrorism*, (3): 377-392.

Said, Edward (1988), "American Intellectuals and Middle East Politics: An Interview with Edward W. Said," *Social Text*, interviewer Bruce Robbins, pp. 37-53.

UNDP (2003), *The Arab Human Development Report 2002: Creating Opportunities for Future Generations* (New York: UNDP Regional Bureau of Arab States).

UNDP (2004), *The Arab Human Development Report 2003: Building a Knowledge Society* (New York: UNDP Regional Bureau of Arab States).

UNDP (2005), *The Arab Human Development Report 2004: Towards Freedom in the Arab World* (New York: UNDP Regional Bureau of Arab States).

UNDP (2006), *The Arab Human Development Report 2005: Towards the Rise of Women in the Arab World* (New York: UNDP Regional Bureau of Arab States).

2. Political Violence or Violent Politics? Libya in Contemporary Times

Amna Sunmbul

Abstract

The political space in the Middle East and North Africa has undoubtedly strived to expand since 2011. However, this expansion has meant neither plurality nor democracy for most of these societies. Rather, terror and violence prevail in the political domain: factionalism, tribal loyalties and repression have led to instability and uncertainty. What has prevented a smooth and civil transition of power in the post-'Spring' Arab world? Two arguments are presented in this chapter. One, it is argued that political violence draws its legacy from the previous regimes and is based on policing and control. Two, violence is instrumentally embedded in regional politics wherein the focus has been on power consolidation and not on stability. In this context, the case of Libya after the overthrow and killing of Muammar Qaddafi in October 2011, has been studied. In the aforementioned setting, the theoretical propositions of control and regulation are consolidated with the practice of brutal authority, thus, making the line of distinction between political violence and violent politics insignificant.

Key Words: Libya; Qaddafi; Mutassim; Political Violence; Human Rights.

The year 2011 was a watershed in the Middle East and North African (MENA) region as it witnessed the overthrow of prolonged authoritarian regimes in Tunisia, Egypt, Libya and Yemen, and protests against rulers in countries such as Bahrain and Syria, where severe state repression had led to the silencing of the people. However, even though the authoritarian regimes were overthrown successfully in at least four countries, political violence has continued unabated. Arbitrary detentions and arrests, non-procedural convictions, torture, custodial deaths and non-arrest of the accused continue to define state power and authority. At the same time, resistance against the ruling regimes has continued, even against those governments which have been set up after 2011, as has been evident in Egypt and Libya.

There is a duality involved in the political movements: a peaceful initiative lapses into undesired antagonism while, at the same time, forceful means are used by the ruling authorities. In this regard, two arguments are proposed. First, there is resistance towards changing the violent political culture in the MENA region because of factionalism in the society. Second, political instability and uncertainty retard economic growth and social welfare: the use of brute force is witnessed wherever there is a threat, to counter the political movement.

The bigger question, however, deals with the continued political malevolence: why has violence been a regular feature in the contemporary politics of the MENA region? It has been observed that rather than settling issues, the ruling governments and the resisting groups start with the aim of bringing tension to the fore. In this regard, the case of Libya is significant. On the one hand, Muammar Qaddafi was criticised for being coercive, authoritarian and corrupt but, on the other, malicious methods of policing continue even after the political change and the brutal death of the Libyan dictator. Political violence, thus, needs to be understood in the backdrop of a tribal society which has corroborated vehemence and ruthlessness ever since Qaddafi came into power in 1969. Even though the Qaddafi regime was overthrown, the political institutions inherited the culture of ruling with coercion. More than anything else, use of force had been the backbone of the Qaddafi rule and had enabled him to maintain his political authority for 42 years.

The acclimatisation to political malevolence has been such that no distinction is drawn between coercion used to ensure state authority and bestiality with no political targets. This can be demonstrated by means of two cases: first, the brutal killing of Qaddafi and the custodial death of Qaddafi's son Mutassim, whose body showed clear signs of physical torture and inhumane treatment as a captive. However, even seven years after these two episodes and substantial evidence of human rights violation, the offenders have neither been arrested on charges of murder nor have trials been conducted. The agenda is geared towards consolidation of power rather than bringing stability to the Libyan state. It is, therefore, evident that politics is drawn along the lines of aggression and depravity.

From the above discussion, it could be argued that violence operates at two levels. The first level is political, wherein repressive state policies, extreme vigilantism and societal deprivation prevail. The second level relates to the operation of violent agendas, use of brute force and perpetual insecurity for the society. The latter impedes any questioning of contemporary state practices from the international community. In this setting, it is argued in this chapter, political violence and violent politics both are present in the region because of which Libya continues to suffer from physical as well as structural atrocities. In other words, the theoretical propositions of control and regulation are consolidated with the practice of brutal authority, thus, blurring the line of distinction between political violence and violent politics.

The main focus of the chapter is on the relation and continuity of violence in Libya, and the manner in which it is reflected in the practical politics of what remains of the Libyan state. There are four sections in the chapter. In the first section, the idea of political violence is discussed briefly, along with its relevance for contemporary politics. In the second section, political violence is seen through a comparison between previous and current policies and practices in Libya. Here, it must be clarified at the outset that the merciless killing and political ouster of Qaddafi is taken as the watershed year. In the third section, the killing of Qaddafi and the custodial death of his son Mutassim are discussed in the light of political violence and violent politics. These are two significant cases, which hitherto have remained uninterrogated, thus, raising the concerns of the international community. There is a critical assessment of the political culture in contemporary Libya. It is argued that violent politics could be observed through specific instances, but there is a more serious issue of political violence which validates the use of brute force. Finally, a brief overview of contemporary Libya is provided to understand the direction in which Libya is moving: stability, failure or alienation in international politics.

Idea of Political Violence

Political violence can be understood as violence inflicted by state as well as non-state actors, and is motivated towards the attainment of certain political goals. According to Patrick O'Neill, "In the case of political violence, we are speaking of a phenomenon that operates beyond state sovereignty, neither war nor crime, and that seeks to achieve some political objective through the use of force" (2010: 261). Here, there is an implication of the act being carried out by groups which are not affiliated to the state institution. The second important feature evident from the above definition is its practice outside state jurisdiction; however, the state can use its information to control and interdict groups which attempt to transgress its authority. It is notable that war does not fall under the rubric of political violence because it is authenticated by the state and there are international laws and regulations governing war, whether offensive or defensive in nature.

The use of physical force is an essential feature of political violence. There are several forms of political violence: uprising, revolution, coup and civil war, to name a few. It also includes policing, vigilance and use of extra-legal authority by the state and its institutions. The involvement of civilians is a regular feature; attacks on government buildings, arson obstructions, etc., are ways in which the common people engage in political violence. At the same time, there are possibilities of the involvement of rival political elites who aim at realising their interests in the politics of the state. Terrorism could also be considered a form of political violence if, firstly, the group has declared political aims and not merely a religious and ideological rationale for the violence inflicted by it; secondly, the target of vehemence is a defined political actor such as state institutions; thirdly, there is some resonance with the local population who support the group because of the ultimate political goal, which is lucrative and sentimental for the people (O'Neill, 2010: 275).

There is a second sense in which the term political violence is used (Hague and Harrop 2004: 134). In this interpretation, political violence is used in the sense of extra-legal authority that the state exerts upon its population due to security concerns or for repressing oppositional activities. In this sense, the state exercises authority over civilians, constitutional opponents, civil society workers and others. The idea is to concentrate authority and repress any form of dissension. It could also be argued that the ruling class uses means to ensure that the regime is not perturbed. This is on account of the fact that its rule is not through popular elections but established as a government by coercion.

As Hague and Harrop (2004) argue, "(p)olitical terror, a subcategory of political violence, occurs when such acts are aimed at striking fear into a wider population" (p. 134). As a necessary corollary, the use of violence is arbitrary and absolute. At the same time, non-state actors could also be participants in the accomplishment of violence. For instance, if a local elite faction has strong regional or tribal ties and intends to exercise exclusive authority, then suppression is done through stringent measures, including vigilance, policing and adherence to traditions and customs which render opposition gruesome. Additionally, "political terror" is a term which connotes violence for inducement of fear in the population, and provides a broader meaning to the notion of political violence (Hague and Harrop, 2004: 135). This is because it recognises that violence may also be carried out by non-state actors on such as a militant organisation, local militias and even the political opposition. In the light of this conceptualisation of political violence, it could be argued that there is a deliberate attempt to dissuade counter-opinion and dissension—therefore, the material ventilation may be seen through the infliction of pain and harm.

The idea of "collective violence", as envisaged by Charles Tilly (2003) is important to discuss because it deals with "contentious politics" and the manner in which some "contentious politics" becomes violent (Tilly, 2003 and 2017). This concept is relevant in the case of Libya, as would be substantiated in the subsequent sections. He observes,

> We can conveniently mark our crossing into contentious politics' territory by noticing when governments—more generally, individuals or organizations that control concentrated means of coercion—become parties to discontinuous, public, collective claims. Governments become parties to contention as claimants, objects of claims or stakeholders.

> Collective violence, then, is a form of contentious politics. It counts as *contentious* because participants are making claims that affect each other's interest. It counts as *politics* because relations of participants to governments are always at stake (Tilly, 2017: 275).

Collective violence clearly reveals that governments are involved in contentions in some role or the other (Tilly, 2003 and 2017). For instance, they could have a vested interest in supporting a cause or in delegitimising it by not according support to it. More importantly, the government can be a direct partisan in the conflict in the eventuality that it has to also defend its structure and political survival. The contest between interest groups is played out by the ruling regime or government, depending upon the stakes the state has. This is an instrumental notion that guides the participation, and the extent of it, of the government, in terms of defending, supporting, protecting or opposing the contest.

It is collective violence that explicates on the manner in which some contestations, albeit politics, lead to violence. This argument could also be logically turned on its head to argue that politics, howsoever noble its intentions, could lapse into violence. This is on account of the competition that the various groups are involved in. Violence may easily be deciphered in politics in the form of legislations, policing, rules, repression of opposing political views, discrimination through structured procedures of governance, de-recognition and even criminalisation. These are ways of formalising exclusion from the public sphere. Censorship of the media, for example, delimits and controls the opinion of the people.

Violence is also imminent in the curtailment of civil liberties that become the cornerstone of state policies. Noticeable is the continuation of violence in politics in spite of a change in leadership or institutions. This is because of the tacit acceptance of politics by means of using violence as well as violence in the conduct of politics which has underlined the state-society relations. Violence manifests in several ways in politics; as a brute force, it reiterates the coercion that the state, its agencies and resourceful elites and sub-state organisations unleash on its people. Rather than engaging in a clinical argument, there is an attempt to assess this point in the context of the Libyan state-society complex, which, since the overthrow of Qaddafi, has not witnessed the abatement of violence.

Continuity of Violent Politics: Before and After 2011

The Libyan case is mostly seen as a continuity of the larger episodes and events that were going on in the MENA region. Libya, just like Tunisia and Egypt, was governed by an authoritarian ruler, with no sign of abdication or even partial democracy, along with a high probability of a hierarchical rule. The overthrow of Qaddafi is mostly located along the spectrum of political upheavals in the region beginning from January 2011 in Tunisia. This approach provides a general framework within which the unprecedented reprisal could be understood. Nevertheless, contextualisation is also important. Rather than generalising, it provides scope for understanding the stimulus to the political upheaval in Libya.

Qaddafi's regime was autocratic, as has been evident in the policies he adopted. The most significant observations in this regard could be spelt out as follows: firstly, Qaddafi supported and channelised funds towards supporting political overthrow in parts of the Arab world; secondly, he did not use the vast Libyan resources towards speeding up economic growth and development—rather the energies of the centralised state were directed towards repression; thirdly, in spite of his dictatorial regime, Qaddafi could not reach out to the Arab region in totality and assume the role of a regional leader (Haseeb, 2011). The aims of the government under Qaddafi were to maximise its control over the people. Haseeb (2011) appropriately points out:

> Instead of transforming Libya, with its huge oil revenues and limited population, through peaceful democratic rule, into a state that might serve as a shining model in the Arab world and elicit positively in the African sphere, the country became an object of scorn and ridicule, representing one of the most viciously repressive Arab regimes and thereby distinguished as most deserving to be brought down. Such was the end of what was optimistically termed the "Libyan revolution" at the outset, but which came to be the despotic regime of an individual and his family practising every shade of corrupt rule to the extent that its being brought down and its passing will not be regretted (Haseeb 2011: 426).

Therefore, Libya was a case where there was general and disproportionate grievance against the Qaddafi regime: it was markedly authoritarian and drew the ire of the Western powers. The United States, in particular, vehemently criticised Qaddafi and his domestic policies. It is a well-known point that President Ronald Reagan was most sceptical of the aims and ambitions of Qaddafi. Pargeter argues that despite the lashing and reprimands inflicted by the West, directed at Qaddafi, the latter confronted, rather than succumbing to, the same. She points out, "With his overextended sense of flamboyance and showmanship, Qaddafi both repelled and fascinated simultaneously" (Pargeter, 2012: 3). The economic policies of Qaddafi were equally problematic because they brought more strain to the Libyan economy than replenishing it. Much of the resources were brought under state control, and private ownership became negligible. Mezran (2012), on the lines of Pargeter (2012: 3), argues that "the first decade" of Qaddafi's rule, after the overthrow of the Sanussi regime and consolidation of power in 1969, was extremely crucial. Qaddafi ensured that all forms of dissension were curbed: overtly, in the form of media censorship and abolition of political opposition, and covertly, through the restriction of external influence and instillation of fear within the citizenry of Libya.

It is not an overstatement to suggest that there was a nationalist anti-imperialist discourse as well that guided Qaddafi throughout the consolidation of his regime. Therefore, the society was controlled not only with outright political force but also semantically through the propagation of a nationalist narrative that legitimised Qaddafi's rule over Libya. The society and people in Libya were controlled through a list of legislations such as outlawing of political parties in 1972; setting up revolutionary committees which were well-known for their repressive actions; press and media censorship, and so on (Haseeb, 2011). These methods were important for bringing the Libyan people under the direct control of the regime, and dependent upon the state for their jobs, living, education, etc. At the same time, there was a security discourse that instilled fear amongst the people that they might be interdicted if they went against the state policies (Kafala, 2011).

There is not an iota of doubt regarding the repression and fear that the Qaddafi regime infused in the society—the violence was both physical as well as structural. The opposition was eliminated systematically. His *jamhariyya*, which was claimed to be a popular representation of the Libyan people's choice for political leadership, was indeed a misnomer. It was anything but the choice of the people and over a period of four decades, the liberties and representation of the people were withdrawn or curtailed (Haseeb, 2011; Kafala, 2011). Hence, there was an increasing sense of suppression that the Libyan people felt. The rebellious spirit in the Libyans did not, therefore, come as a surprise.

In this regard, Haseeb (2011) argues that due to the repressive policies of the Libyan state under Qaddafi, the Libyan people could not oppose openly but had to resort to peaceful revolt as witnessed in other Arab states such as Tunisia and Egypt. He argues,

> ... not all of these conditions were available to the Libyan people, where events compelled some to undertake an "armed *intifada* (uprising)" where, ... the conflict between the opposition and the heavily armed and well-trained forces loyal to Qaddafi ... was still a highly asymmetrical one. (Haseeb, 2011: 426)

This implies two things: there was a general disgruntlement among the people against dictatorial regimes, as was seen in other parts of the MENA region; and the violence corroborated in Libya was indeed a continuity of the Qaddafi regime. The revolutionary spirit, nonetheless, was suppressed until there was an outside stimulus in the form of uprisings in other parts of the Arab world.

The Libyan 'armed conflict' started in February 2011 and there was a movement towards Libyan reforms. However, it was met with stiff resistance from the state which caused riots between the state and the rebel factions. The most affected cities were Benghazi, Baida and Derna. In a tense situation, where the rebels got engaged in an armed uprising, the Libyan violence became unprecedented. According to a research project report, brought out by the Syracuse University College of Law, "The Arab Awakening caught hold in Benghazi in February of 2011 resulting, nearly nine months after the start of peaceful protests, in the toppling of the Gaddafi (*sic.*) regime" (Syracuse University College of Law, *Libya in Conflict: Mapping the Libyan Armed Conflict 2012*: 3). The Qaddafi government unleashed a series of repressive acts, in spite of which the government was overthrown. The report also notes that "indiscriminate killings continued", after three days of the start of the rebellion, by the state and its agencies against the protesting populations (Syracuse University, College of Law, 2012). From a different standpoint, given the complexity of the Libyan state in which rebellion was inevitable but difficult to achieve, the response to state violence came in the form of violent insurrections.

The implications are profound for political violence. In a situation where violence is operational in many forms such as the denial of personal freedom and the concentration of resources in the hands of the state, an uprising may become violent rather than being civic or peaceful. In the absence of a constitutional forum that would provide the people with space to ventilate their grievances, illegitimate and aggressive means of expression remain the only option. Therefore, the political violence unleashed during Qaddafi's regime, breathed the desire for vengeance into the opposing camps. The climax was reached with the Libyan Army opening fire on the people, which further justified the use of force on the part of the rebelling forces.

The killing of Qaddafi was itself a heinous act, especially on the grounds that it might have been possible to reason with him for abdicating his position. Most of his political allies were either dead or in the captivity of the rebels. By the end of September 2011, it was a foregone conclusion that Qaddafi's regime had come to an end, especially after the loss of Fezzan to the National Transitional Council (NTC). His killing on October 20, 2011, was accompanied by the detention of his son, Mutassim Qaddafi, who was leading the convoy, and his ultimate death in custody, evidently on the same day. His body showed signs of torture and his death could have been a result of physical coercion (Human Rights Watch, 2012).

This custodial death was not a singular instance during the Libyan civil war between Qaddafi and the rebels. In fact, the deaths of several political prisoners, including Muammar Qaddafi's sons Mutassim Qaddafi and Saif al-Islam Qaddafi, some other family members and close allies, remain suspicious but have not been investigated. The idea of "collective violence" (Tilly, 2003) is very evident here. The interest-based politics has managed to keep the political murders under cover. The interests of the divergent political groups as well as the current political competitors, lie in veiling these episodes rather than bringing them to light, lest it lead to sympathy for the dead dictator.

Nearly seven years after the fall of Qaddafi, one feature of the Libyan polity remains constant: violence. In the contemporary times, Libya is home to rebels and civil war fighters, with two polarised factions fighting for power. On the one hand, there is a government in Tripoli which is governed by the General National Congress, while, on the other, the House of Representatives aims at consolidating its authority and is based in Tobruk. This civil war has brought about a devastation of the Libyan economy worse than in Qaddafi's time and the country has been experiencing bloodshed and political instability ever since the overthrow of Qaddafi in October 2011. Eriksson (2016) argues that "the existing conflict in Libya could be understood as a multi-layered conflict" (p. 817) which is traversed by actors at different levels and where there is a competition for varied interests. He (2016) succinctly argues that "the election held in July 2012 brought numerous political actors to the political scene, all jockeying for power" (Eriksson, 2016: 821).

Therefore, there is an interest-based contestation for power. During the Qaddafi regime, diversity on the political front was denied and, therefore, the political ambitions of the people and opponents remained under cover. However, after years of denial, the overthrow of Qaddafi provided an opportunity for the political factions to openly contest with each other. This has caused the political strife to be unpredictable and violent.

An Eye for an Eye: Killing of Qaddafi and his Son

The killing of Qaddafi was an event by itself not only because it brought the 42-year-old dictatorship to an end but also for the vengeance reflected in the cruelty towards the former ruler. The panorama of violence was enigmatic in as much as it amply demonstrated the feeling of hatred towards Qaddafi, as he fled for his life from Sirte. According to the Human Rights Watch Report (2012: 28):

> As soon as the militia fighters had custody of Gaddafi, they began abusing him. Blood was already gushing from the shrapnel wound in his head. As he was being led onto the main road, a militiaman stabbed him in his anus with what appears to have been a bayonet, causing another rapidly bleeding wound. Misrata militia fighters surrounded Gaddafi, punching and beating him, and yelling "*Allahu Akbar*!" and "*Misrata*" over and over again.... (Human Rights Watch, *Death of a Dictator: Bloody Vengeance in Sirte*, 2012: 28).

Qaddafi, in any case, had been absconding and hiding from the rebel forces since March 2011. The fight between pro- and anti-Qaddafi forces escalated into a full-scale civil war, with fighting on all fronts. However, the vehemence shown towards the vanquished dictator was clearly a product of the violent political culture that the Libyan society had been experiencing for more than four decades.

The cause of the death of Muammar Qaddafi remains debatable, though it is amply evident that he succumbed to his wounds and repeated physical abuse. The violence unleashed by the militia was a match for the militancy of the pro-Qaddafi militia. The local militias also made inroads into the bastions of Qaddafi. With the fall of the military, the final moments of the civil war were indeed catastrophic. Nevertheless, the ill-treatment of Qaddafi and his subsequent killing seems to be spontaneous and unprovoked (Human Rights Watch, 2012). The situation went out of the control of the leaders of the local militias once Qaddafi was arrested and the rest of his convoy devastated. The frenzied actions of the rebels were a manifestation of the vagaries of a war-torn society which suddenly brought the anxieties of the Libyan people to the fore.

Apart from the terrible death of the dictator, the war crimes committed during the civil war in Libya were also horrific. Not only were the pro-Qaddafi military forces involved in this but also the local militias, "regional stakeholders" (Erikkson, 2016: 823) such as Qatar, Egypt and United Arab Emirates (UAE) as well as North Atlantic Treaty Organisation (NATO) forces (Milne, 2012). These crimes included misconduct with the prisoners of war, torture, detention and attacking civilians on the pretext of defending their respective fortresses (Milne, 2012). An important case relates to the treatment of political prisoners of war, allegedly by the

Misrata-based militias during the Libyan crisis (Human Rights Watch, 2012). The case of Mutassim Qaddafi is an important one in this regard. His custodial death was indeed suspicious. His death revealed the torture techniques being used on, and the inhumane treatment of, the prisoners in Libya during the civil war (Human Rights Watch, 2012). This was a legacy, indeed, of the Qaddafi regime. According to Seeberg (2014), despite the professed state structure in Libya which accorded power to the people through a Congress, "… most of its (Qaddafi's rule) 42 years involved arbitrary detention, torture and assassinations; few are fighting to restore what existed before 2011 …" (Seeberg, 2014: 123).

The killing of Qaddafi highlighted the presence of a violent political attitude that has made inroads into the socio-political complex of Libya. It needs to be exemplified that the regimes of both Idris and Qaddafi were based on "tribal alliances in the administration of power and this recourse always had a role in stirring up tribal and regional sensitivities" (Sawani, 2012: 3). There were attempts to consolidate authority coercively through these tribal relations because of which the use of force became normalised over time. Tribal relations were not formed adequately on the lines of a stolid state structure due to which it was evident that problems and issues would occur over a period.

It has been noted by the Human Rights Watch World Report 2017:

> Militias and armed forces affiliated with the two governments engaged in arbitrary detentions, torture, unlawful killings, indiscriminate attacks, abductions, and forcible disappearances. Criminal gangs and militias abducted politicians, journalists, and civilians—including children—for political and monetary gain. The domestic criminal justice system remained dysfunctional, offering no prospects for accountability, while the International Criminal Court (ICC), despite having jurisdiction over Libya provided by the UN Security Council, failed to open any new investigation into on-going crimes. (Human Rights Watch World Report 2017)

The similarities between the observations of Seeberg (2014) and the Human Rights Watch Report 2017 are not overdrawn. There were clear precedents that were set in the Libyan state under Qaddafi which are witnessing their logical culmination in the contemporary times. The kidnapping of Prime Minister Zeidan in October 2013 bears testimony to the extremely delicate security scenario that is present in Libya; if the political leaders cannot be protected, then the situation is particularly scary for the civilians. The violence is the consequence of not disarming of the local militias after the death of Qaddafi in October 2011 by the NATO forces (Chivvis and Martini 2014). Violence has become the backbone of the Libyan polity and the post-Qaddafi authority remains in continuous jeopardy. The uncertainty is spearheaded by the lack of a formal political structure.

The Human Rights Watch (2012) has indicated that some members of the ruling regime in Libya need to be arrested and tried in the International Criminal Court (ICC) for crimes against humanity for their roles and actions during the crisis in 2011. These include the killing of Qaddafi and suggest investigation into the death of Mutassim. However, there has been very little or no progress in this regard. In a scenario wherein there is no stable governance, the inability to arrest war criminals is obvious. Libya is also not a party to the ICC. However, the ICC was given the jurisdiction to investigate the war crimes committed in Libya since 15 February 2011 by the UN Security Council (UNSC) Resolution 1970 passed on 26 February. Regarding the deaths of Muammar and Mutassim Qaddafi, it has been argued that in the absence of autopsy reports, the cause of their deaths cannot be ascertained (Human Rights Watch, 2012).

As mentioned earlier, there is a climactic lapse of the political structures in Libya which have not been rebuilt and stabilised even after six years. Political violence decidedly comprises that which involves the state, government, elites as well as non-state actors. Libya falls within this bracket. There is another threshold on which the Libyan state is resting: violent politics. The Qaddafi regime was based on autocracy and dictatorship. This was accompanied by the annulment of political parties, along with censorship and the centralised authority of the state. This implied repression by the state. However, post-Qaddafi Libya is confronted with a version of politics that cannot be governed without violence. The line of difference becomes stark— violence has been the order of the day as well as the only means of maintaining governance.

The Security Council, in its meeting held on 14 December 2017 observed that stability in the Libya political set-up is possible only under the guidance of the UN. The statement by the President points out:

> The Security Council reiterates that two years since the signing of the Libyan Political Agreement (LPA) on 17 December 2015 in Skhirat, the LPA remains the only viable framework to end the Libyan political crisis and that its implementation remains key to holding elections and finalising the political transition. The Council emphasises the continuity of the LPA throughout Libya's transitional period and rejects incorrect deadlines that only serve to undermine the UN-facilitated political process.
>
> The Security Council reaffirms its endorsement of the United Nations' Action Plan for an inclusive Libyan-owned political process under the leadership of the United Nations (UN) as presented by the Special Representative of the Secretary-General (SRSG), Ghassan Salamé, in New York on 20 September 2017, in order to deliver the establishment of stable, unified, representative and effective governance under the framework of the LPA. (UNSC, 2017: 1)

This shows that there is no easy or simple solution to the Libyan problem. There is an acknowledgement of its complicated political situation, with militias in different parts of the country competing for authority (UNSC, 2017). The UN needs to take the lead in the post-war reconstruction in Libya, and it has a pivotal role to play in the political reconstruction also. The LPA in this regard could help in the abatement of violence.

Political Violence Versus Violent Politics

The violence in contemporary Libya is two-fold: one, there is a scramble for power among the various political factions which leads to compulsive actions; and two, there is an environment of violence which shows the aggression of the actors involved theretofore. These layers reveal the rapidity with which political violence could become recurrent, almost insurmountable, and, therefore, showcases the violent politics. Addressing, more concretely, the death of Qaddafi and the mistreatment of the political prisoners, it could be argued that rather than being categorised as political violence, these actions were innately violent.

An analogy may be drawn with the arrest, trial, sentencing and hanging of Saddam Hussein. Although it was a war between two countries, the vanquished President was sought, arrested and tried by the new Iraqi government. His trial, however, was not fair wherein most of the defence lawyers of Saddam Hussein were threatened, kidnapped and murdered, despite the appeals for security and protection (Burns and Hauser, 2006). This led to a partial representation of the defence, notwithstanding the predictable judgement passed against Hussein by the interim government of Iraq beginning in October 2005. He was sentenced to death on 5 November 2006 by hanging for the killing of Shias in Dujail in 1982. This example is pertinent for political violence wherein a defeated dictator was neither given a fair trial nor handed over to the International Criminal Court.

In the case of Qaddafi, a similar counterfactual might have been possible. However, the desperation with which he was killed unveiled the violent attitude of the militias. This was not an act that stemmed from political interests: it was emotive and the consequence of an anxious struggle to besiege Qaddafi's stronghold. As the situation deteriorated from riots to a full-scale civil war, the fighting became more aggressive. Mutassim's custodial death, however, may be understood as an act of political violence given that his survival could have been a symbolic rallying point for pro-Qaddafi leaders.

In any case, the situation in Libya hardly seems to be under control. Violence at a multivariant level places the Libyan state in jeopardy. The current situation in Libya is reminiscent of collective violence as envisaged by Tilly. This is because the state, its agencies and various non-state actors are involved in the conflict, each with its own interests and identifying its own tribal solidarities. However, this form of violence is not a break from the past, rather it is a continuity of Qaddafi's time. The political instability and economic stagnation are indeed the foremost problems of the Libyan state—a situation that was missing in Qaddafi's *jamhariyya*.

This has rendered day-to-day politics not only uncertain but also marred in bloodshed. Given that there has been no substantial resolution of the political situation in the last six years, violence is destined to recur in the Libyan polity.

Conclusion

The political and societal circumstances in Libya have reached an all-time low—the ouster of the Qaddafi regime did not even remotely lead to a movement towards a republic. The conflict shows no sign of abating. The Libyans, at the level of global politics, are also confronted with an identity crisis. There is no singular representative of the Libyan people. There is no doubt that Qaddafi was not a revered political leader at the international level. However, the people have not been able to recognise a particular leader or party as representing them. This has severe repercussions for the Libyan state in as much as it could lapse into an unstable war zone, with fighting over possession of resources. This has meant an unabated spate of violent eruptions throughout Libya, with little chance of disappearing absolutely. In order to stabilise the Libyan society, international support is required. Once again, the political violence disrupts international intervention. In a contest between sustaining political structures and establishing a new one, Libya seems to be staring down an abyss.

References

Burns, John F. and Christine Hauser (2006). "Third Lawyer in Hussein Trial is Killed", *The New York Times*, 21 June 2006. Retrieved on 12 August 2018. https://www.nytimes.com/2006/06/21/world/middleeast/21cnd-lawyer.html

Chivvis, Christopher S. and Martini, Jeffrey (2014), "Libya After Qaddafi: Lessons and Implications for the Future" (Santa Monica, CA: RAND Corporation). Retrieved on 10 March 2016. https://www.rand.org/pubs/research_reports/RR577.html

Eriksson, Mikael (2016). "A Fratricidal Libya: Making Sense of a Conflict Complex", *Small Wars & Insurgencies*, 27 (5): 817-836.

Hague, Rod & Martin Harrop (2004), *Comparative Government and Politics: An Introduction* (Sixth Edition), (Basingstoke: Palgrave MacMillan).

Haseeb, Khair El-Din (2011) "Libya…Hopes and Fears", *Contemporary Arab Affairs*, 4 (4): 425-430.

Human Rights Watch (2012), "Death of a Dictator: Bloody Vengeance in Sirte". Retrieved on 30 June 2016. http://www.hrw.org

Human Rights Watch World Report (2017), "Libya: Events of 2016". Retrieved on 3 January 2018. file:///D:/chapter%20for%20book/World%20Report%20 2017_%20Libya%20_%20Human%20Rights%20Watch.html

Kafala, Tarik (2011), "Gaddafi's Quixotic and Brutal Rule", BBC News, 20 October 2011. Retrieved on 12 August 2018. https://www.bbc.com/news/world-africa-12532929

Mezran, Karim (2012), "Libya: The Rise and Fall of Qaddafi", *Middle East Policy Council*, Retrieved on 3 March 2016. http://www.mepc.org/libya-rise-and-fall-qaddafi

Milne, Seumas (2012), "If There were Global Justice, Nato Would be in the Dock Over Libya", *The Guardian*, 15 May 2012. Retrieved on 12 August 2018. https://www.theguardian.com/commentisfree/2012/may/15/global-justice-nato-libya

O'Neill, Patrick (2010), *The Essentials of Comparative Politics* (Third Edition). (London: Norton & Company).

Pargeter, Alison (2012), *Libya: The Rise and Fall of Qaddafi* (Cornwall: Yale University Press).

Sawani, Mohammad Youssef (2012), "Post-Qadhafi Libya: Interactive Dynamics and the Political Future", *Contemporary Arab Affairs*, 5 (1): 1-26.

Seeberg, Peter (2014), "EU Strategic Interests in Post-Qaddafi Libya: Perspectives for Cooperation", *Middle East Policy*, 21 (1): 122-32.

Syracuse University of Law (2012), "Libya in Conflict: Mapping the Libyan Armed Conflict". Retrieved on 5 December 2017. http://insct.syr.edu/wp-content/uploads/2013/02/Mapping-the-Libyan-Conflict.pdf

Tilly, Charles (2003), *The Politics of Collective Violence* (Cambridge: Cambridge University Press).

Tilly, Charles (2017), "The Politics of Collective Violence", in Casteneda, Ernesto and Shneider, Cathy Lisa (eds.), *Collective Violence, Contentious Politics, and Social Change A Charles Tilly Reader* (London and New York: Routledge).

United Nations Security Council (UNSC) (2017), "Statement by the President," No. S/PRST/2017/26, 14 December. Retrieved on 3 February 2018. https://www.un.org/press/en/2017/sc13120.doc.htm

3. From Local to International Conflict: An Assessment of the Syrian Crisis

Lakshmi Priya

Abstract

The Syrian crisis, which began as a local event, transformed into a civil war. The regional political situation, raging domestic protests and fast spread of the uprising made Syria vulnerable, and the fear of being overthrown led to extreme retaliation from the regime. As regional actors got involved in the proxy war and the huge mass of refugees posed a threat not only to regional but also international stability, the crisis became mired in complexities, and the local conflict became an international problem. This chapter will trace the trajectory of the Syrian crisis and discuss the state's response, the Islamic State of Iraq and Syria (ISIS) phenomenon, the refugee problem, and the role of regional and international actors.

Key Words: Syria; Civil War; Bashar al-Assad; Violence; Instability

According to a Jewish legend dating back to 497 AD, Nachman Chatufa, born to the barren couple Rabbi Pincus and Rachel, started reciting verses of the Torah soon after his birth. Anxious, the Rabbi slapped him and Nachman became mute for twelve long years after which he again started speaking. He made five prophecies about Israel in Aramaic which were later compiled as *Nevuat Ha Yeled* (*The Child's Prophecy*) after his death. Some of the prophecies of Nachman Chatufa are believed to have come true (Discovering Islam, 2018). Likewise, the beginning of the second decade of the 20th century witnessed a child's prophecy coming true in Syria when fourteen-year-old schoolboy Naief Abazid (MacKinnon, 2016) was coerced by his seniors to write *Ejak el door ya Doktur* (Your turn, doctor), the doctor being Bashar al-Assad, on the walls of his all boys' school called Al-Banin, situated in the Dara'a province.

On 16 February 2011, Naief unknowingly prophesied doom for Syria and Bashar al-Assad when he wrote these words in black spray paint on the wall under the school principal's office to amuse his seniors. His writing had an explosive effect and the next day he was called to the principal's office, and then was arrested by the dreaded secret intelligence agency of Syria known as the Mukhabarat which subjected him to isolated confinement and severe torture like *al-dullab* in which the victim is tied to a tyre and rolled over. Under pressure, he gave the names of five boys who had coerced him to write on the wall, who were later arrested and they disclosed the names of 23 other boys who were or were not present in the school on the ill-fated day. After a series of protests, followed by strong repression by the state, Naief and the other boys were pardoned. After getting free, he joined the on-going protests, painting President Bashar al-Assad's portrait on the streets of Dara'a, to be stomped and driven on by passers-by which was a grave insult considering the prestige associated by Hafiz al-Assad, Bashar's father and predecessor, in erecting huge portraits of himself in public places (Pipes, 1996: 15). Meanwhile, Naief was hit by a bullet and took refuge in Jordan after which he returned to Dara'a for some time before leaving for a long and tenuous journey to Austria as a refugee (MacKinnon, 2016).

When Naief and the other boys were arrested, the people of Dara'a protested and demanded their release. After waiting for weeks, they approached Atef Najib, a cousin of Assad who was in charge of the security apparatus in Dara'a, but it was a futile exercise. After three weeks, 18 March was declared a day of rage in Dara'a when the residents gathered at the Omari Mosque and the protest march headed towards Najib's office. The protesters hurled stones and the police opened fire, killing two protestors whose funeral marches saw more firing. Thus began a cycle of funeral marches followed by more killings. At last, Assad pardoned the boys and set them free not knowing that their stories of torture would begin a period of chaos in Dara'a and beyond.

As the Naief incident enraged Dara'a, other parts of Syria were not peaceful either. On the day that Naief and the other boys were arrested, demonstrations took place in Damascus against the beating up of a shopkeeper by the police, but dispersed peacefully after the Interior Minister promised an investigation. The following weeks saw more demonstrations and subsequent promises by the government for reforms, including an end to the 48-year state of emergency imposed in the wake of the Hama massacre. Similarly, on the day of rage in Dara'a, there were small demonstrations in Damascus and other cities. Until then, the grievances had been local, and the demand was for the freedom of the boys and getting rid of Atef Najib, but the day the boys got free and their stories of torture became public knowledge, the people torched the Ba'ath Party building in Dara'a, and demonstrations became a daily affair, spreading to other provinces like Homs, Hama, Damascus and Latakia.

State's Response to the Crisis

When Naief Abazid wrote the anti-Assad graffiti on his school wall, there was a prompt and disproportionate reaction by the state, represented by the Chief Mukhabarat officer in Dara'a, Atef Najib, the son of Fatima Makhlouf (sister of Bashar al-Assad's mother Anisa al-Assad). Atef Najib was the ultimate point of contact between the Syrian state and the people in Dara'a, and living up to his reputation (Sands et al, 2014a) of being a brash, ruthless and authoritarian person, he dealt with the graffiti incident with an iron hand. When the local elders reached his office to request for the release of the Dara'a boys, he allegedly insulted them by responding, "Forget your children. Just make more children. And if you don't know how to make more, I'll send someone to show you" (MacKinnon, 2016). He ordered the police to deal with the protestors sternly and was the one responsible for the torture of the Dara'a boys. A member of an influential Dara'a family mentioned that in the beginning it was a revolution against Najib, and everyone wanted Najib gone instead of Assad (Sands et al., 2014b).

Atef Najib was an accomplice of Hafiz al-Assad's eldest son Basel al-Assad and was part of the Syrian intelligence. He was kicked out of the Mukhabarat by Basel as his father did not approve of Najib's arrogant and ruthless behaviour. A year before the death of Hafiz, Najib was reinstated in the Mukhabarat and around 2008, he was put in charge of the political security branch in Dara'a (Lister, 2016). Once in control of Dara'a, he converted it into his fiefdom and a reign of terror engulfed the region.

The imprisonment and torture of the boys enraged the Dara'a residents and led them to protest against the regime. Dara'a is a Sunni majority region where people of the older generation had still not overcome the fear created by the Hama massacre of 1982 (MacKinnon, 2016), but the young blood had no such first-hand experience and was not ready to take atrocities quietly. Anthony N. Celso (2017) emphasises that the role of the Muslim Brotherhood is significant in the Syrian crisis, the roots of which go back to the Hama massacre in which an estimated 25,000 Sunni residents were killed by the regime in order to repress the rebellion (Amnesty International, 2012). Second, the Dara'a residents were aware of the unrest going in Tunisia and Egypt. It would not be wrong to say that their Arab brethren raising voices and taking up arms against their regimes encouraged the Dara'a people to take a stand against the Assad regime.

Other than Atef Najib, there were other officers like Wafiq Nasser in Suweyda (Firas, 2016) who were equally authoritarian and played a crucial role in the beginning of the uprising. It did not take much time for the revolution to graduate its demand from removal of a particular officer to removal of Bashar al-Assad. Under the tutelage of Assad, the Syrian authorities crushed the rebellion by firing on unarmed people. They sent tanks to isolate Dara'a from the other areas, and deployed naval forces, troops, helicopters, soldiers and paramilitary fighters to take control of the cities. The regime gave absolute power to the Mukhabarat and used chemical weapons on its own people, showing the least regard for human rights (MacKinnon, 2016). Apart from these repressive measures, Assad also used the policy of appeasement and promised reforms. He lifted the 48-year-old emergency laws in April 2011 and proposed the draft of a new Constitution that would be put up to a public referendum (Assad, 2013). He abolished the Higher State Security Court and issued a decree regulating the right to peaceful protest as one of the basic human rights guaranteed by the Syrian Constitution (Maktabi et al., 2011).

Assad promised to make the guilty officers accountable for their crimes: and in some cases, he disowned responsibility, while in others, he acted as per his convenience. A special judicial committee was set up in

June 2011 to investigate allegations against the security officers, headed by Judge Mohammed Deeb Al-Muqatran who banned Atef Najib from travelling abroad (Sands et al., 2014b). Faisal Kalthoum was sacked as Governor of Dara'a before the soldiers raided the Omari Mosque claming that it had become a safe haven for foreign conspirators (Ibid.). Similarly, the President earned the support of the Druze community in Sweida province by removing Wafiq Nasser from his post as head of the Military Intelligence Directorate's local branch in Sweida at the behest of Sheikh al-Aql Hammud al-Hinnawi, the leader of the Druze community (Lang, 2014). In his December 2011 interview to Barbara Walters of ABC News (Goldman, 2011), Assad disowned responsibility for the brutality committed by his forces and shifted the blame onto individual officers. He stated, "Every 'brute reaction' was by an individual, not by an institution … there is a difference between having a policy to crackdown and between having some mistakes committed by some officials. There is a big difference" (Goldman, 2011).

Opposition and Other Groups in Syria

When the Syrian regime sent tanks on 24 April 2011 (Shadid, 2011) to encircle Dara'a and crush the uprising by isolating it from other parts of Syria, the Sunni soldiers who had grown up in Dara'a and the neighbourhood registered their unwillingness to fire on their own people. Subsequently, the regime was cautious while using the Army against its own people in Dara'a and it mainly used the loyalist non-Sunni units on the ground while keeping the Arab Sunni units in the barracks (Beauchamp, 2015). These Sunni soldiers began to defect, and it marked the beginning of the opposition in the form of the Free Syrian Army (FSA). Similarly, on 27 March, four days after the Omari Mosque was raided by soldiers, Member of Parliament Yusuf Abu Rumiah demanded that Assad should ensure that Atef Najib was punished for his deeds, though those remarks did not feature in the parliamentary footage telecast on state television (Sands et al., 2014).

The Syrian crisis did not have an organised opposition, leadership or a clear agenda, and this was considered to be one of the reasons for the lack of momentum in the rebellion during the initial days (Sheikh, 2013). Though people under the fragmented opposition demanded the removal of Assad, they did not have a plan or a vision for the aftermath. Meanwhile, several opposition groups emerged in Syria in the course of the civil war with the objective of removing Assad from power but without any common plan. Majid Rafizadeh (2014) has classified the opposition groups into five categories as per their affiliation and ideology: "1. Armed rebel groups and revolutionaries. 2. Oppositional groups. 3. Various governmental forces and groups. 4. Foreign *Salafi-Jihadist* groups, Al-Qaeda affiliated groups. 5. Pro-government foreign armed rebel groups" (p. 48). On the other hand, groups such as the Jaysh al-Muwahhiddin, Kataib Hizbullah and Baath Brigades, among others, emerged in support of the Assad regime (Rafizadeh, 2014).

Among the local opposition, the FSA emerged as the most recognised group. The FSA was founded by Colonel Riyad al-Assad with the aim to protect the people protesting peacefully against the Assad regime and to initiate resistance against his security forces. It comprised the defected Army officers and many former Syrian Army conscripts. Colonel Riyad al-Assad aspired to make the FSA a centrally commanded insurgent organisation but could not succeed. However, the FSA emerged as an umbrella organisation for various rebel groups. The FSA failed to control the militia associated with it due to lack of centralisation, and many of those groups began operating as 'criminal outfits' (Laub, 2017).

The Islamist elements of the FSA began drifting towards the *jihadi* camp in 2012 as the FSA suffered battlefield defeats owing to lack of regional support and resources. Unlike the FSA, groups such as the Jaish al-Islam and Ahrar al-Sham aimed at remaking the state and society as per the principles of Islam. They emerged in mid-2011 when more than a thousand insurgents who had fought in Iraq after 2003 were released by Bashar al-Assad. After their formation, they have often allied with the former Al-Qaeda affiliate Jabhat al-Fatah al-Sham, formerly known as Jabhat al-Nusra, but, at times, have clashed with them. The opposition groups in Syria had a fluid nature and alliances were built and broken in short spells of time, based on local issues and agendas. The extremely dynamic and evolving nature of the opposition groups becomes clear if one traces the graduation of the Jabhat al-Nusra to Jabhat Fatah al-Sham and then evolving into the Hay'at Tahrir al-Sham.

The Jabhat al-Nusra emerged in 2012 as a *jihadist* force and within a year, became an important military actor in the insurgency. It was affiliated with Al-Qaeda and this became apparent when it distanced itself from the ISIS, and its leader Abu Muhammad al-Jowlani declared a 'renewal' of the allegiance to Al-Qaeda leader Ayman al-Zawahiri. However, in 2016, the Jabhat al-Nusra broke its ties with Al-Qaeda and renamed itself as Jabhat Fatah al-Sham. While announcing the break from Al-Qaeda, Abu al-Khayr al-Masri, the deputy of Ayman al-Zawahiri emphasised that necessary steps should be taken to preserve the *jihad* in Syria and bring about unity among all the *jihadist* organisations (Al-Tamimi, 2018). Later, in 2017, the Hay'at Tahrir al-Sham (HTS) was formed as a result of the merger between the Jabhat Fatah al-Sham and factions such as the Jabhat Ansar al-Din, Harakat Nour al-Din al-Zinki, Liwa al-Haqq and Jaysh al-Sunna. The HTS was formed to counter the growing strength of the Ahrar al-Sham which was getting support from several smaller factions. The Harakat Nour-al Din al-Zinki and Jaysh al-Ahrar defected from HTS in early 2018 after HTS established a salvation government with 11 ministries in the areas of its control in late 2017.

As the crisis in Syria continued, several alliances and coalitions were formed in order to present a united front against the Syrian regime. The Syrian National Coalition (SNC) was formed in December 2011 and included people associated with the Damascus Declaration of 2005, Syrian Muslim Brotherhood, various Kurdish factions, representatives of local coordination committees, Alawi and Assyrian communities and independent figures (Pradhan, 2014). The SNC was dominated by Sunni Muslims and struggled to win over the Christians and Alawis. A year later, at the Doha meeting, a more diverse and inclusive Syrian opposition coalition was formed called the National Coalition for Syrian Revolutionary and Opposition Forces (NCSROF). Its blueprint was outlined in a document based on the July 2012 Cairo Conference, published by the dissident Riad Saif who served as its Vice President (NCSROF, 2018). NCSROF was formed to gain more widespread international recognition and increased financial and material support. However, like the SNC, NCSROF was unable to control the *jihadi* forces of Syria, struggled to address the humanitarian crisis due to lack of funding, and was overtly controlled by foreign powers. In July 2013, candidates backed by Saudi Arabia ousted those backed by Qatar, and Ahmed Jarba, with close ties to Riyadh, was elected as the President, defeating Mustafa Sabbagh who had links with Doha.

In the middle of 2017, the Unified National Army (UNA) was created to bring together the armed groups of various ideological and political backgrounds, spread out and fighting in various regions of Syria, including Aleppo, Ghouta and Idlib (Abboud, 2017). The Ahrar al-Sham formed in 2012 was the main group in the UNA. The Ahrar al-Sham was formed by the Seydnaya prisoners, released in 2011 by Bashar al-Assad, who adhered to Salafi Islam. The prisoners formed small groups in villages and came under the umbrella of the Ahrar al-Sham with the aim to establish a civilised Islamic society in Syria after overthrowing Assad. It was led by Abu Abdallah al-Hamawi. It succeeded in capturing Raqqa and Idlib from the regime, and portrayed itself as an independent force, however, it fought alongside the Jabhat al-Nusra during the crisis. It rejected the FSA and SNC but joined the West-backed revolutionary Command Council (El-Yassir, 2016). The Ahrar al-Sham is backed by Turkey and Qatar. On the question of signing the revolutionary covenant declaring a commitment to fight not only against the Assad regime but also the ISIS, it differed from the Jabhat al-Fatah al-Sham which opposed the covenant (Scott, 2014). Though formed with good intentions, the chances of success for the UNA were slim owing to the internal divisions, the geographic distribution of the rebel groups and the involvement of foreign powers (Porter, 2017).

The ISIS Phenomenon

Though the ISIS is not a direct product of the Syrian crisis as it originated as an Al-Qaeda offshoot in Iraq, it certainly played a decisive role in Syria and changed the course of the crisis from a regional to an international challenge. Two years after the formation of Al-Qaeda by Abu Musab al-Zarqawi in 2004, Abu Ayyub al-Masri created the Islamic State of Iraq and proclaimed Abu Omar al-Baghdadi as its leader. In 2010, after the death of Al-Masri and Al-Baghdadi, Abu Bakr al-Baghdadi became the leader of the Islamic State of Iraq. As the Arab Spring reached Syria and a few opposition groups emerged, the Islamic State of Iraq expanded its forte, claimed the Al-Qaeda backed Jabhat al-Nusra as its branch in Syria in 2013 and was renamed as the Islamic State of Iraq and Syria or ISIS.

Within a year, the ISIS took control of Falluja, al-Qaim, Mosul and Tikrit in Iraq, along with Raqqa in Syria and it announced the creation of a borderless Islamic Caliphate and rebranded itself as the 'Islamic State'. Following that, the ISIS occupied Syria's largest oil field and a gas field in Homs, and expanded its control over a 90-mile stretch from Deir Ezzor to the Iraq border. By 2016, the ISIS gained complete hold over large swaths of territory in Syria, including Palmyra, Raqqa, Aleppo and South Damascus and was responsible for the death of many people in other parts of Syria as well as in the world (CNN, 2017).

The ISIS' terror activities, its brutal methods of beheadings, *jihadist* propaganda through digital and social media, ability to attract significant numbers of foreign fighters from the European countries, and ability to inspire a series of lone-wolf attacks across Europe and in the US shocked the world. This proved to be a crucial turning point in the Syrian crisis as the focus shifted from the removal of Assad to defeating the ISIS. The rise of the ISIS not only internationalised the crisis but brought adversarial regional and global actors, including the US, Russia, Iran and Turkey to the Syrian theatre with the agenda to combat the ISIS. By the end of 2015, the US began Operation Inherent Resolve, and around the same time, Russia began its anti-ISIS air strikes in Syria which culminated in the loss of 95 per cent of the ISIS territories, including Raqqa by the end of 2017 (Rowan, 2018). In the beginning of 2018, the ISIS had control over a major portion near the Syria-Iraq border and smaller territories in Deir Ezzor, Idlib, and South Damascus. David Ignatius (2015) has observed that the ISIS was able to have a wide reach and gained momentum as it combined its reverence for Islamic piety with the use of social media platforms and encryption techniques. It depended on taxes, fees, oil, kidnapping, lootings, confiscations, fines, sale of antiquities and foreign donations (BBC, 2018).

The Refugee Crisis

The Syrian crisis which began as a local issue, soon had grave implications for the whole region, and impacted neighbouring countries through a ripple effect. As Syria became unstable, people began to migrate in large numbers to other stable countries which, in turn, generated distinct responses from them. According to the PEW Research Centre, about 13 million Syrian citizens have been displaced over the course of the civil war; while nearly six million are internally displaced, the rest have been forced to migrate to neighbouring countries in the Middle East, with Turkey (3.4 million), Lebanon (1 million), Jordan (660,000), Iraq (250,000), Egypt and Libya (150,000) as the major hosts (UNHCR, 2018). As a spillover from these countries, nearly one million asylum seekers and refugees reached Europe and were distributed among Germany (500,000), Sweden (110,000) and Austria (50,000) (Connor, 2018). France, the United Kingdom, Denmark, Hungary, Spain, Netherlands, Switzerland, Bulgaria, Italy, Greece and Australia too have small numbers of Syrian refugees. Apart from that, around 100,000 Syrian refugees live in North America, especially Canada (52,000) and the US (21,000).

As the refugees were desperately looking for safe havens and the concerned countries took steps to accommodate them, the oil-rich Gulf Arab countries were accused of not accepting the refugees. The Gulf countries are not a party to the 1951 UN treaty on refugees which says that protecting refugees is the primary responsibility of states (Martinez, 2015). Since they are not bound to comply with the treaty, these countries do not differentiate between a common person and a war refugee applying for a visa. It is also important to note that the unwillingness to accept refugees comes from the demographic challenge that the Gulf countries are going through. All the Gulf Arab countries, except Saudi Arabia and Oman have expatriates outnumbering the native population which can pose a threat to their stability. Irrespective of accepting or non-accepting refugees, in both ways, rentier Gulf countries are exposed to the threats of instability caused by the Arab Spring. In their defence, the Gulf countries claim that they have been accepting Syrians fleeing from the war and have provided better living conditions for them. For instance, the Saudi Foreign Ministry claims that it has hosted 2.5 million refugees since the beginning of the crisis and around 100,000 Syrian students are enrolled in Saudi schools (PRNewswire, 2015). The UAE government maintains that it has around 242,000 Syrians and has provided residency permits to more than 100,000 Syrian refugees (Amos, 2015). Similarly, Kuwait too claims that it has provided long-term residency permits to Syrians (Toumi, 2015).

When the Syrians fled to neighbouring Arab and other developed countries, most of their hosts welcomed them, portraying a positive image for themselves, but as various problems due to the imbalance in demography began to emerge (like Lebanon turned into an arena of conflict as Shia individuals as well as Syrian regime critics were killed and riots took place in the Zataari refugee camp in Jordan), they adopted policies to prevent the inflow of the Syrian refugees. For instance, initially Turkey spent US$ 15 million to set up six camps for the refugees, but later, it started building walls along the border with Syria. Lebanon, which had agreed to register refugees in 2013, imposed visa restrictions on Syrian asylum seekers.

In October 2013, 15 Organisation for Economic Cooperation and Development (OECD) countries and Moldova made pledges to the UN High Commissioner for Refugees (UNHCR) to offer resettlement opportunities to Syrian refugees (UNHCR, 2013). Two years later, Hungary closed its border with Serbia to deter migrants and border checks were established in Sweden. Greece and Bulgaria deterred the Syrian refugees by using armed forces to push then back and built fences on their borders. Along with the states, the people of these countries too did not give a positive response to the refugees; for instance, in Hungary, a referendum was held on 2 October 2016 to decide the refugee quotas, but it failed. Similarly, a majority of Germans opposed Angela Merkel's open-door policy (Paterson, 2015). To overcome these challenges, efforts were made to resolve the issue and an International Pledging Conference took place in Kuwait in March 2015, followed by the European Union (EU) summit in Brussels. The same year, the European Commission presented a proposal for the reallocation of asylum seekers across the EU member states. Italy, Greece, Hungary, France, Germany and Spain supported the move, while the others opposed it.

Role of International Actors

The roots of the Syrian crisis certainly lie within the country, but the role of regional and international actors in prolonging it cannot be denied. Seen holistically, one can identify the proxy wars going on between the various groups though the scenario is complicated, and a detailed discussion is beyond the scope of this chapter. However, it is important to underline the complex international involvement in Syria. There is an internal war between the rebels or the Nusra Front which adheres to extremist Islam, and the regime which is an advocate of moderate Islam. Apart from that, there is the conflict between the ISIS and the moderate opposition forces in the Syrian theatre. The regional forces support the respective sides depending on their own interests; for instance, Saudi Arabia, Qatar, Jordan and Turkey support the Islamists as well as moderate opposition groups with diplomacy and logistics but oppose the ISIS with military action. They also oppose the Syrian regime with diplomacy and logistics. Iran supports the Assad regime, and is fighting all the opposition groups, including the ISIS, Islamist and non-Islamist rebels on behalf of the regime. Similarly, Russia supports the Assad regime with military action and opposes the ISIS, Islamists and moderate groups with military action (Shaheen et al., 2015).

On the one hand, Iran and Saudi Arabia are on opposite sides, in line with the Saudi-Iran rivalry, while, on the other, Qatar and Saudi Arabia, though supporting the rebels, disagree on the level of extremism. Saudi Arabia supports the Salafist groups whereas Qatar backs the Muslim Brotherhood, though both support some elements of *jihadist* groups (Khalil, 2015). The rift between Saudi Arabia and Qatar became clear when, in June 2017, Saudi Arabia, supported by Bahrain, the UAE and Egypt, isolated Qatar, accusing the latter of promoting terrorism in the region. Both had looked at the Syrian theatre as a means to enhance their regional influence. For Saudi Arabia, the removal of Assad and the emergence of a Sunni regime would have not only reduced the "Shia crescent" (Meir, 2012), but also strengthened its own position as the leader of Sunni Islam. Qatar, on the other hand, was looking to build on its recent foreign policy activism to emerge as an important regional state with far larger influence than its size.

Turkey too got actively involved in the Syrian theatre, mainly to counter the growing threat to its national security on account of the growing Kurdish gains across northern Syria. It supported the rebels against the Assad regime by backing the ethnic Syrian Turkmen, as its policy in Syria has been based on three pillars that is, replace the Assad regime with favourable opposition forces as part of its "zero problem with neighbours policy"; prevent the refugees from entering Turkey; and push for a safe zone (a part of the troika with Russia and Iran in Astana) in Syria for damage control and to avoid the advances by the Kurdish Democratic Union Party in northern Syria (Tokyay, 2016). Jordan, which got parted from Syria as a result of the Sykes Picot Agreement of 1916, shares socio-cultural similarity with Syria and has been hosting a large chunk of the refugees. It tried to tread a fine line, and in consonance with the US policy, it supported the rebels and a smooth transition of power, along with supporting the political verdict of the citizens (Mahmoud, 2014).

Israel maintained a neutral position as far as the Syrian crisis was concerned though it provided humanitarian aid to the war victims as part of Operation Good Neighbour (Gross, 2017). In the beginning, it supported the regime, wary of what would replace it, but later, keeping in mind the developments beneficial to Iran and the Hezbollah forces, changed its stand (Rabinovich, 2012). Of late, it has become concerned with the growing Iranian military presence in Syria and has successfully undertaken military strikes inside Syria to prevent a build-up of the Iranian military apparatus near the Syrian-Israeli boundary.

Internationalisation of the Conflict

International actors like the US and Russia played a more important role than the regional actors in Syria due to greater availability to them of dispensable resources and their major stakes in the region. The US had a policy of non-intervention and active reduction of its military footprint in the region when President Barrack Obama was in office. He made it clear that the US was not going to take military action against the Syrian regime though it did launch the bombing campaign in 2014 against the ISIS strongholds in Syria to check its spread. Though Obama intended to make a positive move on the ground and use it as a bargaining chip with Assad, the situation did not progress as expected. On the ground, the US was able to push back the ISIS with air raids, but at the negotiation front with the Assad regime, there was hardly any progress.

When President Donald Trump came to office in January 2017, he declared that he would go ahead with Obama's bombing campaign without demanding the removal of Assad but after the chemical bombing in Khan Shaykhun, his stance changed and the US started supporting the removal of Assad from power (Quamar, 2017). Since then, the US has been endorsing a negotiated settlement and transitional government in Syria while supporting the moderate rebels and main opposition group called the National Coalition in Syria. At the same time, it has ensured that its attack on the ISIS does not benefit Assad's forces (BBC, 2015). The US National Security Strategy Report released on 18 December 2017 mentions that the US was willing to collaborate with Russia in settling the Syrian crisis (US Department of State, 2017). The US opposes the ISIS and Islamist groups with military action, as well as opposes the Syrian regime, and supports the moderate groups with diplomacy and logistics (Shaheen et al., 2015).

Russia is a long-term ally of Assad, with historical ties with Syria. It supports the regime with military action and is against the opposition (Shaheen et al., 2015). Its proactive approach in support of the Assad regime can be attributed to the presence of its naval base in Tartus and air base in Latakia which are important for its access to the Black Sea. Politically, Russia supports the Syrian regime and claims that a political solution is the only option. Russia began air raids in September 2015 to eliminate the terrorists, but soon graduated to providing arms to the regime forces (Perry, 2015). From 2011 to 2018, Russia vetoed 12 UN Security Council Resolutions (UNSCRs) that could put Assad in a difficult situation (RTE, 2018). It also participated actively at international fora to bring peace in Syria. Indeed, Russia used the Syrian crisis to emerge as a bigger player in the region, as the US was taking a laid-back approach. It is the most important player in the Syrian peace talks being held in Astana since January 2017 and has a considerable say in the UN-sponsored peace process at Geneva which began in 2012 (Priya, 2017).

As far as the other international actors are concerned, France, which had once colonised Syria, took part in the air strikes against the ISIS as part of the US-led coalition and increased the intensity of those strikes after the

Paris terror attacks in May 2018. The terror attacks made it change focus from the removal of Assad to limiting the ISIS, and it does not hesitate to seek cooperation from the Syrian regime though it still aims to attain a credible political transition. The United Kingdom takes a balance stand: it opposes the regime and Islamist groups with diplomacy and logistics while opposing the ISIS with military force. It supports the moderate rebel groups such as the FSA with diplomacy and logistics (McCormack, 2018).

Conclusion

A year after the Syrian crisis began, in 2012, the UN Secretary General Ban Ki Moon appointed his predecessor Kofi Annan as the Joint UN-Arab League Special Envoy for Syria, showing the UN's intent to work for peace in Syria. Kofi Annan's six-point plan outlined in UNSCR 2042 by the Arab League and the UN became the basis of the Geneva Communiqué which has been reiterated in the Geneva talks (UN, 2018). After various rounds, the Geneva talks came to a standstill, with the regime, as well as the opposition forces not willing to compromise. The major bone of contention was the question of the removal of Assad. As the number of deaths and incidents of violence kept rising and chances of a ceasefire seemed grim, Russia, with Iran and Turkey, proposed to have ceasefire zones through the Astana talks till a viable political solution is found. The Astana talks, held in May 2017, established ceasefire zones. As the ceasefire continued, an attempt was made to discuss the question of a political transition at the Sochi Conference, followed by summits at Ankara and Tehran. Though these summits failed in achieving their objective, the peace talks continue and provide a ray of hope for an end to the crisis and return of stability in Syria.

References

Abboud, Samer (2017), "Who are Syria's Opposition Alliances?", Al-Jazeera. Accessed on 19 September 2018, https://www.aljazeera.com/news/2017/10/syria-opposition-alliances-171010075809951.html

Al Tamimi, Aymen Jawad (2018), "From Jabhat al-Nusra to Hay'at Tahrir al-Sham: Evolution, Approach and Future", Konrad Adenauer Stftung. Accessed on 19 September 2018, http://www.kas.de/wf/doc/kas_52977-1522-1-30.pdf?180629110914

Al-Assad, Bashar (2013), Speech delivered on 6 January 2013 in Damascus, addressed to heads and members of the leaderships of popular organisations and trade unions, Voltaire Network. Accessed on 15 February 2018, http://www.voltairenet.org/article177102.html

Alfifi, Majid, Parisa Kaghazgaran, and James Caverlee (2018), "Measuring the Impact of ISIS Social Media Strategy", Texas A&M University. Accessed on 20 September 2018, http://snap.stanford.edu/mis2/files/MIS2_paper_23.pdf.

Amnesty International (2012), "Syria: 30 Years on, Hama Survivors Recount the Horror", 28 February 2012. Accessed on 11 September 2018, https://www.amnesty.org/en/latest/news/2012/02/syria-years-hama-survivors-recount-horror/

Amos, Deborah (2015), "Gulf States Fend Off Criticism About Doing Little For Syrian Refugees", NPR, 20 September 2015. Accessed on 10 February 2018, https://www.npr.org/sections/parallels/2015/09/20/441457924/gulf-states-fend-off-criticism-about-doing-little-for-syrian-refugees

BBC (2018), Islamic State and the Crisis in Iraq and Syria in Maps". Accessed on 09 February 2018, http://www.bbc.com/news/world-middle-east-27838034

BBC (2015), "Syria Crisis: Where Key Countries Stand", 30 October 2015, BBC. Accessed on 20 September 2018, (2) http://www.bbc.com/news/world-middle-east-23849587

Beauchamp, Zach (2015), "The Syria War: A History", 21 September 2015, Vox. Accessed on 2 February 2018, https://www.vox.com/cards/syrian-refugees-war-assad/free-syrian-army

Celso, Anthony N. (2017), "Hama's Ominous Shadow and the Stalled Jihadist War in Syria", *Mediterranean Quarterly: A Journal of Global Issues*, Vol 28, No 1, March 2017.

CNN (2017), "ISIS: Fast Facts", December 12, 2017. Accessed on 20 September 2018, https://edition.cnn.com/2014/08/08/world/isis-fast-facts/index.html

Connor, Phillip (2018), "Most Displaced Syrians are in the Middle East, and About a Million are in Europe", 29 January 2018, Pew Research. Accessed on 3 February 2018, http://www.pewresearch.org/fact-tank/2018/01/29/where-displaced-syrians-have-resettled/

Discovering Islam, (2018), "Prophecy of Nachman (Chatufa) Pinchas", 20 July 2018, accessed on 12 August 2018, http://www.discoveringislam.org/jewish_signs.htm

El Yassir, Ali (2016), "The Ahrar al Sham Movement: Syria's Local Salafists", Wilson Centre". Accessed on 19 September 2018, https://www.wilsoncenter.org/article/the-ahrar-al-sham-movement-syrias-local-salafists-0

Firas, Al-Ali (2016), "Wafiq Nasser Follows in Atef Najib's Footsteps", Baladi News, Al Suwayda, 15 May 2016. Accessed on 19 February 2018, https://www.baladi-news.com/en/news/details/6137/Wafiq_Nasser_Follows_in_Atef_Najib&;s_Footsteps

Fivedoves.com (2013), "The Prophecies of the Child, Part 1: Nachman Chatupha Whose Name Means Rapture", February 2013. Accessed on 5 February 2018, http://www.fivedoves.com/letters/feb2013/jovial218-2.htm

Goldman, Russels (2011), "Defiant Assad Denies Ordering Bloody Syrian Crackdown", ABC News, 7 December 2011. Accessed on 18 January 2018, http://abcnews.go.com/International/bashar-al-assad-interview-defiant-syrian-president-denies/story?id=15098612

Gross, Judah Ari (2017), "Operation Good Neighbour: Israel Reveals its Massive Humanitarian Aid to Syria", *The Times of Israel*, 19 July 2017. Accessed on 10 January 2018 https://www.timesofisrael.com/operation-good-neighbor-israels-massive-humanitarian-aid-to-syria-revealed/

Ignatius, David (2015), "How ISIS Spread in the Middle East", *The Atlantic*, 29 October 2015. Accessed on 15 December 2017, https://www.theatlantic.com/international/archive/2015/10/how-isis-started-syria-iraq/412042/

Khalil, Abu Asad (2015), "The 8 Proxy Wars Going on in Syria Right Now", 6 March 2015. Accessed on 10 December 2017, https://www.huffingtonpost.com/asad-abukhalil/syria-proxy-wars_b_5874488.html

Lang, Tobias (2014), "Druze Sheikhs Protest in Sweida", Carnegie Middle East Centre. Accessed on 19 January 2018, http://carnegie-mec.org/diwan/55356

Laub, Zachary (2017), "Who's Who in Syria's Civil War", Council on Foreign Relations, updated 28 April 2017. Accessed on 18 September 2018, https://www.cfr.org/backgrounder/whos-who-syrias-civil-war

Lister, Charles R (2016), *The Syrian Jihad: Al-Qaeda, the Islamic State and the Evolution of an Insurgency* (London: Oxford University Press).

MacCormack, Tara (2018), "Why is Britain Funding Jihadis?" *Spiked*, 8 January 2018. Accessed on 20 September 2018, http://www.spiked-online.com/newsite/article/why-is-britain-funding-jihadis/20725#.W6NIP9czbcs

Mackinnon, Mark, 2016, "The Graffiti Kids Who Sparked The Syrian War", *The Globe and Mail*, Vienna, Friday, 2, December 2016. Accessed on 10 September 2018 https://www.theglobeandmail.com/news/world/the-graffiti-kids-who-sparked-the-syrian-war/article33123646/

Mahmoud, Khaled Waleed (2014), "Where Does Jordan Stand on the Syrian Crisis?", *Middle East Monitor*, 24 January 2014. Accessed on 19 November 2017, https://www.middleeastmonitor.com/20140124-where-does-jordan-stand-on-the-syrian-crisis/

Maktabi, Reema, Arwa Damon, Salma Abdelaziz, Yousuf Basil, Nada Husseini, and Hamdi Alkhshali (2011), "Al-Assad Lifts Unpopular Emergency Law, Special Court", 21 April 2011. Accessed on 11 September 2018, http://edition.cnn.com/2011/WORLD/meast/04/21/syria.unrest/index.html

Martinez, Michael (2015), "Syrian Refugees: Which Countries Welcome Them,

Which Ones Don't", CNN, 10 September 2015. Accessed on 19 September 2018, https://edition.cnn.com/2015/09/09/world/welcome-syrian-refugees-countries/index.html

Meir, Alon Ben (2012), "Syria: The Battleground between Sunnis and Shiites", 4 November 2012, *Huffington Post*. Accessed on 20 September 2018, https://www.huffingtonpost.com/alon-benmeir/syria-the-battleground-be_b_1418270.html

Menekse, Tokyay (2016), "How Turkey's Role In Syria's Crisis Has Evolved Over The Past Years", *Al Arabiya*, 15 March 2016. Accessed on 19 December 2017, https://english.alarabiya.net/en/2016/03/15/How-Turkey-s-role-in-Syria-has-evolved-over-the-past-years-.html

NCSROF (2018), "National Coalition for Syrian Revolutionary and Opposition Forces", Carnegie. Accessed on 18 September 2018, http://carnegie-mec.org/syriaincrisis/?fa=50628

Paterson, Tony (2015), "Refugee Crisis: Angela Merkel's Allies Could Desert her Over Germany's Open-Door Policy", 29 October 2018, *Independent*. Accessed on 20 September 2018, https://www.independent.co.uk/news/world/europe/refugee-crisis-angela-merkels-allies-could-desert-her-over-germanys-open-door-policy-a6714151.html

Perry, Tom (2015), "Exclusive: Syrian Army Starts Using New Weapons from Russia: Military Source", 18 September 2015, Reuters. Accessed on 20 September 2018, https://www.reuters.com/article/us-mideast-crisis-syria-russia-exclusive/exclusive-syrian-army-starts-using-new-weapons-from-russia-military-source-idUSKCN0RH15S20150918

Pipes, Daniel (1996), "Syria Beyond the Peace Process", Washington Institute for Near East Policy, Policy Papers, Number Forty, Washington DC.

Porter, Lizzie (2017), "Analysis: Unified Rebel Army Is Too Little, Too Late", 5 October 2017, *Syria Deeply*. Accessed on 19 September 2018, https://www.newsdeeply.com/syria/articles/2017/10/05/analysis-unified-rebel-army-is-too-little-too-late

Pradhan, P. K. (2014), "Syrian Uprising: March Towards Future Instability," in Anwar Alam (ed.), *Arab Spring: Reflections on Political Changes in the Arab World and its Future* (New Century Publications), pp. 119-136.

Priya, Lakshmi (2017), "Astana Talks: A Prelude to Peace in Syria," *IDSA Backgrounder*, https://idsa.in/backgrounder/astana-talks-a-prelude-to-peace-in-syria_lpriya_271117.

PRNewswire, (2015), "Saudi Arabia Received 2.5 Million Syrians since Beginning of Conflict", 11 September 2015, PR Newswire. Accessed on 20 September 2018, https://www.prnewswire.com/news-releases/saudi-arabia-received-25-million-syrians-since-beginning-of-conflict-300141800.html

Quamar, Md. Muddassir (2017), "Will Khan Sheikhoun Reshape the War in Syria?" *IDSA Comment*, April 7, https://idsa.in/idsacomments/will-khan-sheikhoun-reshape-the-war-in-syria_mmquamar_070417. Accessed on 7 August 2017.

Rabinovich, Itamar (2012), "Israel's View of the Syrian Crisis", Saban Centre for Middle East Policy at Brookings, November 2012. Accessed on 18 January 2018, https://www.brookings.edu/wp-content/uploads/2016/06/Rabinovich-web-final.pdf

Rafizadeh, Majid (2014), *The Syrian Civil War: Four Concentric Circles of Tensions*, Graduate thesis, University of South Florida.

Rowan, Mattisan (2018), "ISIS after the Caliphate", 8 January 2018, Wilson Centre. Accessed on 19 September 2018, https://www.wilsoncenter.org/article/isis-after-the-caliphate-0

RTE, (2018), "Russia's 12 UN Vetoes on Syria", 11 April 2018, RTE. Accessed on 20 September 2018, https://www.rte.ie/news/world/2018/0411/953637-russia-syria-un-veto/

Sands, Phil, Justin Vela and Suha Maayeh (2014a), "Syria Conflict: Atef Najib, the Man who Sparked the Uprising, the National", 17 March 2014. Accessed on 15 January 2018, https://www.thenational.ae/world/syria-conflict-atef-najib-the-man-who-sparked-the-uprising-1.328020

Sands, Phil, Justin Vela and Suha Maayeh (2014b), "Joined in Blood", *The National*, 20 March 2014. Accessed on 2 September 2018, https://www.thenational.ae/world/joined-in-blood-1.259560

Scott, Lucas (2014), "Syria Document: Insurgents Issue 'Revolutionary Covenant'", 18 May 2014, EA world view. Accessed on 19 September 2018, https://eaworldview.com/2014/05/syria-document-insurgents-issue-revolutionary-covenant/

Shadid, Anthony (2011), "Syria Escalates Crackdown as Tanks Go to Restive City", 25 April 2011. Accessed on 11 September 2018. https://www.nytimes.com/2011/04/26/world/middleeast/26syria.html

Shaheen, Kareem, Paul Torpey, Pablo Gutierrez, Cath Levett (2015), "Who Backs Whom in the Syrian Conflict", Institute for the Study of War, *The Guardian*, 2 December 2015. Accessed on 13 September 2018, https://www.theguardian.com/world/ng-interactive/2015/oct/09/who-backs-whom-in-the-syrian-conflict

Sheikh, Salman (2013), "The Challenge of Syrian Unity: Reassuring Local Communities and Framing National Consensus", Syria Workshop series, Brookings Doha Centre, June 2013, Doha. Accessed on 9 February 2018, https://www.brookings.edu/wp-content/uploads/2016/06/BDC_Challenge-Syrian-Unity_Eng.pdf

Tisdall, Simon (2015), "US Changes its Tune on Syrian Regime Change as Isis Threat Takes Top Priority", 25 January 2015, *The Guardian*. Accessed on 20 September 2018, https://www.theguardian.com/us-news/2015/jan/25/us-syrian-regime-change-isis-priority

Toumi, Habib (2015), "Kuwait Extends Residency Permits for Syrians", 2 September 2015, *Gulf News*. Accessed on 20 September 2018, https://gulfnews.com/news/mena/syria/kuwait-extends-residency-permits-for-syrians-1.1577117

UN (2018), "Syria". Accessed on 20 September 2018, https://www.un.org/undpa/en/middleeast-westasia/syria

UNHCR (2013), "Finding Solutions for Syrian Refugees", 18 October 2013, UNHCR. Accessed on 20 September 2018, http://www.refworld.org/pdfid/53ad36614.pdf

UNHCR (2018), "Syrian Regional Refugee Response". Accessed on 20 September 2018, https://data2.unhcr.org/en/situations/syria

US Department of State (2017), "National Security Strategy of USA", December 2017. Accessed on 11 January 2018 https://www.whitehouse.gov/wp-content/uploads/2017/12/NSS-Final-12-18-2017-0905.pdf

4. Salafists in Egyptian Politics: Al-Nour since 2011

Paulami Sanyal

Abstract

The Salafists have been involved in the political transformation in Egypt in the wake of the 2011 popular uprising. The Al-Nour Party (Hizb al-Nour), which owes its origin to the Al-Dawa al-Salafiyya (the Salafist Call), was established after the ouster of President Hosni Mubarak, and survived under various governments. While the 2014 Constitution proscribes creation of a political party on religious basis, the Al-Nour Party remained free to participate in the 2015 parliamentary election. The chapter examines the role of the Al-Nour Party in Egyptian politics and analyses the rise of the party, the moderately defused status that it has acquired lately, and whether the government's increasing hostility to political Islam puts the party's future in jeopardy.

Key Words: Egypt; Salafism; Al-Nour; Al-Dawa; Morsi; Abdel Fattah al-Sisi

One of the many changes that appeared in Egyptian politics after the ouster of President Hosni Mubarak was the emergence of Islamist parties. The Muslim Brotherhood secured the largest number of seats in the 2011-12 parliamentary elections and its presidential candidate won the May-June 2012 election. While the Muslim Brotherhood was politically active even prior to the uprising, an unprecedented measure was taken by the Egyptian Salafists. Before 2011, a majority of the Salafists were apathetic towards politics: they condemned politics as heretical or were reluctant to participate due to the fear of state repression. Taking advantage of the post-Mubarak uncertainty and political void, a number of Salafist organisations formed political branches. Al-Nour or the political wing of the Salafist group Al-Dawa al-Salafiyya was prominent among them and obtained the second highest number of seats in the first post-Mubarak parliamentary elections. Some of the other Salafist political parties are the Al-Asala Party or Authenticity Party (formed in July 2011), Al-Fadhila Party or Virtue Party (June 2011) and Al-Bena wa'l Tanmiya Party or Building and Development Party (June 2011), etc. (*Ahram Online*, 2011; Dabbash, 2011; Al-Anani, 2011).

In the years after Mubarak's removal, the political situation of Egypt experienced some unexpected alterations. What seemed to be the arrival of a pro-Islamist government, faltered, and within a year, the Muslim Brotherhood was banned. During this period, Egypt witnessed two parliamentary elections (2011-12 and 2015) and three presidential elections (2012, 2014 and 2018). Taking a different turn from the pro-Islamist course, Field Marshal Abdel Fattah al-Sisi won the presidential election in 2014 and was re-elected in March 2018. Most of the Islamist political parties faced lawsuits under Article 74 of the 2014 Constitution which prohibits religion-based political organisations.

Under these restrictions, not only did Al-Nour survive while other religion-based political groups such as the Freedom and Justice Party (FJP), the Muslim Brotherhood's political wing, were banned but Al-Nour also managed to play a role in the political developments under President Sisi. To survive under different governments and internal challenges, Al-Nour shifted its strategy and changed its planned course of action from being politically apathetic to being politically active.

Egyptian Salafism, Al-Dawa and Al-Nour

Salafism has a strong presence in Egypt and it would not be wrong to argue that the Salafist trend in contemporary Islam has partially originated in modern Egypt (Lauzière, 2015). It is perhaps for this reason that there is greater variation within Egyptian Salafism on important contemporary Islamic questions such as apostasy, political activism and *jihad*. Prior to the Free Officers' Movement of 1952, Salafism was concerned only with increasing the role of the *Sharia* in the British-influenced Egyptian society. Two organisations were created during this time, namely, *Al-Jama'a al-Shari'a li-al-'Amilin bi-al-Kitab wa-alsSunna* (Lawful Association of the Adherents of the Book and the Sunna) in 1912 and Ansar al-Sunna al-Muhammadiya (Society of the Supporters of the Muhammadan Sunna) in 1926. Even though both organisations demonstrated certain political awareness,[1] their primary activities remained in the theological domain (Høigilt and Nome, 2014; El-Sherif, 2015). Gradually the popularity of these institutions grew, and the Ansar al-Sunna became one of the most important Salafi associations, with branches in the lower middle class neighbourhoods of Cairo and in the delta region, such as Damanhur, Mansoura and Alexandria (El-Sherif, 2015).

The next change in the Salafi movement emerged in the 1970s when President Anwar Sadat attempted to coopt political Islam for countering the socialist opposition. After his initial interest, he refused to impose the *Sharia* law and this generated renewed attention in Salafi movements, primarily among university students of Alexandria, Cairo and southern Egypt. Each city's Salafi movement bore different characteristics. The groups of Alexandria and Cairo developed a non-violent approach as against the violence-prone Salafi movement of southern Egypt (Henzel, 2005; Høigilt and Nome, 2014). Students organisations such as the Al-Gama'at al-Islamiyya (Islamic Group) turned against the government and started using violence for political purposes (Heffelfinger, 2007).

Salafism in Egypt, thus, acquired its multifarious character. Although its principal standpoint remained the same, namely, revival of purist Islam, there are differences of attitudes among its followers. Broadly, these can be categorised into three factions: (a) those apathetic to politics; (b) those seeking political participation; and (c) those espousing armed struggle. The first group limits its activities to religious pedagogy and charitable works while the second group believes in being actively involved in politics, sometimes through initiating collective action against the government (Wiktorowicz, 2006). The Ansar al-Sunna al-Muhammadiya, for example, is a group with political apathy. It took the stand during the initial period of the 2011 popular protest that opposing a ruler in

1. Al-Jam'ya al-Sharia was associated with two magazines (*Al-Itisam* and *Al-Tibyan*) which are considered partly political; and Ansar al-Sunna's charter demands an Islamic nation based on the *Sharia* (Høigilt and Nome, 2014)

the present context "is not permissible, even if he (the ruler) transgresses and creates injustice" (Boehmer and Murphy, 2012, p. 29). However, Al-Dawa al-Salafiyya (Salafist Call), the religious wing of Al-Nour, is a group which has preached and attempted legislative actions (El-Sherif, 2015).

The third group calls for violence against the regimes for following an unIslamic path (Wiktorowicz, 2006; Gauvain, 2013; El-Sherif, 2015). The al-Gama'at al-Islamiyya is an example of this category: its beliefs and religious practices are similar to these of Salafism, but it participated in terrorist attacks on tourists and civilians during the 1970s and 1990s and denounced terrorism only in 2003 (Brown, 2011; Lacroix, 2016).[2]

One of the most significant Salafi groups and subsequently the religious wing of Al-Nour is Al-Dawa al-Salafiyya. It was established in the 1970s in Alexandria and its founders were students of the Alexandria University who broke away from Al-Gama'at al-Islamiyya (Lacroix, 2012). The chief founder, Sheikh Mohammed Ismail al-Moqadim, was influenced by Saudi Islamic scholars such as Sheikh Abdel Aziz Bin-Baz and Sheikh Mohammed ibn Saleh al-Othaimin. Unlike the Muslim Brotherhood, Al-Dawa did not possess a formal organisational structure, and in its initial years, limited itself to preaching. Among the students, the group enhanced its presence through Islamic camps, lectures or leaflets. In 1986, the Al-Furqan Institute for Preparing Preachers was established for teaching Salafi ideology, which later built up a religious education network and published a monthly magazine, *Al-Dawa*. In view of its increasing influence on the citizens, the government closed down this institute, dissolved its executive council and banned the magazine in 1994 (Wright, 2012). Even though certain repressive measures were taken against the group, for example, imprisoning its members on several occasions, the organisation managed to continue its social and religious activities because of its secret networks and strong social presence (Lacroix, 2012).

One of the after effects of the 2011 uprising was the formation of several new political parties. Al-Nour emerged during this time as an

2. After some of its leaders were imprisoned for more than two decades, and discussions with Al-Azhar University scholars, members of this group wrote several books renouncing violence. The imprisoned leaders also provided interviews to the press condemning terrorism (Gunaratna and Bin Ali, 2009).

attempt to initiate political action while still maintaining Al-Dawa's religious and social activities. Emad Abdel Ghaffour, an early supporter of the revolution, convinced the Al-Dawa Sheikhs to form a political party. Al-Nour was officially established on 15 June 2011, with Abdel Ghaffour as the first President (Lacroix, 2012). Formation of the party maintained a balance between its Salafi roots and political fluidity which was necessary to develop support beyond Al-Dawa followers (Lacroix, 2012; Ghalwash and Phillips, 2017). For example, a group of academic experts were called upon to build the groundwork of the political party. Many of these academicians were not Salafists but participated alongside the Al-Dawa leaders.

Al-Nour also claimed that it had established a partnership with Japanese experts to reform the education system of Egypt. A party spokesperson was chosen through an open competition. Most of the competitors were relatively young and the youngest one, 27-year-old Nader Bakkar, eventually won the position. The selection of Bakkar, with a degree in management, as the party spokesperson, reflected the image Al-Nour wanted to attain: its support for the revolutionary youth and the changes occurring in the country (Lacroix, 2012).

Ideological Shift

The Salafist doctrine generally conveys the idea of an orthodox Islamic movement but to place such an ideology in the emerging pluralistic politics required maintaining a balance between the Salafi Sheikhs and the largely-secular Egyptian population (El-Sherif, 2015). Assuming a political status meant Al-Nour could not have followed every regulation imposed by Al-Dawa. On several occasions, it showed its willingness to collaborate with political parties of different ideologies. The party also introduced young and new faces as its candidates. Scholars such as Farhad Khosrokhavar (2012) and Stephane Lacroix (2016) opine that by abandoning their erstwhile apathy for politics, the Salafists recognised, and became a part of, a democratic system. Kamran Bokhari and Farid Senzai (2013) believe that attempts by the Egyptian Salafists to become politically active comprised a strategic move at a time of political uncertainty.

Either way, the Egyptian Salafism went through certain changes once it developed political branches. Al-Nour had to demonstrate its support for the revolutionaries and insisted on acquiring a gradual imposition of *Sharia* law which would be acceptable to the different factions of society. It criticised the Muslim Brotherhood for its inability to communicate with the opposition, the National Salvation Front, in 2013;[3] and it even backed the popular demands of the 25 January protesters (Ranko and Nedza, 2016).

The relationship between religion and the state has been a point of disagreement among the party members. Al-Nour's position remained quite unchanged on matters of implementing the *Sharia* law for protecting Egypt's Islamic identity. Even in the drafting committee for the 2014 Constitution, the Al-Nour member called for the removal of the word 'principles' from Article 2. The content of the Article entailed that the principles of *Sharia* law will form the main source of legislation and removing the word 'principle' implied a stricter imposition of *Sharia* law (*Ahram Online*, 2013). However, Al-Nour members have also recommended leniency in the application of the *Sharia* law and argued in favour of gradual imposition of the law to bring moderate changes in the society. A modern state, as per Al-Nour, is not equal to a theocratic state. In fact, Al-Nour's agenda in the 2011-12 parliamentary election emphasised more on the welfare of the citizens.

The party identified the requirement of national economic development and social justice through anti-poverty policies, creating civil societies to represent the diversified population and an environment to enhance the freedom and rights of the citizens (El-Sherif, 2015). Even for the 2015 parliamentary election, Al-Nour tried to maintain a balance by accepting the electoral rules imposed by the regime and not highlighting its religious ideas. By taking these measures, the party wanted to create the impression that it is like any

3. A National Salvation Front (NSF) was created on 24 November 2012 criticising President Morsi's constitutional declaration on 22 November. The front called for the withdrawal of the November declaration. However, instead of initiating a dialogue with the NSF, a draft of the Constitution was passed and President Morsi organised a referendum on the new draft on 15 December 2012 (Ranko and Nedza, 2016).

other political party which participates in the state mechanisms and does not threaten them (Youssef, 2015).

However, on several occasions, Al-Nour or Al-Dawa members have moved away from this pragmatic approach; for example, Al-Nour joined the Democratic Alliance for the 2011-12 parliamentary election but left the coalition in September 2011 due to its concern that the secular parties would have greater representation than their Islamist counterparts (Trager, 2016). Hazem Shouman, a Salafi cleric and an Al-Nour member declared in a speech in Mansoura on 6 November 2011, that Islamic rule is imminent and the secularists can do nothing to stop it. In another incident, he crashed the stage of a concert stating that such affairs are sinful (*Ahram Online*, 2011).

Al-Nour's approach towards religion is also challenged because of its position on the Coptic Christians. It calls for a Muslim male to be the President of Egypt since the majority of the population is Muslim (Cesari, 2013). There were no Coptic candidates in the party list for the 2011-12 parliamentary election. For the 2015 election, it was forced to include Copts in the party list as the electoral law reserved a quota for the Copts (Al-Anani, 2016).

On the question of women, Al-Nour's opinion did not deviate much from that of Al-Dawa. Because of the unwillingness of the Salafists to let women participate in the political system, the party's announcement of fielding 60 female candidates for the 2011-12 parliamentary election created a controversy within the party and among Al-Dawa members. It escalated to the point where the party President Abdel Ghaffour made a statement that fielding women candidates was a necessary measure to win seats as the law stipulated a quota for female candidates in the party lists. For the 2015 parliamentary election, the party laid down the condition that the women candidates needed to have 'good reputations' and should be committed to wearing the *hijab* (*Ahram Online*, 2014). Moreover it refused to display photos of its female candidates, replacing them with an image of flowers, with the name of the candidate in the 2011-12 parliamentary election (El-Sherif, 2015). This practice was repeated in 2015 as well and even the Coptic female candidates of Al-Nour had to follow it (Mikhail, 2015).

While the Coptic female candidates considered the issue to be a trivial one, their action was criticised by the Coptic Christians and the liberal secular factions of the society (Mikhail, 2015). The inclusion of women and Copts in the party list, even with certain limitations, showed Al-Nour's willingness to continue its political participation. Ashraf el-Sherif (2015) argues that in a way, Al-Nour has adopted the Brotherhood's strategy of acting according to necessity rather than within the religious dogma. By this argument, nomination of women in the party list as mandated by the law is considered a lesser evil than not participating in the election altogether.

Relations with Other Islamists

Egypt's largest moderate Islamist group, the Muslim Brotherhood has always had contentious relations with Al-Nour. During the tenure of President Mubarak (1981-2011), the Salafists maintained that the Brotherhood's political goals were making them sacrifice Islamic principles. The Muslim Brotherhood, on the other hand, criticised the Salafists for supporting the authorities instead of criticising or opposing the regime (Maged, 2011). After the ouster of Mubarak, there was a possibility that both would join forces and, indeed, a rapprochement was noticeable for a few months. Salafi leaders made positive statements about the Muslim Brotherhood; for example, Yasser Burhami, one of the founders of Al-Dawa, stated that the Salafists should offer their support to Muslim Brotherhood candidates in the parliamentary election. Muhammad Hassan, a Salafist cleric, also described the Brotherhood as "those who most deserve and are the most competent to enter Parliament" (Arafat, 2018, p. 70). The Muslim Brotherhood reciprocated these sentiments by demonstrating its wish to cooperate with Al-Nour for common political goals. The two groups jointly led the campaign to support the March 2011 constitutional amendments[4] and their effort was considered a success as 77 per cent of the voters approved of the amendments (Lacroix, 2016; Arafat, 2018).

This cooperation, however, was shortlived. The rift between them resurfaced when the Salafists turned up in the Kandahar Friday protest

4. The Constitution of 1971, which existed so far and was suspended on 13 February 2011, was amended and submitted for a public referendum on 19 March 2011 (Bassiouni, 2016).

on 29 July 2011,[5] with posters calling for the implementation of the *Sharia* and chanting in support of creating an Islamic nation (Blair and Awad 2011). The Brotherhood called for a quick transition to civilian rule and trial of the former officials of the Mubarak regime, like the rest of the protesting factions, and criticised the Salafists' action. In the 2012 presidential election, Al-Nour supported Abdel Moneim Aboul Fotouh over Mohamed Morsi. Aboul Fotouh was a former Muslim Brotherhood member campaigning as a moderate Islamist. In his campaign, he supported a *Sharia* law that would respect Egypt's diverse society. His campaign was inclusive of Islamists as well as other factions of the society.

Supporting Aboul Fotouh in the presidential election helped Al-Nour in two ways. First, it created an understanding that more than building an Islamic state following the *Sharia* law, the goal of the party was to elect a president who could represent a wide range of the population (Kirkpatrick and Sheikh, 2012). As its spokesperson Nader Bakkar put it, "We were looking for a President who can be a mere executive manager not an Islamic Caliph". Secondly, supporting Aboul Fotouh meant cutting into the support base of the Muslim Brotherhood, and thereby lessening its probable monopoly over the government (Al-Anani, 2012).

After the victory of Mohamed Morsi, Al-Nour tried to adapt to the situation by avoiding criticism of the President (Lacroix, 2016). The Brotherhood and Al-Nour also coordinated on the subject of drafting a new Constitution during this time. The June 2012 Constituent Assembly consisted of both Brotherhood and Al-Nour members and they had a common interest to make Islam a source of influence in the Constitution. Their joint effort resulted in Article 2[6] and Article 219[7] of the November 2012 Constitution (Lacroix, 2016). Al-Nour even supported President Morsi's controversial decree which prevented the judiciary from

---

5. This was a protest calling for elections as soon as possible, the resignation of the public prosecutor and meeting the demands of the families of the 25 January deceased (Blair and Awad, 2011).
6. Islam is the religion of the state and Arabic is its official language. The principles of Islamic *Sharia* are the principal source of legislation.
7. Principles of *Sharia*: The principles of Islamic *Sharia* include general evidence, foundational rules, rules of jurisprudence, and credible sources accepted in Sunni doctrines and by the larger community.

challenging his decisions, and protected the Shura Council from being dissolved by a court order (*Ahram Online*, 2012).

By the end of 2012, the internal crisis within Al-Nour had escalated. The struggle between the party President Emad Abdel Ghaffour and the Al-Dawa Sheikhs led to the removal of the former. While a group led by the founder of the party, Emad Ghaffour, wanted Al-Nour to be a religious party open to different political alliances and programme, the more religious factions associated with Al-Dawa wanted the party to serve the interests of the Salafi movements. To challenge the group of more politically oriented members, in January 2012, a number of *fatwas* were published on the personal website of Yasser Burhami, one of the founders of Al-Dawa (Lacroix, 2016). In one such *fatwa,* he criticised Emad Ghaffour's statement that Al-Nour was open to alliances with all political parties and in another he condemned Ghaffour for attending the National Day celebration in the Turkish Embassy. The group supporting Emad Ghaffour formed a Reform Front within the party, asking for Al-Dawa's support. However, this tension continued and in December 2012, Emad Ghaffour and his allies left the Al-Nour Party and established a new political party called the Hizb al-Watan (Homeland Party) (Lacroix, 2016).

This internal struggle made the differences between the Brotherhood and Al-Nour prominent. It was announced by Al-Nour that Ghaffour had been expelled because of his intentions of joining President Morsi's advisory team. Al-Nour members in the Parliament were offered only the portfolio of the Environment Ministry, which the party declined, criticising the Brotherhood's attempt to monopolise the Cabinet (Shukrallah, 2013). After the expulsion of Ghaffour, Al-Nour members of the Shura Council were more vocal about the Brotherhood's political tactics. For example, Tarek El-Sehri, the deputy head of the Shura Council, accused Prime Minister Hisham Qandil of being incompetent and demanded the dismissal of his government (Shukrallah, 2012).

In February 2013, Al-Nour criticised the Brotherhood for the state visit of Iranian President Mahmoud Ahmadinejad.[8] Al-Nour members

8. The hostility between Egypt and Iran continued after the removal of Iran's former Shah's regime. Egypt being a Sunni majority country is hostile to the Shia majority Iran. Moreover, Iran supports Syrian President Bashar al-Assad while Egypt has so far called for President Assad to step down (France24, 2013).

also engaged in a dialogue with the National Salvation Front, an alliance of opposition parties against President Morsi (*Ahram Online*, 2013; Shukrallah, 2013). It refused the call of the Al-Gama'at al-Islamiyya on 21 June 2013 for a demonstration in support of the President. The party justified its position by suggesting that such demonstrations were unnecessary and condemned the violence perpetrated by the demonstrators. The Brotherhood retaliated by accusing Khalem al-Din, member of the presidential advisory team, of corruption, and dismissing him. The presidential advisory team comprised only two Salafi members. The other Salafi member, Bassem Al-Zarqa, resigned in protest against this measure, and, thus, the advisory team was left without any Salafi representatives. Moreover, in May 2013, Yasser Burhami, one of the founding members of Al-Dawa, was detained at Alexandria airport while returning from Saudi Arabia (Lacroix, 2016).

As the crisis escalated and the *Tamarod* (Rebellion), a demonstration to unseat President Morsi, began on 30 June 2013, the Muslim Brotherhood called on the Islamist factions to show their support for the President and join counter-demonstration on 26 and 28 June. Al-Nour refused to join this sit-in and argued that demonstrations should be stopped to maintain national stability. It argued that the call to protect the President's Islamic order was unjustified because Egypt did not transform into an Islamic state under Morsi (El-Sherif, 2015). To further strengthen its call for national stability Al-Nour explicitly praised the military institution. The Secretary-General of the party Galal Mora, in the Al-Nour official Facebook page, praised the Egyptian Army as patriotic and honourable and called on politicians to refrain from diminishing the status of the military. Al-Dawa further requested the government to make amends with the opposition. After President Morsi's speech on 28 June, Al-Nour assessed it as lacking any concrete formula to resolve the present crisis (Ghalwash and Phillips, 2017).

Interim Government and President Sisi

President Morsi was removed by the military on 3 July 2013. Al-Nour's decision to back the ouster was met with criticism from the Islamist factions. Not supporting the Morsi regime affected the image and reputation of the party severely and created a rift among the party supporters (El-Sherif, 2015). While most of the Islamist parties including the Al-Watan Party or Homeland Party, headed by ex-Nour President Ghaffour, Salafist Front and Al-Fadhila Party joined an anti-coup alliance, criticising the military intervention, Al-Nour sided with Sisi and the liberal groups (Cook, 2013; Mohie Eldin, 2016). This action left an impression upon some of the party members that Al-Nour had sacrificed its religious principles for its political agenda. Some members even appeared in the pro-Morsi protests or left Al-Nour over its action; for example, Sheikh Ahmed Aboul Enein, a senior official of Al-Nour, resigned in protest aganist the party's stance on the military takeover (Kingsley, 2013). Al-Nour spokesperson Nader Bakkar clarified the situation by saying that 20 per cent of its members were disappointed by Al-Nour's position regarding President Morsi's ouster but the remaining 80 per cent were in favour of its actions (Cook, 2013; El-Rashidi, 2013).

Al-Nour also faced criticism from independent Salafi Sheikhs. For example, Nageh Ibrahim and Osama El-Kousy called on the party to distance itself from politics and stick to social activities (Mohie Eldin, 2016). Al-Nour members, on the other hand, insisted that its primary focus was to safeguard the Egyptian citizens and claimed that the Brotherhood did not pay heed to their request of communicating with the opposition or organising an early presidential election. Moreover, Al-Nour recalled the Army's importance during the ouster of President Mubarak and insisted that aligning with it was beneficial for the citizens (El-Rashidi, 2013). The primary reason behind this unlikely alliance between Al-Nour and the armed forces, as argued by several scholars (El-Rashidi, 2013; Awad, 2014; Mohie Eldin, 2016) was its paranoia that the party and Al-Dawa were being undermined by the Brotherhood. On the other hand, Al-Nour's inclusion helped the Egyptian military to appear as moderately supportive of the Islamists (Mohie Eldin, 2016). However, Stephen A. Cook (2013) and Patrick Kingsley (2013) opine that by taking this step, Al-Nour made a similar mistake like the Muslim Brotherhood, which was alienating its core support base by being politically manoeuvred.

Due to its support of the 2013 military coup, Al-Nour ensured its security from the repression that Muslim Brotherhood members faced in the latter half of 2013. It was also able to escape from the restrictions on religious parties as per Article 74 of the 2014 Constitution which states, "No political activity may be practised, and no political parties may be formed on the basis of religion." Even though this law was not specifically to be imposed on an ex-post facto basis, Al-Nour came under severe scrutiny by a campaign called *No to Religious Parties*,[9]supported by the Egyptian Ministry of Endowments (El-Din, 2015; Mohie Eldin, 2016). Al-Nour even participated in the 2014 constitutional drafting committee to include Articles on the *Sharia* and Islamic identity in the new Constitution (El-Sherif, 2015). However, in an attempt to strike a balance between its religious identity and political activities, Al-Nour has been witnessing increasing difficulties with both the regime and the people since 2013. Most of its Salafi supporters still feel that Al-Nour has betrayed its core values for political gains and the party's support for Sisi in the 2014 presidential election only augmented this notion. The lessening support of the people was reflected in the 2015 parliamentary election in which the party won only 12 out of 596 seats in the House of Representatives (Linn and Linn, 2015; Mohie Eldin, 2016).

On its part, Al-Nour has tried to mitigate this accusation by taking several measures. To maintain its opposition status, it has moderately criticised the regime from time to time. For example, after the security forces dispersed the protesters from the Rabaa and Nahda square sit-in on 14 August 2013, Al-Dawa declared in its website that it had warned the Muslim Brotherhood against the protest and urged the government not to use force against non-violent protesters (El-Rashidi, 2013). Moreover, to show that it did not intend to gain from President Morsi's removal, it refused to accept four portfolios in the interim Cabinet, considering them to be military appointments and claiming that it would accept political involvement only when the government was elected though democratic elections and run by experienced technocrats (El-Rashidi, 2013).

9. This campaign was launched in August 2015 by *Tamarod* participant and political activist Hamdi Al-Fakharani (El-Din, 2015).

During the 2015 parliamentary election, Al-Nour announced that it would contest in a minimal number of seats (two out of four party-list constituencies and 160 out of 448 individual seats). Al-Nour's intransigent position on not including Coptic Christians in the party list also changed in the face of the June 2014 electoral law which requires all political parties to maintain candidate quotas for women and Christians. In the 2015 parliamentary election, Al-Nour fielded a Christian candidate (Lacroix, 2016), but these measures failed to help it appear in a better light among the secular parties and the regime (Linn and Linn, 2015; Lacroix, 2016).

Al-Nour also did not receive its expected support from the regime. In the 2015 election, the party blamed the corrupt election process and electoral laws for its failure (Linn and Linn, 2015). The ongoing anti-Islamism led to several lawsuits being filed against Al-Nour for violating Article 74[10] of the Constitution. The cases were dismissed by the judiciary but Al-Nour remained under constant threat from its own religious status and received little assurance from the regime (Lacroix, 2016; Mohie Eldin, 2016). Under interim President Adly Mansour's decree, Imams were required to be Al-Azhar graduates and those who lacked the criteria had to pass an examination to get a licence for preaching. Unauthorised Imams were threatened with fines and imprisonment. Al-Nour supported this decree because, although most of the Al-Dawa preachers were not Al-Azhar graduates, exceptions were made for the Dawa preachers (Lacroix, 2016). This way, while managing to sustain itself, such steps by the regime subjected Al-Nour to continuous pressure (Fick and Abdelaty, 2014).

Conclusion

Regardless of the consistent challenges, Al-Nour continues to function. Under the anti-Islamist regime, this party has become the largest and most significant Islamist party, in the absence of the Brotherhood. Its continuous pro-regime status has made the regime regard it as a non-threat but the party still faces challenges from the secular liberal factions of the society. Moreover, a significant number of Salafists and Islamists consider the party to be a traitor. While Al-Nour is aiming constantly to win the support of the secular political factions, it is failing to reclaim the

10. No political activity may be undertaken and no political parties may be formed on the basis of religion.

trust of the Islamists. Even though the regime did not enforce repressive measures against the party members, it would not be judicious to think that Al-Nour would receive any favour from it in the immediate future. Nonetheless, the present low key status may be helpful for the party to increase its influence on the grassroots level.

The future of Al-Nour, therefore, depends on its own course of action. The hope for Al-Nour to recreate a viable future depends on how well it can secure the trust of its former supporters. Most of the Islamist parties have been banned and the Sisi administration has made it impossible for a party to thrive on its religious identity. Under these circumstances, an emphasis on social services by the members of Al-Dawa would help the group to regain its previous goodwill among the Islamist electorates. On the other hand, keeping a low profile and shedding its religious identity can bring helpful results for the political wing.

References

Ahram Online (2011), "Egypt's Salafists Proliferate with yet Another Salafi Party in the Works", Cairo, July 11. Retrieved on 18 January 2018, from http://english.ahram.org.eg/News/16075.aspx.

—— (2011), "Al Nour Party, Egyptian Elections Watch", Cairo, December 4. Retrieved on 12 February 2018, from http://english.ahram.org.eg/News/26693.aspx.

—— (2012), "Egypt's Nour Party Backs Controversial Morsi Decree: Spokesman", Cairo, November 28. Retrieved on 5 March 2018, from http://english.ahram.org.eg/News/59389.aspx.

—— (2013), "Salafist Nour Party Meets with Egypt's NSF in Closed-Door Talks", Cairo, February 14. Retrieved on 2 January 2018, from http://english.ahram.org.eg/News/64827.aspx.

—— (2014), "Women Allowed on Egypt's Islamist Nour Party Electoral List, 'on Condition of Wearing Hijab'", Cairo, October 15. Retrieved on 17 February 2018, from http://english.ahram.org.eg/News/113169.aspx

Al-Anani, Khalil (2011), "The New Islamist Scene in Egypt", *Al Ahram Weekly*, Cairo, June 23-29. Retrieved on 2 February 2018, from http://weekly.ahram.org.eg/Archive/2011/1053/op3.htm.

—— (2012), "Islamist Parties Post-Arab Spring", *Mediterranean Politics*, 17(3): 466-472.

Arafat, Alaa Al-Din (2018). *Egypt in Crisis: The Fall of Islamism and Prospects of Democratization* (New York: Palgrave Macmillan).

Awad, Mokhtar (2014), "The Salafi Dawa of Alexandria: The Politics of a Religious Movement", *Current Trend in Islamist Ideology*, 17: 5-39.

Bassiouni, Cherif M (2016), *Chronicles of the Egyptian Revolution and its Aftermath: 2011-2016* (Cambridge: Cambridge University Press).

Blair, Edmund and Awad, Marwa (2011), "Groups Quit Egypt Rally Saying Hijacked by Islamists", Reuters, Cairo, 29 July. Retrieved on 14 June 2018, from https://www.reuters.com/article/us-egypt-protests-idUSTRE76S1T720110729.

Boehmer Daniel A. and Murphy, James P. (2012), "The Politicization of the Egyptian *Salafiyya*: Principled Participation and Islamist Competition in the Post-Mubarak Era", Institute for Middle East Studies, Elliott School of International Affairs, George Washington University, Washington, DC.

Bokhari, Kamran and Senzai, Farid (2013), *Political Islam in the Age of Democratization* (New York: Palgrave Macmillan).

Brown, Jonathan (2011), "Salafis and Sufis in Egypt", Carnegie Endowment for International Peace, Washington, DC, December.

Cesari, Jocelyne (2013), *The Awakening of Muslim Democracy: Religion, Modernity and the State* (Cambridge: Cambridge University Press).

Cook, Stephen A. (2013), "Lights Out for Al Nour?" Council on Foreign Relation,s New York, August 6. Retrieved on 1 March 2018, from https://www.cfr.org/blog/lights-out-al-nour.

Dabbash, Hamdi (2011), "Salafis in Cairo Aim to Establish 'Virtue' Political Party", *Egypt Independent,* Cairo, May 11. Retrieved on 5 February 2018, from http://www.egyptindependent.com/salafis-cairo-aim-establish-virtue-political-party/.

El-Din, Gamal Essam (2015), "The 'No to Religious Parties' Campaign Gains Momentum", *Ahram Online*, Cairo, August 26. Retrieved on 9 February 2018, from http://english.ahram.org.eg/News/138915.aspx.

El-Rashidi, Sarah (2013), "Egypt's Nour: A Party Reborn?" *Ahram Online*, Cairo. August 4. Retrieved on 30 January 2018, from http://english.ahram.org.eg/News/77196.aspx.

El-Sherif, Ashraf (2015), "Egypt's Salafists at a Crossroads: Part 3 of a Series on Political Islam in Egypt", Carnegie Endowment for International Peace, Washington, DC.

Fick, Maggie and Abdelaty, Ali (2014), "Egypt Bans Unlicensed Preachers, Tightens Grip on Mosques", Reuters, Cairo, June 7. Retrieved on 25 December 2017, from https://www.reuters.com/article/us-egypt-religion-preachers/egypt-bans-unlicensed-preachers-tightens-grip-on-mosques-idUSKBN0EI0PV20140607.

France24 (2013), "Ahmadinejad Greeted with Red Carpet, Protests in Egypt", Paris, February 6. Retrieved on 10 June 2018, from http://www.france24.com/en/20130206-iran-ahmadinejad-makes-historic-visit-egypt.

Gauvain, Richard (2013), *Salafi Ritual Purity: In the Presence of God* (Abingdon: Routledge).

Ghalwash, Maha and Phillips, Lawrie (2017), "Jumping Ship: The Nour Party Turns its Back on the Muslim Brotherhood", British Society for Middle Eastern Studies, Edinburgh University, Scotland, July 4-7.

Heffelfinger, Chris (2007), "Trends in Egyptian Salafi Activism", Combating Terrorism Centre, New York, December.

Henzel, Christopher (2005), "The Origins of Al Qaeda's Ideology: Implications for US Strategy", *Parameters*, XXXV (1): 69-80.

Høigilt, Jacob and Nome, Frida (2014), "Egyptian Salafism in Revolution", *Journal of Islamic Studies,* 25(1): 33-54.

Kingsley, Patrick (2013), "Egypt's Salafist Al-Nour Party Wields New Influence on Post-Morsi Coalition", *The Guardian*, Cairo, July 7. Retrieved on 11 February 2018, from https://www.theguardian.com/world/2013/jul/07/egypt-salafist-al-nour-party/.

Kirkpatrick, David D. and Sheikh, Mayy El (2012), "Support from Islamists for Liberal Upends Race in Egypt", *The New York Times*, April 28. Retrieved on 23 January 2018, from http://www.nytimes.com/2012/04/29/world/middleeast/conservatives-in-egypt-back-liberal-to-oppose-brotherhood.html.

Lacroix, Ste'phane (2012), "Sheikhs and Politicians: Inside the New Egyptian Salafism", Carnegie Endowment for International Peace, Washington, DC.

—— (2016), "Egypt's Pragmatic Salafis: The Politics of Hizb Al-Nour", Carnegie Endowment for International Peace, Washington, DC.

Linn, Emily Crane and Linn, Nicholas (2015), "The Nour Party Goes Dim", *Foreign Policy*, November 21. Retrieved on 14 January 2018, from http://foreignpolicy.com/2015/11/21/the-nour-party-goes-dim-egypt/.

Maged, Amani (2011), "New-Found Friends: Islamist Forces are Uniting in Pursuit of Power", *Al Ahram Weekly*, Cairo, July 21-27. Retrieved on 30 January 2018, from http://weekly.ahram.org.eg/Archive/2011/1057/eg8.htm.

Mikhail, George (2015), "Why Some in Egypt are Banning Campaign Photos of Female Candidates", *Al Monitor*, Cairo, October 16. Retrieved on 9 January 2018, from

Mohie Eldin, Fatima (2016), "Can the Nour Party Remain Politically Viable in Sisi's Egypt", *Muftah*, January 20. Retrieved on 10 February 2018, from https://muftah.org/striving-to-remain-relevant-the-nour-partys-political-viability-in-sisis-egypt/#.Wp2ME-hubDc.

Ranko, Annette and Nedza, Justyna (2016), "Crossing the Ideological Divide? Egypt's Salafists and the Muslim Brotherhood after the Arab Spring", *Studies in Conflict & Terrorism*, 39(6): 519-541.

Shadid, Anthony (2011), "Islamists Flood Square in Cairo in Show of Strength", *The New York Times*, Cairo, July 29. Retrieved on 13 February 2018, from http://www.nytimes.com/2011/07/30/world/middleeast/30egypt.

Shukrallah, Salma (2012), "Nour Party Infighting Reveals Wider Cracks Within Salafist Movement", *Ahram Online*, Cairo, September 27. Retrieved on 19 February 2018, from http://english.ahram.org.eg/News/53998.aspx.

—— (2013), "Opposition to Presidency Opens Rifts in Egypt's Islamist Current", *Ahram Online*, Cairo, February 11. Retrieved on 20 January 2018, from http://english.ahram.org.eg/News/64335.aspx.

Trager, Eric (2016), *Arab Fall: How the Muslim Brotherhood Won and Lost Egypt in 891 Days* (Washington, DC: Georgetown University Press).

Wiktorowicz, Quintan (2006), "Anatomy of the Salafi Movement", *Studies in Conflict & Terrorism*, 29: 207–239.

Wright, Robin (2012), *The Islamists are Coming: Who They Really Are* (Washington, DC: Woodrow Wilson Centre Press).

Youssef, Abdelrahman (2015), "Despite Concessions Nour Party Loses out in Parliamentary Elections", Atlantic Council, October 21. Retrieved on 23 February 2018, from http://www.atlanticcouncil.org/blogs/menasource/despite-concessions-nour-party-loses-out-in-parliamentary-elections.

5. The Green Movement in Iran

Rashmi Muraleedhar

Abstract

The Green Movement is one of the most significant instances of contentious politics playing out in Iran since the 1979 revolution. The movement saw massive crowds of people thronging the streets of Iran in spontaneous outrage against what was perceived to be a stolen election. This chapter seeks to give a brief outline of how the Green Movement unfolded, the main categories of the political actors involved, and locates the development of the movement in the context of the reform movement in Iran. Lastly, the chapter is concluded by reviewing the literature on the impact made by the Green Movement in Iranian politics.

Key Words: Iran; Green Movement; Democracy; Civil-Political Rights

Political violence as a concept is understood as politically motivated acts of violence that take place outside the realm of state control. The Weberian concept of the state having a monopoly over the use of violence is employed in distinguishing political violence from instances when the state uses force. In this chapter, the Green Movement in Iran is examined. It was a non-violent protest movement which was sparked by allegations of fraudulent vote counting in the presidential elections held on 10 June 2009 (Tait and Weaver, 2009). Due to the distinctive commitment to non-violence, the Green Movement does not readily fall under the category of political violence, but the response of the state has been violent and repressive. It can be argued that the Green Movement is an interesting case of 'contentious politics' in modern Iranian politics.

Contentious politics is defined as,

> .... episodic, public, collective interaction among makers of claims and their objects when (a) at least one government is a claimant, an object of claims or a party to the claims; and (b) the claims would, if realized, affect the interests of at least one of the claimants. (McAdam, Tarrow and Tilly, 2001: 5)

In contentious politics, the actors make claims on the authorities, use public performances to do so, draw on inherited forms of collective action and invent new ones, forge alliances with influential members of their respective polities, take advantage of existing political regime opportunities and make new ones, and use a combination of institutional and extra-institutional routines to advance their claims (McAdam, Tarrow and Tilly, 2001).

In the following sections, a better understanding of the Green Movement and the reasons behind its emergence will be examined. It is viewed as a contemporary of the Arab Spring protests that emerged in different parts of the Middle East. It will be contextualised in the development of Iranian politics since the Islamic revolution of 1979. Lastly, an attempt will be made to analyse its impact on contemporary politics.

What was the Green Movement?

Massive crowds of Iranians came spilling out on to the streets of Tehran and other cities in a spontaneous protest against the results of the presidential election held in June 2009 (Tait and Weaver, 2009). The mass demonstrations questioned the legitimacy of the declared results and have since been referred to as the Green Movement (Lackner-Gohari, 2009). At its height, the Green Movement gathered up to three million peaceful demonstrators on the streets (Milani, 2010).

In 2009, the Islamic Republic was to hold the 10th presidential elections in which the contest was mainly between the incumbent President Mahmoud Ahmadinejad and alternative candidates Mir Hossein Mousavi, Mehdi Karroubi and Mohsen Rezaei (Press TV, 2009). The campaigning prior to the elections had reenergised the electorate, and, as Farhi (2012) contends, it seemed to be an election between candidates who were 'real alternatives' to the incumbent President. The voter participation rate recorded in the 2009 election was among the highest since the establishment of the Islamic Republic in 1979:

> If the total number of votes announced by the Interior Ministry is to be accepted, it brought into the electoral process at least an additional 11 million voters out of the announced total eligible electorate of 46.2 million and raised voter turnout from close to 60 percent in the first round of 2005 to about 85 percent, the highest in the history of presidential elections in the Islamic Republic (Farhi, 2012: 11).

Most notably Mousavi, as the leading reformist candidate, had managed to mobilise supporters through his deftly run campaign trails, televised debates and savvy networking strategies (Esfandiari, 2009). Because of the fever-pitch that the reformist candidates had been able to stir up prior to the elections, the announced result of the conservative Ahmadinejad's landslide victory came as a shock to the voters (Lackner-Gohari, 2009). Calling it a fraudulent vote count, Mousavi described Ahmadinejad's victory as an "electoral coup d'état", effectively lending support to the grassroots movement (Haghighatjoo, 2009: 15). Pari Esfandiari (2009) argues that the campaign of the reformist alternative candidates had been so effective that a substantial number of supporters had formed a collective identity, and, hence, reacted as strongly as they did, thronging the streets and chanting the slogan, "Where is my vote?" (Tohidi, 2009: 7).

Reportedly, millions sported the colour green, by waving flags and banners or wearing wristbands (Milani, 2010). Mir Hossein Mousavi's pre-election campaign was associated with the colour green, so his supporters sported the colour during the movement to reject the announced election results (Moruzzi, 2009). With the scale the post-election protests had taken, the colour green moved beyond Mousavi's campaign, and came to represent the colour of protest and persistence that questioned the legitimacy of the election results (Esfandiari, 2009).

The state's reaction to the movement was swift and sought to shut it down as completely as possible. This involved mass arrests of activists, students, journalists, bloggers, intellectuals and all those who were accused of provoking unrest (Jeffrey, 2009). The Basij were deployed to dispel the crowds that thronged on the streets, by violent means, if deemed necessary. The protest movement was largely described as non-violent in nature, and the employment of violence in order to shut it down has been documented in the form of photos, videos, weblogs (Esfandiari, 2009). Within the first six weeks of the post-election demonstrations, official figures claimed that 2,500 arrests were made in Tehran alone, as many as 150 were placed in jail and 30 people died (Jeffrey, 2009).

On 20 June 2009, Neda Agha-Soltan was shot in the chest in Tehran, videos and images of which were shared extensively through the internet. She came to symbolise the tragic use of violence against the people and was "mythologised as a martyr" to the movement's cause (Tait and Weaver, 2009). Sohrab Arabi, a 19-year-old male student, who was reportedly killed while being detained by the Basij, emerged as another icon of the protest movement (Tohidi, 2009).

Along with the physical crackdown on the protestors, the state also curbed reportage of the events. Reporters and journalists were either arrested or warned to stay indoors and keep away from the protest movement. News of the movement, hence, depended heavily on citizen journalism (Esfandiari, 2009). The Iranians actively utilised the cyber space to mould a makeshift public sphere for themselves (Golkar, 2017). They actively shared images, videos, reports and stories through the use of Information and Communication Technology (ICT) in the face of the state-led shutdown. However, it has not been possible to verify and confirm all such information. In such circumstances, it was acknowledged that reliable reporting of the events was a difficult task.

> Interpreting events as they occur is a tricky affair, in part, because it is difficult to obtain both reliable sources of information and the means to independently and immediately verify those sources. In the case of the 2009 elections, the main press was largely controlled by those in power. There were also reports and comments from weblogs and pictures taken with mobile phones by the protesters, which could not be confirmed (Adelkhah, 2012:18).

The Iranian state has slowly woken up to the challenge that ICT presents, and has been steadily augmenting its own capacities in this field.

Since 2003, the conservative establishment acquired sophisticated filtering programmes (Smartfilter) from other authoritarian regimes such as China, and U.S. companies based in Dubai. It began a systematic strategy to block internet websites (Gheytanchi and Rahimi, 2009). Internet Protocol (IP) blocking became the filtering policy after 2003, which resulted in an increase in the number of filtered websites. According to an Iranian newspaper, the number of filtered websites increased from 5 million in the year 2008, to 10 million in 2009 (*Sarmayeh* newspaper, 2009; Golkar, 2017: 58)

During the Green Movement, the state was alert to the mobilisation taking place in the cyber space. In addition to blocking and filtering of websites, the state resorted to significantly lowering the internet bandwidth to effectively impede the sharing of videos, photos and emails (Golkar, 2017). Besides restricting access to the cyber space, the state allotted resources to develop advanced website hacking, virus spreading, monitoring and espionage systems as well:

> Besides restricting access to the Internet, another regime strategy has been to apply this technology against activists and engage in information warfare, such as website hacking and virus spreading (Kalathil and Boas, 2001: 3). Intelligence agents, especially the IRGC Cyber Force, also arrested many weblog writers and activists by means of advanced monitoring and espionage systems (Golkar, 2017: 60).

In the aftermath of the mass arrests after the Green Movement demonstrations, the trials of several prominent reformist intellectuals were televised and publicly broadcast. The defendants, more than 100 in number, were accused of provoking unrest and undermining the Islamic Republic (Hardy, 2009). Iranian officials publicly admitted that the protesters who were arrested were tortured while in custody in a prison in the Kahrizak area of Tehran (Tisdall, 2009). The opposition claimed that there were widespread instances of torture, abuse and rape of political prisoners. At least in the case of three prisoners, the Iranian judiciary ruled that such torture led to their death (Associated Press, 2009).

Within a year of the protests, official records suggest that an estimated 5,000 people were arrested and 115 executed, however, the actual death toll is estimated to be much higher (Tait, 2010). The participation in the demonstrations had dropped visibly in response to the government's heavy-handedness (Tait, 2010). Occurring nearly two years prior to the Arab Spring, the Green Movement had characteristics that had a distinct resemblance to the popular protests in Tunisia and Egypt in early 2011. In both the Arab and Iranian contexts, the uprisings were unexpected and unprecedented. They were largely leaderless, with the initial organisational work carried out by small groups in urban centres using social media (Kurzman, 2012). In support of the uprisings in Tunisia and Egypt, Mousavi and Karroubi called for demonstrations in Iran in February 2011. After that, Mousavi, Karroubi and their wives were placed under house arrest (Reuter Staff, 2011).

Reformist Movement in Iran

Mahmood Monshiuri and Ali Assareh (2009) claim that the root causes of this spontaneous spilling of the Iranian people onto the streets reflected a deeper discontent that had been brewing over the decades. Nader Hashemi (2014) argues that the Green Movement protests were an attempt to bring back the reform movement agenda in Iran. The Green Movement was the second attempt to renegotiate post-revolutionary social contract through democratic means (Hashemi 2014). To gain a long-term perspective on why the Green Movement emerged, it would be useful to look at the development of Iranian politics since the establishment of the Islamic Republic after the 1979 revolution.

Monshipouri and Assareh describe the 1979 revolution as a powerful event that challenged the "post World War II zeitgeist" of secular democratisation of the Third World (2009: 27). The Iranians went against the tide and established for themselves a "semi-democratic, semi-divine form of government" instead (Monshipouri and Assareh, 2009: 27). The revolution was also strongly rooted on a nationalist and anti-imperialist basis (Bayat, 2011). The anti-imperialist characteristic stemmed from the deep-seated resentment against two centuries of foreign intervention by the British and Russians as part of the 19th century 'Great Game' and the more recent US machinations that led to the downfall of the democratically elected government led by Mohammad Mossadegh in 1953 (Benjamin, 2018: 6). The revolution saw nation-wide support, bringing people from different walks of life onto the streets (Bayat, 2011). It was the result of a historically incongruent alliance among the modernising middle and technocratic classes, urban poor, women's and students' groups, new industrialist class, members of the bazaar, and religious hardliners (Milani, 2010). However, this incongruous alliance was clearly led by the Shia cleric, Ayatollah Khomeini. After the successful revolution, Khomeini insisted that the Shia clergy be given the role of 'guardianship' of Iranian society:

> The traditional "guardianship" role of the Shiite clergy was to oversee religious foundations and protect the weakest members of society, especially children, widows, and the mentally ill. Khomeini reinterpreted this guardianship, or *velayat-e faqih*, to cover society at large. He wanted to ensure that all government laws conformed to the tenets of Islam, extending religious jurisprudence to allow direct clerical rule of society. (Benjamin, 2018: 29)

The Islamic Revolution, thus, established a theocratic republic, with an elected Parliament and President subordinated to the non-elected clerical authority.

> The country is divided into a small clerical elite of religious jurists (*mojtaheds*), which maintains its power through the system of conciliar rule and is supported by a 'second stratum' of lay civil servants in control of the administration, and a huge lay population which has no share of political power but votes once a year for the president, the Majles, or the local and municipal councils that confront, and are often effectively neutralized by, the structures of clerical domination (Arjomand 2005: 506).

Clerical supremacy in the new republic was inscribed in the Constitution and is described by the phrase Mandate of the Jurist (*Vilayat-e Faqih*). The Supreme Leader is in practice the *de facto* executive head in Iran (Bruno, 2008). The Guardian Council consists of 12 members, six of whom are appointed by the Supreme Leader, and the remaining six by the Parliament (Bruno, 2008).

In the early 1990s, steps were taken to strengthen the role of the conservative clergy in Iran's political institutions. In 1991, the Guardian Council reinterpreted the law for eligibility of candidates for the Assembly of Experts and Article 99 in the Constitution (Farhi, 2012). In one fell swoop, the Guardian Council attributed to itself the responsibility of 'approving' candidates to the Assembly of Experts, to the office of President, and to the Islamic Consultative Assembly (Farhi, 2012).

Fariba Adelkhah (2012) contends that this increasing authoritarianism was rooted in the experience of the 1979 revolution but got strengthened due to the Iran-Iraq War and the onset of the economic crisis in the early 1990s. Along with the conservative stance on the role of the clergy, the Islamic Republic's political survival has depended on "defending itself against 'real' or 'imagined' enemies" (Monshipouri, 2009: 27). The conservative foreign policy stance has been strongly anti-imperialist and extremely sensitive to perceived external intervention in domestic affairs. The devastation after the Iran-Iraq War, the emerging contradictions between revolutionary ideals and the aspirations of the expanding youth population may all have led to the 'establishment' turning more conservative and acutely sensitive to political dissent (Ladier-Fouladi, 2012; Adelkhah, 2012). The clergy in Iran successfully leveraged the inbuilt legal bias that allowed it to curb any form of political dissent (Hashemi, 2014). This entailed closing down of opposition publications, jailing prominent journalists and intellectuals, banning prominent opposition candidates from contesting elections or even the drastic measure of political murders committed by the secret services (Arjomand, 2005; Hashemi, 2014; Farhi, 2012; Adelkhah, 2012).

The roots of the reform movement itself can be traced to the intra-Islamist ideological split that emerged between right-wing and left-wing Islamists in the 1980s (Hashemi, 2014). The origin of the reform movement took place with the discussions carried out in two centres: *Kiyan*, an independent monthly, which revolved around the religious scholar Abdolkarim Soroush, and the Centre for Strategic Studies, a think-tank affiliated with the office of the President (Nabavi, 2012). *Kiyan* was involved in exploring the relationship between religion and politics and advanced "a broad non-ideological approach to Islam on a theoretical level" (Nabavi, 2012: 44). While the Centre was more preoccupied with the issues of the political structure, political culture and behaviour. The turn that political developments in Iran had taken since the early 1990s had led to the need for considering such issues. With Mohammad Khatami's election victory in 1997 to the office of President, the reformist movement had been opened up to the society at large (Nabavi, 2012).

Khatami was elected into office on his campaign promise of promoting the "rule of law" (Farhi, 2012). The objective of the movement was to bring changes to the political system through what was termed 'political development', rather than to dismantle the system (Nabavi, 2012). Hence, reform was what revolution was not. The reform movement advocated the rule of law, gradualism, non-violence, greater political openness, tolerance, transparency, human rights and democracy (Arjomand, 2002; Hanghighatjoo, 2009; Nabavi, 2012).

Omid Payrow Shabani (2013) accredits the reform movement to the growing class of 'post-Islamist' intellectuals who sided with the left-wing Islamists and initiated modernisation in describing the inter-relatedness between religion and politics. This has been described as a "post Islamist turn" as a decentralised project to bring together "religiosity and rights, faith and freedom, Islam and liberty" (Bayat, 2005:1). Initially using the term "post-Islamism" to describe the reform movement in Iran, Bayat (2011) has since then cited the Arab Spring movements in Tunisia and Egypt as other examples of the "post-Islamist" trend.

The enthusiasm that Khatami's presidency raised for supporters of the reformist movement, soon waned. The reformist commitment to pursue the agenda within the rules proved fruitless, as the very rules in place allowed the non-elective institutions to obstruct attempts of "political development" through reform (Farhi, 2012; Nabavi, 2012). The rise of Mahmoud Ahmadinejad and Iran's "neo-conservatives" in 2005 officially marked the reform movement's denouement (Hashemi, 2014).

Monshipuri and Assareh (2009) argue that it wasn't the failure of the reformists' political agenda, but rather the economic factor that proved to be decisive in bringing the reform movement to a close:

> Iranians [were] suffering from double-digit unemployment rates and rampant inflation… Iranian voters in 2005 sent a strong signal to the religio-political establishment that there were serious cultural and economic gaps in society, and that some civil and political issues must take a backseat to the people's overall economic security. (p. 31)

Nevertheless, Khatami's presidency and the reform movement he was at the helm of made a lasting impression in Iran's public sphere. His initiatives to give more space to the press, socio-cultural freedom for women and the youth provided an opening for the development of 'civil society'. It has been argued that the Khatami era (1997–2005) powerfully "altered the relationship between the state and society in ways that made the Green Movement possible" (Adelkhah, 2012: 22).

Main Actors in the Green Movement

Shabani (2013) lists three main categories of political actors who shaped the Green Movement: youth, women and reformists. In the previous section, the evolution of the reformist movement in Iran, and its proponents were described briefly. This section looks at the other two categories of political actors who were involved in the protest movement.

The "youth bulge" had a very significant role during this protest movement. More than 70 per cent of the Iranian population is below the age of 30 (Asemi, 2006). After the revolution, the state had embarked on a socio-economic development programme that substantially improved literacy rates and educational and health outcomes (Ladier-Fouladi, 2012).

> The emergence of the "youth" category in the early 1970s, indeed, expressed a new form of individualization that extended to a broad social stratum in urban areas. These young people, who were becoming aware of their common characteristics, began to consider themselves as a distinct social group and, thus, sought to assert their points of difference. They were, in principle, opposed to the patriarchal system of the family, which rested on two pillars: young male subordination to elders, and, girl-women subordination to male members. (Ladier-Fouladi, 2012: 144)

It is notable that the generations of Iranians born and socialised after the 1979 revolution did not share the values that the Islamic Republic tried to propagate (Ladier-Fouladi, 2012; Tait, 2010). While literacy rates have been steadily improving, registering at 79 per cent, employment prospects have not shown as promising a trend (Asemi, 2006). Official estimates in 2004 suggested that 3.5 million working-age Iranians were unemployed. Unemployment hit the youth and women especially hard, with figures as high as 30 per cent (Esfandiari, 2004; Dhillon and Egel, 2009). This group was frustrated by the bleak economic prospects and Ahmadinejad's record of not delivering on promises to revive the Iranian economy (Adelkhah, 2012). This group actively participated in, and supported, the reformist candidates, especially Mousavi, during the pre-election campaigning period (Moruzzi, 2009).

This group's participation in the movement also brings to attention a distinct characteristic of the Green Movement. While Iranians have been active in cyber space for a while, technology became a critical tool in challenging the government only with the emergence of the Green Movement (Golkar, 2017). The number of Iranians entering cyber space has increased dramatically, from 600,000 internet users in 1996 to 33,200,000 in 2010 (Johari, 2002). According to these statistics, in 2010, Iran had a penetration rate of 43.2 per cent, which was one of the highest internet-user growth rates in the world (Golkar, 2017). Additionally, using ICT, Iranian internet users have sculpted a 'virtual public space' for themselves where they could exercise more freedom to follow their interests and personal desires than in the real world (Golkar, 2017). The protestors' wide use of ICT helped to keep the Green Movement alive in the face of governmental repression. The Green Movement has been dubbed by journalists in the West as the 'Twitter Revolution' (Stockher, Neumann and Dorting, 2009; Keller, 2010).

Women have also emerged as a significant category of political actors in Iran. Women now make up 63 per cent of university enrolment (Tohidi, 2009). Along with educational attainments, factors like decline in fertility rates, improvement in primary health care and increase in women's contribution to economic, scientific, and cultural spheres have led to their more self-asserting participation in the public sphere (Tohidi, 2009).

However, these developmental advances have not necessarily translated into economic progress:

> After the revolution, the Islamic government embarked on a wide socioeconomic development program… The rise in women's schooling has allowed them to attain a level of education similar to that of men… Despite the significant progress in the education of young women, however, the labour market has remained virtually closed to them. In 2006, only 14.4 percent of women aged 15–64 years participated in the labour force (Ladier-Fouladi, 2012:142).

Women cutting across ideological backgrounds are bristling against the lower status that is accorded to them in Iranian society (Moruzzi 2009). Some aspects of the lower status of women are described as follows

> With its many uncertain and paradoxical social features, Iranian society is fast approaching a gender conundrum. Iranian women constitute 64 percent of university graduates…Despite these achievements, no woman held any key position in President Khatami's or President Ahmadinejad's first Cabinets; women's court testimony is worth half that of men; women cannot travel abroad on their own without the permission of their husbands; a woman's life is worth half that of a man under Iran's blood-money law; and men continue to have a unilateral right to divorce. (Monshipouri, 2011: 35)

Under President Khatami, from 1997 to 2004, certain restrictions against women were relaxed (Haghighatjoo, 2009). However, during the post-reform movement of Ahmadinejad's presidency, women faced many challenges, such as the "No-Choice Dress-Code" and a multitude of similar restraining codes that require women to submit to outdated gender-based restrictions (Lackner-Gohari, 2009: 18). Instead of changing the previously established discriminatory laws, the Parliament added more patriarchal ones to strictly regulate the personal and social conduct of women (Haghighatjoo, 2009).

The political atmosphere during the election campaigns in 2009 propelled an increasing number of women's groups and activists to push the women's agenda. Three months before the date of the election, they formed a diverse coalition called 'Convergence of Women' that represented 42 women's groups and 700 individual activists in an attempt to press presidential candidates to take up women's issues seriously and assert themselves as an important constituency (Tohidi, 2009: 6). Excluding the incumbent Ahmadinejad, all the candidates in the 2009 presidential election promised to promote and elevate the status of women (Haghighatjoo, 2009). Women also voted in large numbers, and later joined the post-election protests to demonstrate against the perceived 'electoral coup', standing side by side with their male peers (Tohidi, 2009: 4). During the Green Movement, it became amply clear that women had emerged as an important class of political actors and were fully committed to actively engage in the public sphere. They were willing to get fully involved in street protests against a government that they no longer perceived as being legitimate (Moruzzi, 2009).

Impact on Iranian Politics

The crisis following the declaration of the presidential election results in June 2009 is considered as the most significant event in the history of the Islamic Republic, since the 1979 revolution itself (Farhi, 2012). The street confrontations and violence following the results signify a profound failure in the Iranian electoral system to effectively regulate politics within the current system.

Although the motivations behind the movement were not in pursuit of class-based demands, but rather universalist civil-political rights for all citizens of Iran, there was an apparent divide in the public sphere on class-based and urban-rural lines (Dabashi, 2017). As was witnessed in 2005, perhaps, the economic factor indeed was decisive in testing the people's commitment to the movement in the face of brutal repression. However, if the Interior Ministry's estimates on voter participation are to be accepted, the 2009 presidential election marked the highest ever voter turnout at 85 per cent (Farhi, 2012). This has been understood as one of the most clinching pieces of evidence that the outrage that propelled the Green Movement might have some basis.

Victor H. Sundquist (2013) is of the view that the Green Movement did not succeed in its stated goals, and faults it for its inability to challenge the political system by working within the system. He argues that the movement encountered several social (religious), economic, and political barriers, which included the inability to connect the movement to Islamic ideals and effectively incorporate national labour organisations into the movement's cause, as well as the absence of leadership (Sundquist, 2013).

Further, the movement's commitment to the principle of non-violence ultimately led to its downfall. The effectiveness of revolutionary activity is premised on the appropriate use of violence against a repressor (Sundquist, 2013). However, Chenoweth and Stephan (2011) argue that use of violence is not the decisive factor in making a movement successful. They argue that non-violent movements are often better placed to successfully achieve the goals of political change and affect post-revolutionary societies that are more committed towards the principles of democracy and equality.

The ability of non-violent campaigns to mobilize a higher number of participants with a more diverse array of skills, abilities, and perspectives explains why they have been successful at activating local mechanisms of change in their societies, including shifts in loyalty from the regime to the resistance, and the ability to make regime repression backfire. The historic tendency of non-violent movements to effectively compel regime loyalists to switch to their side underscores the primacy of participation in generating the mechanisms that determine campaign victory or defeat (Chenoweth and Stephen, 2011: 61).

Shabani (2013) introduces another criterion for evaluating the Green Movement. Instead of looking at it as a movement led by disgruntled voters who made claims on civil political rights as citizens, he focusses on the development trajectory of the political culture. He argues that Iranian politics is characterised by two strands: the entrenched power base of the Islamist regime constitutes the dominant strand, while the non-violent and democratic proponents of the reformist movement constitute the emerging and still nascent strand in the Iranian political ethos. Shabani (2013) argues that the regime has had to face a deepening legitimacy crisis, as increasing reports of rampant use of violence against political dissidents emerge in public. The regime's handling of the Green Movement has been telling.

Navid Nikzadfar (2011) in his introduction to Hamid Dabashi's book on the Green Movement, argues that the Green Movement was a significant indicator of the internal changes taking place in the Iranian society. It was not merely an "impulsive explosion of collective dissent against a tainted election", rather, was reflective of the popular responses in a post-revolutionary Iranian society that is weighing the previous experience of secular authoritarianism against the current experience of an Islamist authoritarian regime (Dabashi, 2011:12). Nikzadfar raises the question of whether the emergence of the Green Movement signalled a transition towards a more post-Islamist, post-ideological pluralist Iranian society.

References

Adelkhah, F. (2012), "The Political Economy of the Green Movement: Contestation and Political Mobilization in Iran", in N. Nabavi (ed.), *Iran: From Theocracy to the Green Movement* (New York: Palgrave Macmillan), pp. 17-38.

Arjomand, S. A. (2002), "The Reform Movement and the Debate on Modernity and Tradition in Contemporary Iran", *International Journal of Middle East Studies*, 34(4): 719-731.

Arjomand, S. A. (2005), "The Rise and Fall of President Khatami and the Reform Movement in Iran", *Constellations: An International Journal of Critical & Democratic Theory*, 12(4): 502-520.

Asemi, A. (2006), "Information Technology and National Development in Iran," Hybrid Information Technology, ICHIT'06, International Conference. 1: 558-565.

Associated Press (2009), "Iran Admits Protestors were Murdered", *The Guardian*, 20 December. Retrieved from https://www.theguardian.com/world/2009/dec/20/iran-admits-protesters-murdered

Bayat, A. (2005), "What is Post-Islamism?" *ISIM Review*, *16*: 1.

Bayat, A. (2011), "Arab Revolts: Islamists Aren't Coming!" *Insight Turkey*, 13(2): 9-14.

Bruno, G. (2008), "Backgrounder: Religion and Politics in Iran", Council on Foreign Relations, June 19. Retrieved from https://www.cfr.org/backgrounder/religion-and-politics-iran

Chenoweth, E., and Stephan, M. J. (2011), *Why Civil Resistance Works: The Strategic Logic of Nonviolent Conflict* (New York: Columbia University Press).

Dabashi, Hamid (2011), *The Green Movement in Iran* (New Brunswick: Transaction Publishers).

Dhillon, N. and Egel, D. (2009), "The Many Crises of Iranian Youth", Brookings, June 25. Retrieved from https://www.brookings.edu/opinions/the-many-crises-of-iranian-youth/

Esfandiari, G. (2004), "Iran: Unemployment Becoming a 'National Threat'", *Radio Free Europe Radio Liberty*, 12 March. Retrieved from https://www.rferl.org/a/1051866.html

Esfandiari, P. (2009), "Reporting Chaos," in *Women in the Iranian Elections Campaign and Protest* [Occasional Paper Series], *Middle East Program*, Woodrow Wilson International Center for Scholars, Fall: 20-23.

Farhi, F. (2012), "The Tenth Presidential Elections and Their Aftermath", in N. Nabavi (ed.), *Iran: From Theocracy to the Green Movement* (New York: Palgrave Macmillan), pp. 3-16.

Haghighatjoo, F. (2009), "Women in Iran's Green Movement: Their Role in the 2009 Presidential Election Protests," [Occasional Paper Series], *Middle East Program*, Fall 2009: 15-17.

Hardy, R. (2009), "Iran 'Show Trials' Make Sorry Spectacle", BBC News, 27 August. Retrieved from http://news.bbc.co.uk/2/hi/middle_east/8223239.stm

Hashemi, N. (2014), "Renegotiating Iran's Post-Revolutionary Social Contract: The Green Movement and Struggle for Democracy in the Islamic Republic", *Beyond the Arab Spring: The Evolving Ruling Bargain in The Middle East*, 191-216.

Jeffrey, S. (2009), "Iran Election Protests: The Dead, Jailed and Missing", *The Guardian*, 20 June. Retrieved from https://www.theguardian.com/world/blog/2009/jul/29/iran-election-protest-dead-missing

Johari, A. (2002), "Internet Use in Iran: Access, Social and Educational Issues", *Journal of Educational Technology Research and Development*, 50(1): 81-84.

Keller, J. (2010), "Evaluating Iran's Twitter Revolution," *The Atlantic*, June 18, Retrieved from: http://www.theatlantic.com/technology/archive/2010/06/evaluating-irans-twitter-revolution/58337/

Kurzman, C. (2012), "The Arab Spring: Ideals of the Iranian Green Movement, Methods of the Iranian Revolution", *International Journal of Middle East Studies*, 44(1): 162-165.

Lackner-Gohari, J. (2009), "The June Elections and the Change in Political Culture", [Occasional Paper Series], *Middle East Program*, Fall 2009: 18-20.

Ladier-Fouladi, M. (2012), "Sociodemographic Changes in the Family and Their Impact on the Sociopolitical Behavior of the Youth in Postrevolutionary Iran", in N. Nabavi (ed.), *Iran: From Theocracy to the Green Movement* (New York: Palgrave Macmillan), pp. 137-165.

McAdam, D. T., & Tarrow, S. S. and Tilly, C. (2001), *Dynamics of Contention*. (Cambridge: Cambridge University Press).

Milani, A. (2010), "The Green Movement," *The Iran Primer: Power, Politics, and US Policy*: 41-44.

Monshipouri, M., and Assareh, A. (2009), "The Islamic Republic and the 'Green Movement': Coming Full Circle", *Middle East Policy*, *16*(4): 27-46.

Moruzzi, N. C. (2009), "Quiet Leadership and Pressure from Below," [Occasional Paper Series], *Middle East Program*, Fall 2009: 10-14.

Nabavi, N. (2012), "From 'Reform' to 'Rights': Mapping a Changing Discourse in Iran, 1997–2009," in N. Nabavi (ed.), *Iran: From Theocracy to the Green Movement* (New York: Palgrave Macmillan), pp. 39-54.

Payrow Shabani, O. (2013), "The Green's Non-Violent Ethos: The Roots of Non-Violence in the Iranian Democratic Movement", *Constellations: An International Journal of Critical & Democratic Theory*, 20(2): 347-360.

Press TV (2009), "War of Words in Iran's Presidential Elections", *Payvand*, 4 June. Retrieved from http://www.payvand.com/news/09/jun/1041.html

Reuter Staff, (2011), "Iran Arrests Two Opposition Leaders: Opposition Website," *Reuters*, 28 February. Retrieved from https://www.reuters.com/article/us-iran-opposition-arrest/iran-arrests-two-opposition-leaders-opposition-website-idUSTRE71R5BX20110228

Stockher, C., Neumann, C. and Dorting, T (18 June 2009), "Iran's Twitter Revolution: Ahmadinejad's Fear of the Internet", *Spiegel*, http://www.spiegel.de/international/world/iran-s-twitter-revolution-ahmadinejad-s-fear-of-the-internet-a-631170.html

Sundquist, V.H. (2013), "Iranian Democratization Part I: A Historical Case Study of the Iranian Green Movement", *Journal of Strategic Security*, 6(1): 19-34.

Sundquist, V. (2013), "Iranian Democratization Part II: The Green Movement-Revolution or Civil Rights Movement?," *Journal of Strategic Security*, 6(1): 35-46.

Tait, R. and Weaver, M. (2009), "How Neda Agha-Soltan Became the Face of Iran's Struggle", *The Guardian*, 22 June. Retrieved from https://www.theguardian.com/world/2009/jun/22/neda-soltani-death-iran

Tait, R. (2010), "Iran Election Anniversary Protests Face Severe Crackdown", *The Guardian*, 9 June. Retrieved from https://www.theguardian.com/world/2010/jun/09/iran-election-demonstration-green-repression

Tisdall, S. (2009), "Iran Admits Election Demonstrators Were Tortured", *The Guardian*, 10 August. Retrieved from http://www.guardian.co.uk/world/2009/aug/09/iran-protesters-torture-election

Tohidi, N. (2009), "Iran's Presidential Elections: Women's Role in the Pre- and Post-Election Politics," [Occasional Paper Series], *Middle East Program*, Fall 2009: 4-9.

Washington Times (2009), "Iran's Twitter Revolution," *The Washington Times*, 16 June. Retrieved from https://www.washingtontimes.com/news/2009/jun/16/irans-twitter-revolution/

6. Egypt at Crossroads: Muslim Brotherhood and Post-Mubarak Political Process

Arshad

Abstract

The post-Mubarak political process was dominated by a fragmented polity as there was no consensus for a unified political system to herald the democratic transition. The major cause behind the fractured political system was the hegemony of the military, the agenda of Islamisation of the Muslim Brotherhood (MB), the mistrust between secularists and Islamists and the intervention of the 'deep state' to circumvent liberal democracy. Under such a pretext, a tacit agreement between the Islamists and the military-led Supreme Council of the Armed Forces deepened the polarisation of Egyptian society as the secularists and liberals got further disenchanted with the promotion of the Islamists and military as a counter-revolutionary measure. This chapter, therefore, focusses on the newly surfaced political dynamics in post-Mubarak Egypt and how it prevented a successful democratic transition.

Key Words: Muslim Brotherhood; SCAF; Morsi; Egypt; Mubarak; Arab Spring

The rise of the Muslim Brotherhood (MB) in the post-Mubarak political process in Egypt was embedded in Islamism as a socio-economic phenomenon. Making Islam the principal source of inspiration for the functioning of its organisation, the Brotherhood was able to deeply penetrate the Egyptian politics and society. As a result, the MB became the second largest political force in the country, although it remained banned until the January 25 revolution. However, following the removal of President Hosni Mubarak, the Brotherhood was able to openly participate in the political transition. Consequently, having a strong organisational base, with Islam as the core pillar of its ideology for the mobilisation of common Egyptians, the MB-led Freedom and Justice Party (FJP) was successful in contesting and winning the first democratically-held parliamentary and presidential elections in the history of Egypt. It had a coalition with the Salafists who gained a substantial number of seats in the election to the Parliament on 28 November 2011.

The political process was uncertain because Egypt has had a legacy of military-security rule since the Free Officers Movement in 1952. The military, through a series of decrees, had protected its core interests such as foreign affairs, security and defence budgeting that weakened the 'civilianisation' of the armed forces during the transition process. In addition, the failure of the Islamists to make the transition process inclusive by bringing the secularists, liberals, youths, and women onto a single platform led to the irreversible fissure that created two camps—dividing the people between the Islamists and secularists. Closing this opportunity, the military staged a coup on behalf of the secularists, youth, Copts, and Al-Azhar against President Mohammed Morsi and obstructed the first democratic political transition.

A Government Movement

The Society of the Muslim Brothers was the predecessor of the Muslim Brotherhood (MB). It believed that Islam is an 'all inclusive' and 'total system' that can offer the guidance that Egypt needed to emerge from its spiritual, social and political malaise (Mitchell, 1993: 24). The MB was founded by Hassan Al-Banna in 1928 and had gained recognition by focussing on Islam to attract educated Egyptians. It was able to deepen its networks and connections at the grassroots level by raising social consciousness, and undertaking charitable work and education programmes (Langhor, 2001: 199). According to the Ministry of Social Solidarity, there were around 30,000 charitable organisations in Egypt, with one of the oldest and largest of these being the Al-Gamiya al-Shariya, founded in 1912 (Allam, 2012: 3). The enhanced Islamist social services and populism had provided promising ground for the MB for its social activism.

The Brotherhood movement had expanded to include civil servants, students, urban professionals, workers, peasants and Army officers (Mitchell, 1993: 24). The MB and Islamists realised that they could not challenge the military regime directly and, hence, they had been working proactively at the grassroots level for a long time without questioning the authority of Mubarak (Bayat, 2007: 191). They were able to religiously radicalise the civil society, but they were not able to supersede all other opposition, particularly the secularists, leftists, Nasserites, feminists, etc. At the regional level, the MB has always been divided into national chapters, a far cry from the fantasy of the "Islamist International" (Roy, 2008: 83).

The MB is not a monolithic organisation and its members have a generally accepted ideology. Historically, many generations from different schools of thoughts have joined the MB. Internally, the MB adopted some general principles such as Islam as an omnipotent belief, non-violence for political reform, and democracy as the only channel to achieve power (El-Houdaiby, 2011). It has always focussed on both internal and external factors for its survival. The 'Social Movement Theory' explained why the MB remained a coherent unit despite having divisive members. According to Asef Bayat, an 'imagined solidarity' was propagated by MB leaders for the social transformation. Thus, what brought the Islamists together in Egypt were not shared interests and values in totality but partially shared interests and values that provided them 'imagined solidarity'. Hence, the Islamists movement in Egypt was able to incorporate groups like the modern middle class, businessmen, peasants of upper Egypt, students, youth, and women, all of whom wanted to change the system (2005: 902).

The neo-liberal economic policy based on the Washington Consensus had destroyed the state-controlled structure of the economy and replaced it with a market economy which had created a small coterie of elites while depriving the majority of the people of their basic needs (Farah, 2009: 17). This resulted in the dominance of Islamists in those vacuums and gaps which were left unattended as the state had retreated from them, and the Islamists became the sole 'providers' or 'allocators' of resources (Al-Awadi, 2004: 106). The neglect of the regime also gave an impetus to the charitable works of civil society groups (Darwisheh, 2014: 117). Knowing that Egyptians needed more basic services than Islam, they focussed on social, political and economic reforms, but keeping Islam as the guiding principle behind their activities (Zubaida, 2001: 242). To garner support, the Islamists never talked about Islam as the solution but always brought in the issues of dignity and self-empowerment which the regime had failed to provide for the common Egyptians (Ayoob, 2004: 11).

The Islamic banking system has also played a major role in providing support to the poor Egyptians (Ibrahim, 1988: 641). Even the regime had to consider the Islamic services because it had to placate the masses in a positive manner (Morsy, 1988: 359). The increasing Islamic capital was supposed to improve the prospects for Islamist politicians, becoming more moderate, institutionalised and democratic. In addition, the Islamic finance in Egypt is less dependent on a neo-liberal economic policy as it has a meagre focus on export trade which was why one of the major businessmen related to the MB, Khairat al-Shater, emphasised on domestic retail sales services to garner funding (Henry, Ji-Hyang and Lee, 2013: 261). Hence, until the 1980s, the private sector was dominated by people who were associated with the Brotherhood (Beinin, 2005: 120). Wealthy people like Hassan Malek and Khairat al-Shatter from the MB dominated the private sector of the Egyptian economy.

Islamic banking increased due to the withdrawal of the state from the social sphere. It was termed by Raymond Hinnebusch as the "post-populist development of an authoritarian-modernising state" (Hinnebusch, 1985: 162). It was started by President Anwar Sadat and the Mubarak regime had totally institutionalised the 'post-populist' neo-liberal economic policy (Hinnebusch, 2000: 129-130).

MB in Egyptian Politics

When the Free Officers Movement captured the Egyptian state, the military had realised that the MB was a formidable political opponent. The MB not only had the numbers but also an attractive ideology that was deeply connected to Egyptian history and culture (Gordon, 1996: 31). To enhance its stronghold, since Nasser's rule, the military created its own networks of people from the military, security, bureaucracy, education system, media, professional syndicates, trade unions, rural governance, and the Shaykh of Al-Azhar, and gradually, the whole society under the garb of the 'command economy' (Vatikiotis, 1978: 127). Thus, the political system was based on a tacit political compact, supported by de-politicisation of the Egyptians in exchange for jobs, education, health facilities, cheap housing and a symbolic sense of dignity (Basheer, 1999: 5).

The Arab defeat in the June 1967 War and the death of Nasser in 1970 left a gigantic ideological and power void which was occupied by new Islamist youth activists such as Khairat al-Shatir, Abd al-Munin Abdul Futuh, Hazim Salah Abu Ismail and Mohammed Morsi under the name of Al-Gamat al-Islamiyya, without any formal institution until they started to operate under the MB (Darwisheh, 2014: 112). Subsequently, in April 1974, Sadat's *infitah* policy pitched for economic restructuring and partial political liberalisation which helped to establish the 'nucleus' of the Islamic movement under the Brothers, coupled with the rise of a new Islamic business class. The MB's third supreme leader Umar al-Timisani was the main architect behind the participation in the parliamentary and syndicate elections (Kotob, 1995: 323). Hence, it followed internal reconstruction, consolidation of the structure (*tanzim*) and social activism, and engagement with the state apparatus to expand its reach in society (Darwisheh, 2014: 113).

The gradual deepening of the social, political and economic influence of the MB developed a notion of a 'state, within a state' alarming the regime, prompting it to shift the policy from accommodation to repression (Campagna, 1996: 280-281). Now, the MB realised the need for human rights norms against the onslaught of the military on its members, and in the ploy to protect human rights, it used the "charm offensive" (Osman, 2013: 101) against the regime. It also changed its slogan from "Islam is the Solution" to "Constitution is the Solution" (Shehata, 2010: 55-56). New documents were outlined to restructure its policy such as the Citizenship Paper (1994) and Reform Initiative (2004) (Hawthrone, 2004: 16). As a result, the leaders of the MB, on the one hand, maintained social conservatism but, on the other, adopted liberal democracy and freedom (Dalacoura, 2011: 123).

Despite the continuous victory of Mubarak in fraudulent and rigged presidential elections until 2010, the protests against him by the youths, secularists and Islamic groups continued under the banner of the 'Kifaya' movement. This ultimately became the 'mid-wife' for the January 25, 2011 revolution that toppled Mubarak in February (Beinin and Vairel: 245). Officially, the MB did not support the protests in the beginning and asked its members to follow the means of constitutional reforms and elections (Maugiron, 2011: 47). However, its members were free to take part on an individual basis. In addition, the youth branch of the MB participated fully in the revolution, right from its beginning (Blaydes and Kayser, 2011: 853). In addition, the MB confirmed that it would neither contest in the presidential election nor in more than 35 per cent of the seats in both the Legislative Assembly and Shura Council in the parliamentary elections (Shahin, 2014: 63).

With the removal of Mubarak, the military had created the Supreme Council of the Armed Forces (SCAF) comprising twenty members of the military, in March 2011, to govern Egypt until the conduct of election. It made a tacit agreement with the MB since it was the strongest opposition (Brown, 2012). At the domestic level, when the nationalist-secular military regime was not able to achieve satisfactory economic development, a counter-elites group comprising businessmen, professionals, intellectuals, unemployed educated youths and the common masses who were not able to meet their basic needs, joined the Islamists like the MB. Thus, the Islamists were able to tap the anti-regime sentiments to mobilise an emerging political community (Darwisheh, 2014: 110). The SCAF realised that for decades, the MB had consolidated its position and, hence, it could win the elections. Later, the SCAF made constitutional amendments on March 30 that helped the MB to gain support from the masses, the military and Western governments, yet keeping the military as the supreme political entity (Darwisheh, 2014: 127).

The nexus between the SCAF and the MB deliberately excluded the genuine opposition which was protesting against the Mubarak regime from the beginning, namely, the secularists, liberals, leftists, Copts, and women. The MB leaders focussed more on the procedure of transition rather than on building political alliances because it was the strongest organisation in post-Mubarak Egypt (Darwisheh: 128). Fearing the hegemony of the Islamists-led MB in the Parliament, the non-Islamists groups realised that they would not be able to win the elections in this quick transition process and, thus, wanted a Constitution before the elections. The inverse sequencing of the political transition in Egypt split up the already divided opposition which ultimately helped the military to reinforce itself.

Parliamentary Elections, 2011

In the run-up to the elections for the Parliament that began on 28 November 2011, and ended on 11 January 2012, 31 new parties, including but not limited to, Freedom and Justice Party (FJP),[11] New Wafd Party, Al-Nour Party, Justice Party, Wasat Party and Youth Party were formed. As a result, in the absence of a Constitution, greater freedom prevailed in the electoral politics which implicitly recognised that no single popular party could represent the fundamental interests of a diverse population (Asad, 2012: 281). Since the MB had the strong national base, it won 45 per cent seats in the Lower House and 58 per cent seats in the Upper House (Lenze, 2016: 57).

The Salafi movement,[12] led by Al-Nour Party, was able to grab 25 per cent of the seats in both Houses which surprised many because it was a highly conservative Islamist movement and had not been involved in politics before 2011. The remaining 32 per cent of the seats were divided among 15 other parties, independents, and state-appointed MPs

11. It was established in June 2011 by MB. The FJP had disguised itself as a civil society but religion remained the centre of its activities. It remained ambiguous and inconsistent because, on the one hand, it considered '*shura*' (consultation) as a broader and more inclusive term than democracy and, on the other, '*shura*' and 'democracy' were used interchangeably to suit its electoral gains. It also lacked internal democratisation because its members such as Mohammed Morsi, Essam el-Erian and Mohammed Saad el-Katatny were not chosen through elections (see: Anani, 2015: 229-230).
12. Many Salafis were recruited in the past by the state security forces to counter the MB. Many were against the revolution and sided with the forces of the Ministry of Interior but not all Salafists identified with the regime. They represented some genuinely traditional and ultra-conservative phenomena. Their financing came from Salafis outside of Egypt, particularly from the conservative forces in the Saudi regime. They increased their visibility after the 2011 revolution but still played into the hands of the SCAF and the military (see: Shafeeq, 2015: 212).

(Anderson, 2013: 43). The largest liberal party which came third was the Wafd (Delegation) Party which won only 7.5 per cent of the seats in the Lower House and 8 per cent in the Upper House. The other liberal party was an alliance of liberal groups called the Egyptian Bloc which won 6.7 per cent seats in the Lower House and 4.5 per cent in the Upper House (Rutherford, 2013: 44). Interestingly, the Islamists had emerged as the winners and, subsequently, the dominant players in Egyptian politics, and ultimately excluded the secular and liberal forces from the political process (Darwisheh, 2014: 118).

The MB's victory in the elections deeply divided the Islamists-led government and the secular opposition composed of liberals, leftists, and secularists, along with the support of the remnants of Mubarak's cliques and revolutionary youth activists. Hence, the political discourse in Egypt quickly metamorphosed from "Muslim Brotherhood versus the Opposition" into "Islamist versus Secularist", creating a deeply polarised polity. The division diverted the youth activists' attention from the original goals of the revolution and they became increasingly involved in the pitched battles taking place between the government and the opposition, based on the Islamist versus secularist discourse. However, the discourse among youth activists did not replicate the simple binary narrative of the older generation of politicians, which was overwhelmingly focussed on the Islamist versus secularist issue (Laiq, 2013: 8-9).

The Brotherhood continued to advocate the fusion of religion with politics after February 2011, but the major task of the Islamists-led Parliament was to control the prominent political institutions of Egypt (Abdou and Zaazou, 2013: 95). The Islamist-dominated Constituent Assembly argued that the Islamic character of Egypt was preserved in the 1923 Constitution through Article 2 (Saleh, 2012). As a result, the Assembly speedily carried forward the drafting of the Constitution, resulting in deeper political polarisation. The secular/liberal groups complained that their demands for a 'secular' state, protection of minority rights, equality of the sexes, and women's education were not included in the Constitution that would ultimately undermine the state's secular or "civil" character (Landolt and Kubicek, 2014: 99). Establishing an Islamic state was the preconceived agenda of the MB, and its political wing, the FJP, had mentioned in its founding document its commitment to the official relationship between Islam and the state (IkhwanWeb, 2011).

The Islamists also supported the SCAF-endorsed constitutional declaration of 30 March 2011, voted for by 77.2 per cent of the registered voters. Later, unofficial campaigns for the presidential election were started by many aspiring candidates. Despite the removal of Mubarak, several anti-democratic electoral rules for the presidential election remained such as the candidate should be born in Egypt, the candidate's parents should be Egyptians, the candidate must not hold dual nationality and he or she should not have married a non-Egyptian. The decisions of the Supreme Presidential Electoral Commission (SPEC) were final and could not be challenged in the court (Rabou, 2012: 2). The judiciary had collaborated with the military to frustrate the attempts of the MB to grab power through its SPEC and Supreme Constitutional Court (SCC) institutions (Laremont, 2014: 155). As a result, the President's election was marred by confusion and ambiguities that hindered the transition process. The first instance occurred on 14 April 2012, when the SPEC ruled that ten of the presidential candidates (including Khairat el-Shater, Omar Suleiman, Hazem Salah Abu Ismail)[13] were debarred from contesting in the presidential elections (Kirkpatrick, 2012).

The next attack was launched on 11 May 2012, with the announcement of General Ahmed Shafik (who was the last Prime Minister under Mubarak), as a presidential candidate, supported by the SCAF. Several cases of corruption were pending against him because of his deep complicity with Mubarak's cliques. Moreover, he was supported by the SCAF and SCC, the old regime's petty capitalists, and the privately-owned media that reinvented Shafik into a revolutionary figure (Greene, 2012). During the

13. Khairat el Shater was the leading strategist and financier of MB, and Hazem Salah Abu Ismail represented the ultra-conservative Islamist forces. Omar Suleiman was notorious, had served as Vice President of Egypt and Chief of the Intelligence Services. By removing the candidatures of these candidates, SPEC claimed that it wanted to eliminate both the remnants of Mubarak's regime and Islamists. The result was that the commission diminished its credibility and displayed judicial *legerdemain* by unilaterally narrowing the number of candidates for presidents (see: Laremont, 2014: 155).

presidential election, the biggest dilemma for the secularists and liberals was to choose between supporting the old order led by Shafik or to vote for the anti-secular Islamist candidate (El Fadl, 2015: 259).

Presidential Election, 2012

Under the SCAF watch, the first multi-party presidential elections took place in two rounds: the first on 23-24 May and the second on 16-17 June. Among the five run-up candidates, Mohammed Morsi of the MB-led Freedom and Justice Party (FJP) won by a narrow margin over Ahmed Shafik. Other influential candidates were Abdel Moneim Aboul Fotouh who was a former Nasserist, Hamdin Sabbahi, the politician, journalist, poet, and leader of the Egyptian Popular Current and co-leader of the National Salvation Front, and Amr Moussa, a politician and diplomat (Darwisheh, 2014: 126).

The outcome of the first round resulted in two finalists, Mohammed Morsi and Ahmed Shafik, for the second round, with the approval of the SPEC. On 13 June 2012, just three days before the second round of the election, the military unilaterally restored a martial law that had been despised by the Egyptians for long (Brown, 2012). The next day, the SCC, mostly staffed by Mubarak's appointees, outlawed the Parliament by claiming that at least one-third of the elected parliamentarians had been unconstitutionally elected, and the independent candidates faced discriminatory electoral laws (Kirkpatrick, 2012). Rather than dismissing the one-third that was unlawfully elected, the SCC outlawed the entire Parliament (BBC News, 2012). This action of the SCC injected a high degree of cynicism among the Egyptians and eroded the overall legitimacy of the transition process.

Another blow to the transition process came on 17 June, when the SCAF amended the Egyptian Constitution and stripped the President and Parliament of any real power by issuing constitutional amendments, transferring the legislative and war-making power to the SCAF. Now the military, not the President, had the power to wage war or send troops to cull the protests (El-Fadl, 2015: 259). In other words, the power of the Parliament and President was overridden by the SCAF (Rutherford, 2013: 45). On 25 June 2012, the SCC not only challenged the legitimacy of the Upper House of Parliament but also made it clear that it needed to be dissolved and, above all, the SCAF appointed a 100-member committee to draft the Constitution (*Al-Ahram*, 2012).

The second round of elections was held only after these deep military interventions. Now the President was reduced to a nominal head, with the military usurping all the constitutional powers of the presidency to protect its own core privileges (Khorshid, 2012). The reality was that the SCAF broke its pledge of relinquishing power within six months because it had to secure economic, financial and legal profits from the revolution. In other words, the privileges of the 'deep state' were to be protected at any cost. These privileges were considered the 'red-line' by the military which was beyond the negotiation table, irrespective of the ideological background of the new regime (Anani, 2015: 231).

The constitutional coup was justified by the SCAF on account of the state-sponsored tradition of the Egyptian 'rule of law' along with the questioning of the principle of legitimacy of the MB rule (Kamrava, 2014: 176). The outcome of the result was in favour of Mohammed Morsi who gained 52 per cent of the vote against Shafik with 48 per cent (*The Guardian*, 2012). The share of the percentage of votes of both the final candidates indicated how divisive the country had become (Esposito, Sonn and Voll, 2015: 219). President Morsi promised to be the leader of all Egyptians and to build a new Egypt that is "civil, national, constitutional and modern" (IkhwanWeb, 2012). Although Morsi was in the presidential palace without a Constitution in place, his powers were ill-defined. As a result, after the behind the curtain agreement with military, Morsi first dismissed the SCAF leader Tantawi and Army Chief of Staff Lieutenant Colonel Sami Anan from their posts on 12 August 2012, but two days later, awarded them Egypt's highest honours: Tantawi was given the Order of the Nile, Anan was awarded the Order of the Republic, and Abdul Fatah al-Sisi was appointed the Defence Minister of Egypt (Fahim, 2012; *Al-Jazeera*, 2012; *The Washington Post*, 2012).

To re-start the drafting of the Constitution after the dissolution of the People's Assembly, President Morsi issued a decree on 22 November 2012 which gave him some controversial extra-constitutional powers such as his declarations could not be scrapped until a new Constitution was drafted and started functioning. With the SCC's power breached by Morsi, it could not dissolve the Upper House and the President had the final authority to take any action to protect, preserve and safeguard the revolution, national unity or national security (*Al Masry Al Youm,* 2012). This process became chaotic as Morsi's powers were considered to be 'quasi-dictatorial' before the announcement of the referendum (Kirkpatrick and Sheikh, 2012). The Constituent Assembly dominated by the MB and Salafi members approved the new Constitution on 30 November 2012, and it was passed in a referendum held during 15-22 December 2012, with 64 per cent support that had a voter turnout of just 33 per cent. Later, on 26 December, President Morsi finally signed the Constitution (Kirkpatrick and Sheikh, 2012).

The fall of the authoritarian regime exposed the fragile political system to antagonistic forces. From the beginning, the MB and the Salafists had marginalised the liberal secularists and Copts; for instance, when the committee to draft the Constitution was established, it was dominated by the Islamists which provoked criticism from the Copts, liberals, and women (Brookings, 2012). The revolutionary forces saw in the MB's tendency to act unilaterally, a shift from pluralist, inclusive politics towards a monopoly of power (Darwisheh, 2014: 130). In other words, there was the intensive '*Brotherhoodisation*' of the Egyptian Constitution (Momani, 2013). The non-Islamists tried to meet several demands such as extensive negotiations before the drafting of the Constitution, a civilian presidential council, a committee to amend the Constitution and new rules for the parliamentary and presidential elections. Thus, the Islamist and non-Islamist forces were irreconcilably divided (Kirkpatrick and Fahim, 2012).

Morsi had spoken about a civil state, rather than a secular one, based on democracy and a Constitution that was not theocratic (*Egypt Independent*, 2012). Parallels between the *shura* (consultation) and democracy are a core aspect of the FJP's political reform, focussing on citizens' participation (Freedom and Justice Party, 2011). A new Article 4 was included which declared that the clerical authorities (officials at Al-Azhar University) would be consulted on the application of the *Sharia* throughout the review of the legislation, governmental policy and judicial decree, thereby creating a 'quasi-theocracy' in Egypt (Laremont, 2014: 159). Having a prominent position in the Sunni Muslim world, the Shaykh of Al-Azhar, Ahmed al-Tayyib issued a statement on 16 February 2011, wherein he stated that Al-Azhar called for a system of governance that respects the rights of all citizens and that despotism is inherently and fundamentally a breach of the *Sharia*. Thus, for the Shaykh, the Egyptian revolution and its goals were the Islamic and proper normative expression of the *Sharia* laws (Moussa, 2015: 248). Since the Egyptian transition process was undertaken with 'reverse logic' (Hessler, 2017), a great amount of confusion crept into the transition which created a deep social division.

The Egyptian public remained clear that the Brotherhood's ultimate motive was to make the country an exclusivist political-religious system (Henry et al., 2013: 260). The Islamists and the secularists were taken hostage by the 'uncertainty' of the transition process because the Islamists realised that the newly appointed secular-military regime would ban them as it had done earlier, and the revolutionary bloc was concerned over the fact that the Islamists and military would collaborate against the revolution. The fast-moving transition, with the underlining uncertainty of all the stakeholders, turned the democratisation process in Egypt not only chaotic but also stagnant as the opposition started fighting among themselves rather than challenging the military that was the root cause of the problems (Brown and Waller, 2016).

As a result, there was no central platform which could have managed the transition from an 'Egyptian Spring' to a stable democracy, unlike the case of Tunisia where several stakeholders came onto a platform for the successful implementation of the transition process (Wittes, 2014). The result was that the fight for freedom, dignity, human rights and equality against the military was reduced to a fight between the Islamists and non-Islamists which ultimately diverted the focus of the uprising from battling the state to fighting among themselves, from striving for "substantive democratization" to engaging in an "electoral competition" (Darwisheh, 2014: 129).

Another inherent weakness of the Egyptian transition process was that the revolutionary forces did not have any clear plan or strong collective institution. They could not move towards a radical change (Bayat, 2013:

591). According to Bayat, "It was not a revolution but a 'refolution', or an uprising that asserted to reform Egypt through the institutions of the existing regime" (2013: 53). The biggest debate in post-Mubarak Egypt was on what should come first: a Constitution or elections. It can be contextualised in Fareed Zakaria's views on consolidation of liberal democracy—whether "liberal" or "democracy" will be the starting point for the transition is debatable. Consequently, the Egyptian people chose elections first, and ended up having a democracy without liberalism which threatened the liberals, minorities and secularists through persecution under the majoritarian Islamist Constitution (Culbertson, 2016: 272). The MB, however, was able to strengthen itself through the election. The Generals probably feared that the MB leaders would support a free market economy based on neo-liberal policies that would undermine the military's monopoly over the resources. Thus, it can be understood that the SCAF was not motivated by only a single factor, namely, defending the revolution, but was reacting to various pressures: the ever-active radical revolutionaries, the increasing political confidence of the MB, the financial and diplomatic manoeuvring of the US and Saudi Arabia, and its own institutional privileges (Asad, 2012: 276).

The protest against Morsi was triggered by his 22 November 2012 constitutional decree which was seen by the opposition such as the secularists, women and liberals as an agenda to create a 'quasi-theocratic' state, hence, they launched a new coalition, the National Salvation Front (NSF), led by Amr Moussa, comprising many secularists and *fulool* (relics of Mubarak) (Al-Amin, 2012). Since several elements of *fulool* had joined the NSF, it was boycotted by youth activists such as Abdel Moneim Abdou Fotou (Strong Egypt Party), Akram Ismail (Socialist Popular Alliance Party), and Khaled Dawoud who resigned as the spokesperson of the NSF (Al-Ahram, 2013). In such a fluid political situation, the opposition groups were forced to regularly examine their aims and collide with even the Army to achieve them. The country's Constitution, which was supposed to be the crowning achievement of the revolution, and the judiciary, which was supposed to guarantee that the historic transition would evolve in a lawful manner, became two of the country's most controversial aspects and causes for division (Esposito, Sonn and Voll, 2015: 225).

There was a division even among the liberals which resurfaced during the appointment of Mubarak's successor; for instance, there was a conflict between El Baradei's National Association for Change and Saad Eddin Ibrahim. The splits and fissures among the prominent opposition leaders became more critical when Egypt was on the verge of succession and the opposition could have had an opportunity to shape the politics. The opposition was so notoriously fractious that it even provided help to the regime-friendly intellectuals (Cook, 2012: 208). The disgruntled youths created another movement under the banner of *Tamarod* or "rebellion" as civil disobedience against Morsi. It comprised Shayfeencom, Kefaya, the NSF, April 6 movement, and members of the NDP, Strong Egypt Party and ex-Prime Minister Ahmed Shafik (Gjorvad, 2013). Tamarod was a prime example of a nascent youth-inspired movement that played a pivotal role in the military ouster of President Morsi in July 2013. It was supported by the military under the command of General Fatah al-Sisi (Laiq, 2013: 55).

The trajectory of Egypt's political history and the fractured opposition confirmed that whether it had overthrown Mubarak or Morsi, the struggle to define Egypt was not over yet. The authoritarian structure run by the deep state was intact. There was news of bloodshed from all sides: the Brotherhood, Tamarod (rebellion) and the Army. The removal of Morsi sowed the seeds of divisiveness in the society based on sectarianism and political ideology as well the political maturity of the Egyptian people (International Crisis Group, July 2013).

Conclusion

According to Lisa Anderson (2013), five major political factors significantly affected the transition process in Egypt: one, the MB "civil state" was opposed to fully endorsing the civil rights and liberties of women and minorities; two, the process of institution building was opaque and dictated, top-down, by the SCAF and MB; three, the military, through constitutional decrees remained the arbiter and manager of the transition process; four, the design of the electoral system resulted in a majority for the Islamists; and five, there was less evidence of prior bridge building between the opposition forces in Egypt. In sum, the challenges to democratisation in Egypt seemed altogether fatal (p. 45). In addition, there were the impediments of the structural legacies and the role of the military as arbiter; neo-corporatism of the regime; and politicisation of the judiciary.

The incompetence of Morsi as President, firmness of the military-security structures and deliberate exclusion of different ideological groups from the constitutional drafting process stunted the Egyptian political system. As a result, the frustration of the common masses was exploited by the military with the help of the youth, Al-Azhar, Al-Nour Party, women, etc. Hence, the removal of President Morsi choked the transition process. The opposition against the regime, marred by its own ideological, political and social differences, provided enough scope for the military to step in in the name of secularism, democracy, freedom, and justice. Structurally, Egypt's military as the guardian of the republic was able to remove the individual from the political system, yet the praetorian nature of Egyptian politics remained intact, coupled with the continuous support of external actors such as the US and European Union.

The Brotherhood had followed the same neo-liberal policy that was continuously widening the socio-economic gaps between the rich and the poor. As a result, it failed to resolve the basic problems such as shortage of fuel and rations. In addition, Morsi never tried to negotiate with the regime to scrap the 'emergency law' which was one of the major causes of the uprising. The political prisoners who were arrested by the security forces during the Arab Spring were not released by him. He even allowed violence against the Tamarod protestors by his supporters just as Mubarak had against the protestors. The security sector was not reformed, and it regularly violated human rights, perpetrating extra-judicial killings and torture of protestors (Blunt and Faulks, 2018). Politically, the Egyptians were not able to generate a consensus to have either the election or Constitution first, ultimately establishing a political system that was democratic without the liberal values. The result was that a fragmented polity emerged that helped the military, Mubarak's cliques and deep state to sustain their control over Egypt. The MB, therefore, was not able to continue its rule in Egypt as it was not able to maintain its tacit agreement with the military. The historical mistrust between the secular military and the Islamists remained the major fault-line that overrode the unholy embrace of the Islamists and the military in post-Mubarak Egypt. In addition, the lack of governance and administrative experience created further hurdles for the Islamists in ruling the country as they were reluctant to synchronise the traditional values and modern institutions. With all these inherent structural problems of the Egyptian political system, driven by the incompetent leadership skills and their negative attitudes towards the transition process, the process of democratic transition under the Islamists leadership failed to reap any positive fruits for democracy building.

References

Abdou, S Doaa and Zaazou, Zeinab (2013), "The Egyptian Revolution and Post Socio-Economic Impact", *Topics in Middle Eastern and African Economies,* 15(1): 92-114.

Ahmed Abd Rabou (2012), "Egypt After Elections: Towards the Second Republic?", *Insight Turkey,* 14(3), https://www.insightturkey.com/author/ahmed-abd-rabou/egypt-after-elections-towards-the-second-republic.

Al-Ahram Online (10 March 2013), "Egypt's Morsi To Reach Out to NSF, Youth Groups: Presidential Source". Retrieved on 12 January 2018, http://english.ahram.org.eg/NewsContent/1/64/66576/Egypt/Politics-/Egypts-Morsi-to-reach-out-to-NSF,-youth-groups-Pre.aspx

_________. (18 June 2012), English Text of SCAF Amended Egypt Constitutional Declaration, 18 September 2017, http://english.ahram.org.eg/NewsContent/1/64/45350/Egypt/Politics-/URGENT-English-text-of-SCAF-amended-Egypt-Constitu.aspx.

Al-Awadi, Hesham (2004) *In Pursuit of Legitimacy: The Muslim Brothers and Mubarak, 1982-2000* (London: Tauris Academic Studies).

Al-Jazeera (13 August 2012), "Crowds in Cairo Praise Morsi's Army Overhaul". Retrieved on 13 September 2017, http://www.aljazeera.com/news/middleeast/2012/08/201281215511142445.html.

Allam, Rabha (May 2012), "Engaging with Traditional and Modern Islamic NGOs in Egypt", Netherlands-Flemish Institute in Cairo, Policy Brief-3, 1-6. http://media.leidenuniv.nl/legacy/policy-brief---islamic-ngos-in-egypt.pdf.

Al-Masry, Al-Youm (22 November 2012), "Morsy Issues New Constitutional Declaration". Retrieved on 12 September 2017, http://www.egyptindependent.com/node/1260136.

Anani, Khalil (2015), "The Anguish of the Muslim Brotherhood in Egypt", in Larbi Sadiki (ed.), *Routledge Handbook of the Arab Spring: Rethinking Democratization.* (London: Routledge), pp.227-240.

Anderson, Lisa (2013), "Early Adopters and the Neighborhood Effects", in Clement Henry and Jang Ji-Hyang (eds.), *The Arab Spring: Will it lead to Democratic Transitions?* (New York: Springer), pp. 27-33.

Asad, Talal (2012), "Fear and the Ruptured State: Reflections on Egypt after Mubarak", *Social Research*, 79 (2): 271-298.

Ayoob, Mohammed (2004), "Political Islam: Image and Reality", *World Policy Journal,* 21(3): 1-14.

Basheer, Tahseen (1999), "The Egyptian State in Transition", in Phebe Marr (ed.). *Egypt at Crossroads: Domestic Stability and Regional Role* (Washington: National Defence University Press), pp. 3-16.

Bayat, Asef (2005), "Islamism and Social Movement Theory", *Third World Quarterly,* 26 (6): 891-908.

__________ (2007), *Making Islam Democratic: Social Movements and the Post-Islamist Turn* (Stanford: Stanford University Press).

__________ (2013), "The Arab Spring and Its Surprises", *Development and Change,* 44 (3): 587-601.

__________ (2013), *Life as Politics: How Ordinary People Change the Middle East* (Stanford: Stanford University Press).

BBC, News (14 June 2012), "Egypt's Supreme Court Calls for Parliament to be Dissolved". Retrieved on 14 October 2017, http://www.bbc.com/news/world-middle-east-18439530.

Beinin, Joel and Vairel, Frederic (2011), "Afterward: Popular Uprisings in Tunisia and Egypt", in Joel Beinin and Frederic Vairel (ed.), *Social Movements, Mobilization, and Contestation in the Middle East and North Africa* (California: Stanford University Press), pp. 237-255.

__________ (2005), "Political Islam and the New Global Economy: The Political Economy of an Egyptian Social Movement", *The New Centennial Review,* 5(1): 111-139.

Blaydes, Lisa and Kayser, Andreas Mark (2011), "Counting Calories: Democracy and Distribution in the Developing World", *International Studies Quarterly*, No.55, No.4, 889-908.

Blunt, Crispin and Faulks, Edward (8 April 2018), "If Mohamed Morsi's Treatment in Egypt Tora Prison Doesn't Improve Soon, He Could Face a Premature Death", *Independent.* Retrieved on 12 June 2018, https://www.independent.co.uk/voices/mohamed-morsi-egypt-tora-prison-treatment-early-death-health-diabetes-latest-a8287856.html.

Brookings (14 November 2012), “Drafting the Constitution: Defining Post-Revolutionary Egypt”. Retrieved on 22 November 2017, https://www.brookings.edu/events/drafting-the-constitution-defining-post-revolutionary-egypt/.

Brown, J Nathan (14 June 2012), “Cairo's Judicial Coup»”, *Foreign Policy*. Retrieved 23 February 2017. http://foreignpolicy.com/2012/06/14/cairos-judicial-coup/.

________ (10 December 2012), “Islam in Egypt's New Constitution”, *Foreign Policy*. Retrieved on 28 July 2017, http://foreignpolicy.com/2012/12/13/islam-in-egypts-new-constitution/.

________ (1 October 2012), “Still Hope for Egypt's Constitution”, *Foreign Policy*. Retrieved on July 27, 2017, http://foreignpolicy.com/2012/10/01/still-hope-for-egypts-constitution.

________ and Waller G. Julian (1 October 2016), “Constitutional Courts and Political Uncertainty: Constitutional Ruptures and the Rule of the Judges”, *International Journal of Constitutional Law*, 14(1): 817-850.

Campagna, Joel (1996), “From Accommodation to Confrontation: The Muslim Brotherhood in the Mubarak Years”, *Journal of International Affairs*, 50(1): 278-304.

Cook, A Steven (2012), *The Struggle for Egypt: From Nasser to Tahrir Square* (Oxford: Oxford University Press).

Culbertson, Shelly (2016), *The Fires of Spring: A Post-Arab Spring Journey Through the Turbulent New Middle East: Tunisia, Turkey, Iraq, Jordan, Qatar, Egypt* (St. Martin's Press).

Dalacoura, Katerian (2011), *Islamist Terrorism and Democracy in the Middle East* (Cambridge: Cambridge University Press).

Daragahi, Borzou. (15 June 2012), “Egypt Court Orders Parliament Dissolved”. *Financial Times*. Retrieved on 15 October 2017, https://www.ft.com/content/02c5e588-b61c-11e1-a511-00144feabdc0.

Darwisheh, Housam (2014), “Survival, Triumph and Fall: The Political Transformation of the Muslim Brotherhood in Egypt”, in Khoo Boo Teik, Vedi R Hadiz and Yoshihiro Nakanishi (eds.), *Between Dissent and Power: The Transformation of Islamic Politics in the Middle East and Asia* (Basingstoke: Palgrave-Macmillan), pp. 108-134.

Egypt Independent (25 September 2012), “Egypt Is Civil, not Secular State”, *22* October 2017, http://www.egyptindependent.com/news/morsy-egypt-civil-not-secular-state.

El-Fadl, Abou Khaled (2015), “Failure of a Revolution: The Military, Secular Intelligentsia and Religion in Egypt's Pseudo-Secular State. In Larbi Sadiki (eds.), *Routledge Handbook of the Arab Spring: Rethinking Democratization* (London: Routledge), pp. 240-253.

El-Houdaiby, Ibrahim (23 April 2011), "The Muslim Brotherhood's Trail of Pluralism". *Ahram Online*. Retrieved on 23 July 2017, http://english.ahram.org.eg/NewsContentP/4/10662/Opinion/The-Muslim-Brotherhoods-trial-of-pluralism.aspx.

Esam, Al-Amin (2012, November 2012). "Egypt's Political Showdown," *International Policy Digest*. Retrieved on 23 December 2017, https://intpolicydigest.org/2012/11/30/egypt-s-political-showdown/.

Esposito, L John, Sonn, Tamara, and Voll O, John (2015), *Islam and Democracy After the Arab Spring* (Oxford: Oxford University Press).

Farah, Ramsis Nadia (2009), *Egypt's Political Economy: Power Relations in Development* (Cairo: American University in Cairo Press).

Freedom and Justice Party (4 December 2011), "FJP 2011 Program on Freedoms and Political Reform. Freedom and Justice Party", 4 July 2017, http://www.fjponline.com/article.php?id=197.

Gjorvad, Nicholas (12 October 2013), "The Evolution of Tamarod", *Daily News Egypt*. Retrieved on 15 June 2018, https://dailynewsegypt.com/2013/10/12/the-evolution-of-tamarod/.

Gordon, Joel (1996), *Nasser's Blessed Movement: Egypt's Free Officers and the July Revolution* (Cairo: American University in Cairo Press).

Greene, Allen Richard (15 June 2012), "Ahmed Shafik: Egypt's Counter-Revolutionary Candidate", *CNN*. Retrieved on 12 July 2018, https://edition.cnn.com/2012/05/22/world/africa/egypt-election-shafik/index.html.

Hawthrone, Amy (2004), "Political Reform in the Arab World: A New Ferment", *Carnegie Papers*, No.52. http://carnegieendowment.org/2004/10/17/political-reform-in-arab-world-new-ferment-pub-15989.

Henry, Clement; Ji-Hyang, Jang, and Lee, Peter (2013), "Democratic Transitions in the Arab World", in Clement Henry and Jang Ji-Hyang (eds.), *The Arab Spring: Will it lead to Democratic Transitions?* (New York: Springer), pp. 256-270.

Hessler, Peter (2 January 2017), "Egypt's Failed Revolution", *The New Yorker*, retrieved on April 12, 2018, https://www.newyorker.com/magazine/2017/01/02/egypts-failed-revolution.

Hinnebusch, A Raymond (2000), "Liberalization Without Democratization in Post-Populist Authoritarian States: Evidence from Syria and Egypt", in Nils Butenschon, Uri Davis and Manuel Hassassian (eds.), *Citizenship and the State in the Middle East: Approaches and Applications* (New York: Syracuse University Press), pp. 123-146.

__________ (1985) *Egyptian Politics Under Sadat: The Post-Populist Development of an Authoritarian-Modernizing State* (Cambridge: Cambridge University Press).

Ibrahim, Eddin Saad (1988), "Egypt's Islamic Activism in the 1980s", *Third World Quarterly*, 10(2): 632-657.

International Crisis Group, "A Difficult Way Forward in Egypt", 3 July 2013. Retrieved on 12 November 2017, https://www.crisisgroup.org/middle-east-north-africa/north-africa/egypt/difficult-way-forward-egypt.

Ikhwanweb (1 June 2011), "The Founding Statement of the Freedom and Justice Party". Retrieved on 22 January 2018, http://www.ikhwanweb.com/article.php?id=28662&ref=search.php.

________ (30 June 2012), "President Morsi's Remarks Upon Taking the Oath of Office". Retrieved on 29 July 2017, http://www.ikhwanonline.com/new/president3/Article.aspx?ArtID=112981&SecID=470.

________ (12 November 2012), "Sobhi Saleh: Article 2 in Current Constitution Not Written by Islamists, but Liberals". Retrieved on 23 December 2017, http://www.ikhwanweb.com/article.php?id=30378.

Kamrava Mehran (2014), *Beyond the Arab Spring: The Evolving Ruling Bargain in the Middle East* (Oxford: Oxford University Press).

Kareem Fahim, Kareem (August 2012), "In Upheaval for Egypt, Morsi Forces Out Military Chiefs", *The New York Times*. Retrieved on 23 July 2017, http://www.nytimes.com/2012/08/13/world/middleeast/egyptian-leader-ousts-military-chiefs.html.

Khorshid, Sara (18 June 2012), "The Betrayal of Egypt's Revolution". *The New York Times.* Retrieved on 18 November 2017, http://www.nytimes.com/2012/06/19/opinion/the-betrayal-of-egypts-revolution.html.

Kirkpatrick, D David and Fahim Kareen (2012, 25 May), "In Egypt's Likely Runoff, Islam Vies with the Past", *The New York Times,* 22 May 2017 http://www.nytimes.com/2012/05/26/world/middleeast/egypt-presidential-election-runoff.html.

__________ (14 April 2012), "Authorities Bar 3 Leading Candidates in Egypt Race", *The New York Times*. Retrieved on 22 April 2017. http://www.nytimes.com/2012/04/15/world/middleeast/ten-candidates-barred-from-egyptian-election.html.

_________ (14 June 2012), "Blow to Transition as Court Dissolves Egypt's Parliament", *The New York Times*. Retrieved on 23 August 2017, http://www.nytimes.com/2012/06/15/world/middleeast/new-political-showdown-in-egypt-as-court-invalidates-parliament.html.

____________ and Sheikh El Mayy (23 December 2012), "As Egypt Constitution Passes, New Fights Lie Ahead", *The New York Times*. Retrieved on 2 December 2017, http://www.nytimes.com/2012/12/24/world/middleeast/as-egypt-constitution-passes-new-fights-lie-ahead.html.

_____________ and Sheikh El Mayy (22 August 2012), "Citing Deadlock, Egypt's Leader Seizes New Power and Plans Mubarak Retrial", *The New York Times*. Retrieved on 12 July 2017, http://www.nytimes.com/2012/11/23/world/middleeast/egypts-president-morsi-gives-himself-new-powers.html.

Kotob, Abed Sana (1995), "The Accommodationists Speak: Goals and Strategies of the Muslim Brotherhood of Egypt", *International Journal of Middle East Studies*, 27(3): 321-339.

Laiq, Nur (2013), *Talking to Arab Youth: Revolution and Counter-Revolution in Egypt and Tunisia* (New York: International Peace Institute).

Landolt, K Laura and Kubicek, Paul (2014), "Opportunities and Constrains: Comparing Tunisia and Egypt to the Coloured Revolutions", *Democratization*, 21(6): 984-1006.

Langhor, Vickie (2001), "Of Islamists and Ballot Boxes: Rethinking the Relationship Between Islamists and Electoral Politics", *International Journal of Middle East Studies*, 33(4): 591-610.

Laremont, Rene Ricardo (2014), "Moving Past Revolution and Revolt: Transitions to Democracy in North Africa", in Ricardo Laremont (ed.), *Revolution, Revolt and Reform in North Africa: The Arab Spring and Beyond* (New York: Routledge), 148-172.

Lenze, Paul Jr (2016) *Civil-Military Relations in the Islamic World* (Lanham: Lexington Books).

Maugiron, Bernard (2011), "Egypt's Path to Transition: Democratic Challenges Behind the Constitution Reform Process", *Middle East Law and Governance*, 3(1-2): 36-49.

Mitchell, Richard Paul (1993), *The Society of the Muslim Brothers* (New York: Oxford University Press).

Momani, Bessma (21 August 2013), "In Egypt, 'Deep State' vs. 'Brotherhoodization'", *Brookings*. Retrieved on 2 April 2018. https://www.brookings.edu/opinions/in-egypt-deep-state-vs-brotherhoodization/.

Morsy, A Soheir (1988), "Islamic Clinics in Egypt: The Cultural Elaboration of Biomedical Hegemony", *International Journal for the Analysis of Health:* 355-369.

Moussa, Mohammed (2015), "Contemporary Islamist Discourses on the State in Egypt: Before and After the Arab Spring", in Larbi Sadiki (ed.), *Routledge Handbook of the Arab Spring: Rethinking Democratization* (London: Routledge), pp. 240-253.

Osman, Tarek (2013), *Egypt on the Brink: From Nasser to Mubarak* (New Haven: Yale University Press).

Roy, Oliver (2008), *The Politics of Chaos in the Middle East* (New York: Columbia University Press).

Rutherford, K Bruce (2013) *Egypt After Mubarak: Liberalism, Islam, and Democracy in the Arab World* (Princeton University Press).

Shafeeq, Ghabra (2015), "The Egyptian Revolution: Causes and Dynamics", in Larbi Sadiki (ed.), *Routledge Handbook of the Arab Spring: Rethinking Democratization* (London: Routledge), pp. 199-215.

Shahin El-din Emad (2014), "The Egyptian Revolution: The Power of Mass Mobilization and the Spirit of Tahrir Square", in Ricardo Laremont (ed.), *Revolution, Revolt and Reform in North Africa: The Arab Spring and Beyond* (New York: Routledge), pp. 53-75.

Shehata, Dina (2010), *The Return of Politics: New Social Movements in Egypt* (Cairo: Al Ahram Centre for Political and Strategic Studies).

Shull, Henry and Hassieb, Ingy (14 August 2012), "Egypt's Morsi Decorates Generals He Dismissed", *The Washington Post,* 23 August 2017, https://www.washingtonpost.com/world/middle_east/egypts-dismissed-generals-decorated/2012/08/14/d30b9c24-e637-11e1-9739-eef99c5fb285_story.html?utm_term=.eae5c0f94266.

The Guardian (24 June 2012), "Muslim Brotherhood's Mohamed Morsi Wins Egypt's Presidential Race", 23 September 2017, https://www.theguardian.com/world/middle-east-live/2012/jun/24/egypt-election-results-live.

Vatikiotis P. J. (1978), *Nasser and His Generation* (Hastings: Croom Helm).

Wittes Cofman Tamara (2014, 18 March), "Why Democracy in Egypt Still Matters", *Brookings.* Retrieved on 12 March 2018, https://www.brookings.edu/opinions/why-democracy-in-egypt-still-matters/.

Zubaida, Sami (2001), "Civil Society, Community and Democracy in the Middle East", in Sudipta Kaviraj and Sunil Khilani (eds.), *Civil Society: History and Possibilities* (Cambridge: Cambridge University Press), pp. 232-250.

7. The Role of Hezbollah in Syrian Civil War

Hirak Jyoti Das

Abstract

Hezbollah is a politico-military organisation which premises its politics on anti-imperialism and the fight against Israeli occupation in Lebanon and Palestine. It occupies a predominant position in Lebanon's domestic politics and achieved regional popularity due to its armed struggle that forced the Israeli military withdrawal from South Lebanon in 2000. After the outbreak of protests in Syria in 2011, Hezbollah sided with President Bashar al-Assad and this transitioned into open military support in 2013 and has continued since then. The chapter analyses the role of Hezbollah in Lebanon from a historical perspective, underlines the links between the movement and Syria, and examines its role in the Syrian crisis.

Key Words: Syria; Bashar al-Assad; Israel; Taif Accord; Iran; National Defence Force

The origins of Hezbollah can be traced to the culmination of national and regional events such as the Shiite Islamic revival in the 1960s and 1970s after the failure of pan-Arabism in the June 1967 Arab-Israeli War and the growing popularity of the clerical leadership; the Lebanese civil war between 1975 and 1990; the Islamic Revolution of 1979 in Iran which resonated among the Lebanese Shiite community to revitalise their political and social consciousness; and Israel's military invasion of South Lebanon in 1982 that submerged the ideological and tactical differences within the Shiite community, culminating in a loose coalition of members to counter the Israeli offensives (BBC News, 2016; El Affendi, 2010: 211-21; Shalaby, 2015: 15).

Eventually, after operating clandestinely as a loose collection of underground cells and conducting resistance against the Israeli forces for two and half years, Hezbollah or the "Party of God" came to the surface and released its Open Letter Manifesto in 1985, specifying its objective to establish an Islamic state,[1] to deter Israel's military intervention in Lebanon and to resist the US dominance in the region (Masters and Laub, 2014; Lebanese Renaissance Foundation, 2009; Moussawi, 2010: 213). Hezbollah's role and tactics comprised a series of kidnappings, suicide attacks, bombings and hijackings throughout the 1980s and 1990s. Prior to the 1985 Open Letter, the group gained notoriety for its attacks on the Israeli military base in Tyre on 11 November 1982[2] and 4 November 1983; the suicide car bomb attack on the US Embassy in Beirut on 18 August 1983, that killed 63 people; and the attacks on the US and French military targets in Lebanon on 23 October 1983, killing 241 American and 58 French security personnel (CIA, 2018; CNN, 2017; *USA Today*, 2013; Moussawi, 2010: 212; Australian National Security, 2018). It is important to note that several attacks on the Western targets in Lebanon were blamed on the Iran-linked militias which came to be associated with Hezbollah, which the latter has denied.

The National Unity government of Lebanon, formed on 24 December 1990, following the conclusion of the Taif Accord that ended the Lebanese civil war (1975-90), under Prime Minister Umar Karami pushed for the dissolution of all the militia groups, barring Hezbollah, by 30 April 1991. Crucially, the accord permitted initiatives to liberate all Lebanese territories from the Israeli occupation (UN, 2018). It, thus, offered formal recognition to the armed wing of Hezbollah as a legitimate resistance movement. The accord drew an important distinction between Hezbollah and other militias that participated in the civil war and were, therefore, obliged to disarm. In the case of Hezbollah, although it evolved under the shadow of the civil war, its military actions were focussed on resisting Israeli occupation, which has been reiterated in the successive Cabinet and ministerial policy statements (Moussawi, 2010: 215).

---

1. The New Hezbollah Manifesto announced in November 2009 underplayed its goal to establish an Islamic state and specified that they only aspire to preserve Lebanon's unity and independence without seeking federalism and partition (Lebanese Renaissance Foundation 2009).
2. Israel denies terror links to the explosion in Tyre and attributes it to gas leakage (Israel Ministry of Foreign Affairs, 2018; Shabak 1983).

Hasan Nasrallah assumed the position of General Secretary of the movement after the assassination of Abbas al-Musawi by the Israeli forces on 16 February 1992 (Haberman, 1992; Masters and Laub, 2014). During the 1990s, Hezbollah intensified its social welfare functions, undertook rebuilding efforts and continued military operations against the Israeli occupation in South Lebanon. The unilateral Israeli military withdrawal in May 2000, is widely attributed to the movement. After six years of relative calm, on 12 July 2006, Hezbollah killed eight Israeli soldiers and kidnapped two more which sparked a month-long war with Israel. Despite the death of more than 1,000 fighters, Hezbollah claimed the conflict as a success due to the failure of Israel's objective to uproot the movement (BBC News, 2006).

In the 2010s, Hezbollah invested considerable military resources to stabilise the government of President Bashar al-Assad and emerged as a major strategic player in the Syrian crisis. It began its military involvement with the purported aim of erasing the presence of radical Sunni Islamist groups in Syria and diluting their potential effect on the Lebanese polity.

Hezbollah's Relations with Syria

Syria's policy towards Lebanon has been traditionally conditioned by the view that the latter was artificially created and separated under the French mandate but represented a natural sphere of influence (Fildis, 2017; *The Telegraph,* 2003; Global Security, 2018; Black, 2008). After the civil war engulfed Lebanon in June 1976, Lebanese President Suleiman Franjieh invited the Syrian forces to intervene and diffuse the crisis (Salloukh, 2005). By the end of the 1970s, Syria's attempts at arbitrating between the rival communities backfired, as it emboldened the Christian militias and strengthened their alliance with Israel (Al–Jazeera, 2007).

Syria, therefore, focussed its policy on fuelling the Muslim and, especially, the Shiite resentment against the Israeli occupation and the Maronite domination within Lebanon. It was also during this period that Hezbollah evolved as a military organisation (Gambill and Abdelnour, 2002; Ward, 2016). From the Syrian perspective, the emergence of Hezbollah was fortuitous for preserving its interests since it paved the way for narrowing the strategic parity vis-à-vis Israel and intensifying pressure for the latter's withdrawal from Lebanese territory. The presence of a parallel Shiite organisation helped Syria to maintain control over other Lebanese allies such as Amal. It allowed the Syrian government to strengthen its ties with the Iranian regime and crucially entrench its military presence in Lebanon. On the regional level, Syria's involvement in the civil war in 1976 strained its relationship with the secular Arab and Sunni groups. In this case, the Shiite community, which has been politically organised since the 1970s, served as a crucial ally for Syria (Hinnebusch, 1998: 145-146). The Syrian government's overall plans, however, were aimed at controlling Hezbollah and exploiting the inter-sectarian polarities within the Lebanese society to extract strategic benefits. It also utilised its alliance with Amal to counter-balance the growth of Hezbollah.

After the end of the civil war, the Taif Accord called for the withdrawal of the Syrian forces from the Bekaa Valley after two years of constitutional reforms. However, Israel's continuing occupation in South Lebanon, the failure of the post-Madrid Syria-Israel negotiations and the eruption of the Al-Aqsa *intifada* delayed the full implementation of the Taif Accord and the withdrawal of Syrian forces (Global Security, 2018; UN, 2018; Al-Jazeera, 2017). After Israel's withdrawal from South Lebanon, Syria and Hezbollah insisted that the Israeli state was continuing its presence in Sheba Farms (Al-Jazeera, 2017).

In terms of Hezbollah in the post-Taif Accord period, the Syrian government allowed the movement to remain armed and continue its military campaign against Israeli presence in South Lebanon to maintain pressure on Israel to withdraw from the Golan Heights (Gambill and Abdelnour, 2002). Damascus, however, placed political and military constraints on the movement's autonomy and viewed it largely as an instrument to engage with Israel during the peace negotiations in the 1990s (Blanford, 2017: 1). The Syrian government engineered the movement's representation in the Parliament roughly on par with Amal. It maintained strict control and prohibited airlifts of arms shipments directly from Iran to Lebanon. The armaments were allowed to land in Syria after which they were transferred overland to Hezbollah bases in the Bekaa Valley (Gambill and Abdelnour, 2002).

After Bashar al-Assad's succession to power on 17 July 2000, the relationship improved and Hezbollah's military operations against Israel were conducted in close cooperation with the Syrian government. Under the Syrian umbrella, Hezbollah succeeded in widening its influence in Lebanon and while most sectarian groups opposed the Syrian occupation, Hezbollah continued to support the regime, arguing that it was a regional and internal necessity (Gambill and Abdelnour, 2002). However, the assassination of Rafiq Hariri on 14 February 2005 ignited nation-wide opposition to the Syrian occupation, leading to its hasty withdrawal completed on 30 April 2005 (Global Security, 2018). Syria's continuing influence in Lebanon after its withdrawal was linked to Hezbollah's political prominence.

Hezbollah's Role in the Syrian Civil War

After the outbreak of the Arab Spring in 2011, Hezbollah adopted a 'wait and watch' approach and initially did not align with any opposition force (Choucair, 2016: 3; Pollak, 2016: 2). The movement elucidated its views on the states undergoing pro-democracy protests and supported the aspirations of the people in Egypt, Tunisia, Bahrain, and Yemen which were classified as regimes backed by the US and the West. In its view, the protests in these states represented true national movements (Choucair, 2016: 3). On the other hand, the movement was cautious about applying the same logic to Syria. According to the movement, the Syrian regime was being targeted due to its opposition to the US policy in the region, hostility against Israel, and friendly ties with Iran (Choucair, 2016: 3).

Regarding the Syrian opposition groups, Hasan Nasrallah in his speech on 25 May 2013, admitted that there were sections among the opposition groups with genuine demands and it was within their rights to seek reforms (Nasrallah, 2013). He, however, suggested that most of the opposition groups were serving the interests of the Western powers and oil-rich Arab states (Nasrallah, 2013). Hezbollah, he elaborated, intended to hasten a political dialogue between the government and the opposition that would facilitate political reforms and lead to reconciliation between the opposing groups and differing Islamic factions (Nasrallah, 2013; Harb, 2017). He also argued that, while the Assad government has adopted flexibility to reach a political solution and implement fundamental reforms, the opposition, backed by external powers had repeatedly rejected dialogue due to the perceived weakness of the Syrian regime. Therefore, the Syrian people became the victims of strategic miscalculations which were complicated by the US and its allies, leading to the conflict (Nasrallah, 2013).

From Hezbollah's perspective, the crisis in Syria is seen as part of a Western plot to replace Assad's regime by bandwagoning with opposition forces (Nasrallah, 2013; Choucair, 2016: 3; Blanford, 2017: 8). Nasrallah has argued that Syria is not an arena of political revolution, but part of a Western effort to destabilise the region and entrench its hegemony. The movement claimed that it extends support for the regime based on ideological reasons and blamed the media campaigns and foreign actors for colouring its intent and activity on narrow sectarian lines. In fact, there have been intentional efforts, according to Hezbollah, at utilising sectarianism to undermine its policies (Harb, 2017). Hezbollah made an explicit commitment that it would not agree to a fundamental change in Syria. Moreover, as a result of the movement's deepening strategic investment over time, its fate has been increasingly intertwined with the future of the Assad regime (Nasrallah, 2013; International Crisis Group, 2017; Pollak, 2016: 2).

In the early phase of the civil war, Hezbollah's assistance was covert at best. It was more or less limited to an advisory role, minor military coordination and assistance primarily focussing on safeguarding Lebanese villages close to the Syrian border, security for the sensitive military sites and protection of the holy shrines in Syria (Pollak, 2016: 3; Tokmajyan, 2014: 108-109; Harb, 2017; *Mediterranean Affairs*, 2015). The movement at this stage did not foresee any real danger to the regime and believed that the government could contain these rebel groups. At the same time, due to the context of the Arab Spring, it did not intend to be perceived as counter-revolutionary by standing up against a popular movement (Pollak, 2016: 3; Sullivan, 2014: 11).

The stability of the Assad regime reached a critical stage in late 2012 and early 2013 with an overall pessimism about its survival as the rebel forces made significant inroads in Aleppo and northern Syria (Sullivan, 2014: 13). The Iranian forces involved in the conflict also suffered a severe blow during this period (Sullivan, 2014: 13; Perry and Bassam, 2018). On 9 January 2013, the Syrian government released 2,130 rebels in exchange for 48 Iranians captured since August 2012 (*The Times of Israel*, 2013; Mostaghim and Parker, 2013). The Iranian efforts received a setback after the death of Islamic Revolutionary Guard Corps (IRGC) Commander General Hassan Shateri on 13 February 2013 on the way between Damascus and Lebanon (*The Guardian*, 2013).

Consequently, Iran readjusted its military strategy by redirecting the Syrian Army to focus on selected key areas instead of fighting battles on multiple fronts simultaneously (Sullivan, 2014: 13; Perry and Bassam, 2018). It, therefore, sought to secure Damascus and the areas connecting Homs and the coastal region, link routes connecting Lebanon and areas close to the Syria-Lebanon border (Sullivan, 2014: 13). The objective to secure the Bekaa Valley, adjacent to the Syrian border, and preserve the route linking to Damascus was shared by Hezbollah.

Hezbollah finally announced its full military involvement in the Syrian War after the siege of Al Qusayr, located close to the Lebanese border, in May 2013 (Pollak, 2016: 3; Harb, 2017; Mishra, 2018). On 25 May, Nasrallah announced the decision to support the Syrian government, elevating Hezbollah's position by placing the movement on a partnership with the Assad regime. It was also during this period that the rebel forces achieved significant gains in the conflict that was threatening the regime and Hezbollah strongholds (Pollak, 2016: 3; Harb, 2017).

Domestically, the movement succeeded in utilising the political vacuum after President Michel Sleiman's term ended on 25 May 2014, to launch its military operation in Syria. During this period, it aligned with Michel Aoun's Free Patriotic Movement. Under Prime Minister Tammam Salam, who served as the acting President between 25 May and 31 October 2014, Jibran Bassil from the Free Patriotic Movement, an ally of Hezbollah, assumed the Foreign Ministry portfolio (Choucair, 2016: 5). After assuming the presidency on 31 October 2016, Aoun refrained from antagonising the movement, and on 21 September 2017, claimed that any solution to Hezbollah's growth would have to come from wider solutions affecting the region and refused to ask Hezbollah to dismantle due to the existence of the Israeli threat (*Al-Monitor*, 2017).

The movement has in the process evolved politically and militarily, affecting its overall strategic outlook, capabilities and role and thereby undergoing a transition as a result of the war. The reasons for Hezbollah's military intervention in Syria lie in the historical strategic alliance between the movement and the Syrian regime; the desire to preserve the geo-strategic alliance of the so-called 'Axis of Resistance' with Syria and Iran; to deter the presence of extremist rebel groups for Syria and Lebanon; and to maintain the arms flow (Berti, 2015; Porter, 2018; Perry and Bassam, 2018; Alami, 2017). Benedetta Berti (2015) has noted that the personal relationship between Assad and Nasrallah adds to the equation for Hezbollah's involvement in Syria.

Syria is seen by Hezbollah as an integral part of the Axis of Resistance. During the 25 May 2013 speech, Nasrallah claimed that Hezbollah and the Syrian regime constitutes the backbone of the resistance. He stated that Syria's stability is essential for Lebanon, the Middle East region, the Arab-Israeli conflict, the Palestinian cause and other resistance movements. The loss of Syria, therefore, would empower the US and its allies, Israel and extremist rebel groups to dominate the region, endanger Lebanon's security and weaken their crucial alliance (Nasrallah, 2013; Pollak, 2016: 2; Porter, 2018; Alami, 2017).

Nadav Pollak (2016) notes the importance of Syria as Hezbollah's logistical lifeline. The former has served as a crucial channel and transit hub for the transfer of weapons by the Quds Force of Iran's IRGC to Lebanon. The Syrian government has contributed by providing anti-tank missiles and rockets imported from Russia (Pollak, 2016: 2). The movement has reportedly maintained training camps and weapons storage inside Syria (Scharf, 2010; Alami, 2017). The fighters have regularly utilised Syrian routes to proceed forward to Iran for training purposes (Pollak, 2016: 2; Harb, 2017).

During the war, the entry of the Islamic State (IS) and groups like *Jabhat al-Nusra, Ahrar al-Sham and Hay'at Tahrir al-Sham* provided further incentive for the movement to fight. It cautioned against the growing influence and territorial control of these extremist rebel groups that are categorised as *takfiris*, groups that identify other Muslims individuals or groups as *kafirs* (non-believers) and, hence, justify their persecution (Blanford, 2017: 8; Tokmajyan, 2014: 109; Porter, 2018). According to Hezbollah, these groups reject dialogue, priorities, commonalities and plurality, and it accused IS and other extremist rebel groups of harming the Sunni community in Syria, Iraq, Pakistan and elsewhere, and destroying religious and historical relics of all the major religions in the region (Tokmajyan, 2014: 109; Perry and Bassam, 2018). From Hezbollah's point of view, the control of these rebel groups close to the Lebanese border poses a threat not only to Hezbollah but also to the state of Lebanon and a society based on the principle of coexistence. It can, therefore, be observed that due to the entry of extremist rebel groups, Hezbollah's war objectives expanded by changing the rhetoric from stabilising Assad's regime to combating these groups to defend Lebanon. The movement, at the same time, through repeated usage of the term *takfiri* has managed to simplify the totality of the opposition forces (Tokmajyan, 2014: 110; Harb, 2017).

Impact on Hezbollah

Militarily, the conflict in Syria is Hezbollah's first experience in sustained expeditionary warfare and has posed a major challenge to its organisational structure, command and combat forces (White, 2014). The Hezbollah fighters, in this case, are fighting outside the paradigm of the resistance struggle and facing unfamiliar rivals in foreign territory (White, 2014). It formed a major component of disparate forces composed of the regular Army, Air Force and Navy, irregular forces such as the National Defence Force (NDF), combat forces from Iran, and allied forces from Iraq and other states (White, 2014; Reuters, 2013). The movement's forces in Syria are essentially light infantry and embedded in the Syrian Army and paramilitary regiments as force multipliers to execute both offensive and defensive warfare (Berti, 2015; Sullivan, 2014: 12-13).

According to Jeffery White (2014), Hezbollah has conducted four types of military approaches in Syria. Firstly, it began with a combat advisory role and minor military coordination. It also deployed technicians and operatives to carry out non-combative functions. Secondly, it is responsible for training fighters aligned to the Assad regime such as the NDF, Liwa Fatemiyoun, the Afghan volunteer force and Liwa Zeinabyoun, the Pakistani volunteer force, and defending the Syrian Army's strategic bases (Pollak, 2016: 1-3; Blanford, 2017: 7; Sullivan,

2014:14; White, 2014). It has learned to work effectively with regime irregulars and allied forces. The training has largely focussed on small unit and counter-insurgency tactics for the regular Syrian Army. Thirdly, it has undertaken operations in which Hezbollah fighters are deployed with regime irregulars to improve their combat capabilities. Fourthly, it has engaged in direct combat operations (White, 2014).

In terms of the command structure, the movement coordinates with IRGC and the Syrian Army personnel who are then assigned specific geographic areas of responsibility. The Hezbollah forces are further organised on a territorial basis with separate command forces (White, 2014). In several cases, the movement has undertaken command positions working alongside the IRGC and Syrian Army during military operations. It has set up communication lines and logistical routes among various units fighting on different fronts (Blanford, 2017: 7-8; Porter, 2018).

The Syrian Army's and Hezbollah's military capabilities in Syria involve a large special forces unit, a signals intelligence unit, an amphibious warfare unit and an armoured brigade consisting of armoured personnel carriers, tanks and mobile anti-aircraft systems for ground support purposes (Blanford, 2017: 6-7). In terms of weapons, Hezbollah fighters have been seen using assault rifles, recoilless rifles, light mortars, general purpose machine guns, truck-mounted heavy machine guns, Anti-Tank Guided Missiles (ATGMs), Rocket-Propelled Grenades (RPGs) and armoured vehicles (White, 2014). According to estimates, there are approximately 8,000 fighters at any one time, depending on the operational goals (Blanford, 2017: 7; Alami, 2017).

On 29 May 2013, Hezbollah collaborated with the Syrian forces for a joint attack in Al-Qusayr in Homs province, located close to the Lebanese border. The rebel stronghold disrupted the main communication lines to Lebanon, access to the Mediterranean Sea and allowed the supply of weapons to the anti-Assad forces. The Hezbollah fighters cordoned off the area to halt resupply, reinforcement of manpower and withdrawal. The Syrian Army followed up by conducting heavy artillery firing and air attacks (Sullivan, 2014: 15). The takeover of the area in June 2013 restored the Syrian regime's control over this region and is marked as a definitive entry point for the movement's involvement in the crisis (Blanford, 2013; O'Bagy, 2013:1-3; Choucair, 2013).

After the battle of Al-Qusayr, Hezbollah proceeded to combat support missions in South Deraa, Idlib and Aleppo provinces in North Syria and areas close to Damascus (Blanford, 2013; Perry and Bassam, 2018). The Syrian forces thereafter easily regained Tel Kalakh near Al-Qusayr in June 2013 and Khaldiya in Homs province in July, utilising similar tactics of cutting off resupply, and bombardment. In Dara'a and Damascus region, Hezbollah coordinated with the Iraqi groups aligned to the Assad regime such as Bosra al-Sham, Suwayda, Abu Fadl al-Abbas, Kataib Hezbollah and Asaib ahl al-Haq (Blanford, 2013). In May 2015, it focussed its attention on recapturing the Qalamoun mountain range from the Jabhat al-Nusra and Islamic State. After almost two weeks of fighting in June, it took over significant areas and reopened the corridor linking to Syria (Stanford University, 2016). In April 2016, it was engaged in Tal al-Ais, located close to Aleppo, fighting against the Ahrar al-Sham, Jabhat al-Nusra and Free Syrian Army (FSA). It has participated in both joint and combined offensive and defensive operations with the government's heavy armour and artillery forces, Air Force units and surface-to-surface units (White, 2014).

As the war entered its seventh year, the Assad regime gained the upper hand with the seizure of eastern Aleppo in December 2016. Since mid-2017, Hezbollah's aim has been to recapture eastern Syria from the Islamic State's control and deny the militias supported by the US any foothold in these areas. In October 2017, Hezbollah's attempts were focussed on regaining the Deir Ezzor region, Euphrates Valley and Abu Kamal close to the Syria-Iraq border (Blanford, 2017: 8). On 3 November, the regime forces backed by Hezbollah recaptured Deir Ezzor (Alami, 2017).

For a militarily overstretched Iran, Hezbollah's role has become indispensable to support its objectives and secure victories for the Assad regime. Hezbollah also benefited from Russia's involvement in the conflict on the side of the Assad regime since 30 September 2015 (Perry and Bassam, 2018). However, despite the convergence of interests among the sides supporting the Assad regime, Russia's involvement has curtailed the movement's freedom to manoeuvre due to Moscow's relationship with Israel and the red lines agreed upon by both Russia and Israel.

In terms of gains, it has strengthened its military capability and enhanced its political prominence, with the Syrian battleground serving as a crucial training ground. The movement has gained crucial battle experience in different types of terrain ranging from urban settings in Al-Qusayr, hilly areas such as the Qalamoun region and deserts near Palmyra (Harb, 2017; Porter, 2018). Moreover, the movement's collaboration with traditional state Armies has enriched it in battle tactics. During the fighting process, Hezbollah benefits from the regime's firepower, a secure base area, firm command and control centre, operational manoeuvrability and extensive logistics which grant it significant advantages over its opponents. It has adopted a *pro-rata* strategy by selecting a number of strategic targets to protect its assets with a limited number of fighters. The Syrian Army has adopted Hezbollah's hybrid warfare doctrine with a mobile Army focussing on anti-tank missiles, air defence systems and surface-to-surface rockets and limited usage of mass armoured assault weapons such as tanks and aircraft (Blanford, 2017: 9).

At the same time, due to the protracted nature of the conflict, it runs the risk of sinking itself in a never-ending war, drawing on its resources and mounting human cost. Due to its involvement in the war in Syria, the movement has lost its position as a resistance movement on a national and pan-Arab level that focusses on challenging the US hegemony, Israeli military superiority and occupation of the Palestinian territories and internal reconciliation (Choucair, 2016: 2; White, 2014). As a result of the war, it has become involved the Saudi-Iran proxy war and Arab citizens and regimes have raised doubt about the credibility of the movement. Its proactive role in Syria and regional motives serving Iran and Syria, some have argued, would lead to a redefinition of the Shiite community as a sectarian minority by dividing the wider Muslim community in Lebanon (Choucair, 2016: 2; Atrache, 2017). It can, therefore, intensify sectarian tensions within the state and the wider region (Harb, 2017).

Hezbollah derives its legitimacy from the firm domestic base within Lebanon. The decision of the movement to intervene has become unpopular among different communities, and suffered a further jolt due to the drawn-out nature of the conflict which has negatively affected its domestic political standing, with political repercussions (Berti,

2015; Harb, 2017). Many within the Lebanese state are opposed to its relationship with the Assad regime and its action in Syria and Lebanon. It has escalated the potential for an influx of extremist rebel members, weapons, increased number of refugees and their attached human and economic costs, communal conflict and political deadlock in the leadership within Lebanon (Ward, 2016; Porter, 2018). In July and August 2015, there were protests over the government's perceived failure to address waste-management. The members of Parliament belonging to Hezbollah suffered criticism for their inability to overcome political differences, and their neglect of environmental and health concerns (Al-Jazeera, 2016).

During the municipal elections held on 8 May 2016, in the Eastern Bekaa Valley region, Hezbollah and its allies competed in 80 out of 143 municipal seats and managed to win most of its constituencies (Macaron, 2016). The polls, however, indicated that Hezbollah's popularity had, in fact, witnessed a decline, with the voters expressing discontent over its performance in improving the state of the economy, tackling corruption and Iran's growing entrenchment (Rassmussen and Osseiran, 2018). In the Hezbollah dominated constituency of Baalbek, it won the polls with a narrow 700 vote margin, with the opposition candidate securing 46 per cent of total votes (Hashem, 2018). The movement, along with its ally, Amal, however, managed to improve its political position and succeeded in winning 29 seats in the National Assembly elections held on 6 May 2018, providing it a firm position in the national decision-making (Ajroudi, 2018; IPU, 2019).

At the same time, Hezbollah's actions in Syria have incited violent reactions and its strongholds have been attacked on several occasions. On 15 August 2015, a car bomb was exploded by the Brigades of Aisha in the Roueiss neighbourhood in South Beirut, causing 20 fatalities and 250 injuries (*The Guardian*, 2013). On 19 November 2013, the Iranian Embassy in Beirut was attacked by the Abdullah Azzam Brigade (Aneja, 2013), killing 23 and injuring 146. On 3 December, Hezbollah commander Hassan Lakkis was assassinated in the town of Hadath. The movement blamed Israel and Saudi Arabia for the attack (BBC News, 2013).

On 2 January 2014, the Hezbollah dominated Haret Hreik area in Beirut was attacked, killing four people and wounding 65 (NDTV,

2014). Hermel, located in the Bekaa Valley and a major stronghold of the movement, was attacked on three occasions in 2014: 16 January, 1 February and 22 February (*The Guardian*, 2014; Al-Jazeera, 2014; *Daily Star*, 2014). The Iranian Cultural Centre was attacked in Beirut by the Abdullah Azzam Brigades on 19 February 2014, killing five people (Atassi, 2014). The Hezbollah checkpoint near Khraibeh village in the Bekaa Valley was attacked on 20 September 2014 (Reuters, 2014). A convoy carrying Hezbollah fighters was attacked in the Bekaa Valley bordering Syria on 5 October 2015 (*Al Arabiyah*, 2015). Moreover in a major incident, the IS claimed responsibility for the bombing in the Hezbollah dominated Bourj el-Barajneh neighbourhood in south Beirut, killing 43 people and wounding more than 100 (Buchanan, 2015). The direct attacks on Hezbollah targets have decreased in 2018 due to the weakening presence of the IS and other radical groups in the Syrian battleground, and the Syrian government forces, Iranian forces and the movement have succeeded in reclaiming major part of the territory.

Hezbollah has continued to justify its position by arguing that its preemptive actions have, in fact, secured the state from what would have been an inevitable conflict within the Lebanese territory (Harb, 2017; Atrache, 2017; Mishra, 2018). According to Al Alfoneh, Senior Fellow at the Arab Gulf States Institute in Washington, the movement suffered an estimated loss of 1,233 fighters in the conflict between January 2012 and October 2018 (Alfoneh, 2018). According to Alfoneh's study, of the total casualties, 77 were officers. He has categorised the number of fatalities on the basis of the natal governorates between January 2012 and October 2018 that is, 385 from Nabatiyah region, 288 from Baalbek-Hermel region, 271 from South Lebanon, 72 from Beqaa, 32 from Mount Lebanon area, 16 from Beirut, 8 from Akkar, 3 from North Lebanon, 22 from Syria and 136 are unknown (Alfoneh, 2018). As of 2018, it maintained a force of 7,000 to 10,000 fighters who are deployed on a rotational basis (Ward, 2016). As a result of the public response over the movement's role in Syria, it has maintained a policy of official ambivalence and has refused to divulge details about the number of total fatalities in the conflict.

The presence of Hezbollah in Syria has provided a new battleground for its efforts against Israel. However, the movement's policy also suffers from certain risks in terms of a military confrontation with the Jewish state. The conflict has complicated the movement and Iran's manoeuvring and surveillance capabilities near the southern border. Escalation of the conflict would lead to a situation of protracted warfare with heavy damage on both sides. Hezbollah's military capability and resources are overstretched due to its presence in Syria (Rossi, 2018). Therefore, Hezbollah is unlikely to engage in an open conflict with Israel.

On 23 July 2018, Russia informed Israel that pro-Iranian forces has agreed to pull back to a distance of 85 km from the Golan Heights border. Israel, however, rejected the offer and demanded the withdrawal of all pro-Iranian forces from Syria's territory (Ahren, 2018; Khoury, 2018). The signs of confrontation have become a new reality as air raids and retaliatory attacks have been occurring on a regular basis. Israel has admitted to conducting air raids to halt weapons transfers and destroy Hezbollah's supplies and bases as well as Iranian assets. Israel has expressed its fear over the movement's access to long-range and medium-range ballistic missiles and rocket systems. On the condition of anonymity, Hezbollah members on separate occasions have privately boasted about its role in the decision to shoot down an Israeli F-16 fighter jet in the Golan region on 10 February 2019 (Anderson, 2018; BBC News, 2018).

On 13 January 2019, outgoing Israeli Defence Force (IDF) Chief Gadi Eisenkot admitted that the Israeli Air Force (IAF) has been carrying out attacks on Hezbollah targets and convoys since its active participation in 2013 and against Iranian assets since January 2017, following the Cabinet's approval (Haaretz, 2019). IDF spokesperson Jonathan Conricus announced on 13 January 2019 that under Operation Northern Shield, launched on 4 December 2018, Israel has detected and destroyed underground tunnels built by the movement along its border with Lebanon (Al-Jazeera, 2019). Nasrallah, on 27 January 2019, warned the Jewish state to halt its air campaigns in Syria to avoid turning the conflagration into a full-fledged conflict (*The Times of Israel*, 2019). Under such circumstances, the presence of the movement in Syria has unlocked its engagement against Israel and the state of confrontation is, therefore, likely to continue.

Conclusion

Hezbollah entered the civil war in Syria initially covertly in an advisory and training role, and after 2013, participated in joint and direct combat campaigns. The motivations for its involvement lie in preserving the geo-strategic alliance with Syria and Iran, to retain its supply routes and deter the spread of extremist rebel groups in Syria and Lebanon. Hezbollah's contribution to the war has been mixed. It was a blessing for the Assad regime as it has remained one of the most formidable forces on the ground to counter the rebel groups. Due to its involvement in Syria, Hezbollah has gained crucial combat experience in different types of terrain and emerged as a regional power. At the same time, the cost in human lives in this protracted conflict, as well as a changing perception of its role from a resistance movement to an expeditionary force allying with Assad's dictatorial regime, may aggravate political tensions within Lebanon and the wider region, and drag the movement into an open conflict with Israel.

Hezbollah is aware of the uncertainty of the political transition but is highly unlikely to accept a change of regime. For Hezbollah, the stakes are high as the collapse of the Syrian regime or political transition would affect its status, political control and legitimacy within Lebanon and boost the domestic opposition to the movement. Therefore, due to the military investment, the movement has developed a symbiotic relationship with the Syrian regime, which requires the Hezbollah fighters on the ground for which the movement requires the Assad regime to stay in power.

References

Agence France-Presse (2014), "Car Bomb Kills Four in Hezbollah Beirut Bastion: Minister," NDTV, 3 January. Retrieved from www.ndtv.com/world-news/car-bomb-kills-four-in-hezbollah-beirut-bastion-minister-546590.

Ahren, Raphael (2018), "Israel Rejects Russian Offer to Keep Iran 100 Km from Syrian Border," *The Times of Israel*, 23 July. Retrieved from www.timesofisrael.com/israel-rejects-russian-offer-to-keep-iran-100-km-from-israels-border/.

Ajroudi, Asma (2018), "Hezbollah, Amal and Allies Biggest Winners in Lebanon Elections,"Al-Jazeera, 8 May. Retrieved from www.aljazeera.com/news/2018/05/hezbollah-amal-allies-claim-lebanon-election-sweep-180507160524402.html.

Alami, Mona (2017), "Hezbollah Emerges from the Syrian War Ready for Action," *Newsweek*, 12 June. Retrieved from https://www.newsweek.com/hezbollah-emerges-syrian-war-ready-action-730918

Alfoneh, Ali (2018), "The Heavy Price of Lebanese Hezbollah's Military Engagement in Syria," Arab Gulf States Institute in Washington, 11 October. Retrieved from agsiw.org/the-heavy-price-of-lebanese-hezbollahs-military-engagement-in-syria/.

Al-Arabiya (2015), "Roadside Bomb 'Targets Hezbollah Van' in Eastern Lebanon," *Al Arabiya*, 5 October. Retrieved from http://english.alarabiya.net/en/News/middle-east/2015/10/05/-Explosion-heard-in-eastern-Lebanon.html

Al-Jazeera (2007), "Syria's Role in Lebanon," 14 October. Retrieved from https://www.aljazeera.com/focus/lebanon/2007/07/200852517306599517.html

Al-Jazeera (2010), "Assad 'To Attend' Summit in Lebanon," 29 July. Retrieved from https://www.aljazeera.com/news/middleeast/2010/07/201072962514334582.html

Al-Jazeera (2014), "Deadly Car Bomb Strikes Eastern Lebanon," 1 February. Retrieved from america.aljazeera.com/articles/2014/2/1/deadly-car-bomb-strikeseasternlebanon.html.

Al-Jazeera (2015), "Lebanese Protest against Waste-Disposal Crisis," 26 July. Retrieved from www.aljazeera.com/news/2015/07/lebanon-beirut-trash-rubbish-crisis-150725060723178.html.

Al-Jazeera (2019), "Israel Says It Has Found All Hezbollah Tunnels on Lebanon Border," 13 January. Retrieved from www.aljazeera.com/news/2019/01/israel-hezbollah-tunnels-lebanon-border-190113080229019.html.

Al-Monitor (2017), "Aoun Sees Role for Hezbollah Until Threats to Lebanon cease," 21 September. Retrieved from: https://www.al-monitor.com/pulse/originals/2017/09/lebanon-president-aoun-unga-hezbollah-threat-syria-israel.html

Anderson, Sulome (2018), "Israel and Hezbollah Are Girding for War—and the Next Round Could Be Horrific," *The Nation*, 5 April. Retrieved from www.thenation.com/article/israel-and-hezbollah-are-girding-for-war-and-the-next-round-could-be-horrific/.

Aneja, Atul (2013), " Iranian Embassy in Lebanon Attacked," *The Hindu*, 20 November. Retrieved from www.thehindu.com/todays-paper/iranian-embassy-in-lebanon-attacked/article5370281.ece#.

Associated Press (2013), "Beirut Car Bomb Rips through Hezbollah Stronghold," *The Guardian*, 15 August. Retrieved from www.theguardian.com/world/2013/aug/15/beirut-car-bomb-hezbollah-stronghold.

Associated Press (2014), "Car Bomb Blasts Lebanese Town near Syria Border," *The Guardian*, 16 January. Retrieved from www.theguardian.com/world/2014/jan/16/car-bomb-blasts-lebanese-town-hermel-syria.

Atassi, Basma (2014), "Civilians Paying the Price for Beirut Attack," Al-Jazeera, 19 February. Retrieved from www.aljazeera.com/indepth/features/2014/02/

civilians-paying-price-beirut-attack-201421912353644323.html.Atrache, Sahar (2017), "Hizbollah's Pyrrhic Victories in Syria," International Crisis Group, 3 July. Retrieved from https://www.crisisgroup.org/middle-east-north-africa/eastern-mediterranean/syria/las-victorias-pirricas-de-hezbola-en-siria

Bahout, Joseph (2014), *Lebanon at the Brink: The Impact of the Syrian Civil War* (Waltham. Massachusetts: Brandeis University). Retrieved from https://www.brandeis.edu/crown/publications/meb/MEB76.pdf

Barnes-Dacey, Julien (2013), "Syria: The View from Lebanon," European Council on Foreign Relations, 19 June. Retrieved from http://www.ecfr.eu/article/commentary_syria_the_view_from_lebanon140

BBC News (2006), "Hezbollah Seizes Israel Soldiers," BBC News, 12 July.Retrieved from http://news.bbc.co.uk/2/hi/middle_east/5171616.stm

BBC News (2013), "Hezbollah Commander Hassan Lakkis Killed in Beirut," BBC News, 4 December. Retrieved from www.bbc.com/news/world-middle-east-25211759.

BBC News (2014), "Syria Shoots Down Israeli Warplane as Conflict Escalates," BBC News, 10 February. Retrieved from www.bbc.com/news/world-middle-east-43014081.

BBC News (2017), "Lebanon Profile – Timeline," BBC News, 6 December. Retrieved from http://www.bbc.com/news/world-middle-east-14649284Berti, Benedetta (2015), "The Syrian Civil War and its Consequences for Hezbollah," Foreign Policy Research Institute, 28 December. Retrieved from https://www.fpri.org/article/2015/12/the-syrian-civil-war-and-its-consequences-for-hezbollah/

Biondi, Charles Brian (2013), "The Impact of the Syrian Crisis on Lebanon: Local and Regional Rationales for Hezbollah's Involvement in Syria," Istituto Affari Internazionali, 28 December: 1-9. Retrieved from http://www.iai.it/sites/default/files/iaiwp1331.pdf

Black, Ian (2008), "Syria and Lebanon to Establish Diplomatic Relations," *The Guardian*, 14 October. Retrieved from https://www.theguardian.com/world/2008/oct/14/syria-lebanon

Blanford, Nicholas (2017), (ed.), *Hezbollah's Evolution from Lebanese Militia to Regional Player* (Washington D.C.). (N. Blanford, Trans.) Middle East Institute. Retrieved from https://www.mei.edu/sites/default/files/publications/PP4_Blanford_Hezbollah.pdf

Buchanan, Rose Troup (2015), "Beirut Bomb: 'At Least 43 Dead' in Twin Isis Suicide Blast in Lebanese Capital," *Independent*, 12 November. Retrieved from https://www.independent.co.uk/news/world/middle-east/beirut-bomb-scores-killed-in-twin-suicide-blast-in-lebanese-capital-a6732156.htmlByman, Daniel & Saab, Bilal Y. (2014), "Hezbollah in a Time of Transition" Centre for Middle East Policy at Brookings. Retrieved from https://www.brookings.edu/wp-content/uploads/2016/06/Hezbollah-in-a-Time-of-Transition.pdf

Central Intelligence Agency (2014), "FLASHBACK: April 18, 1983: U.S. Embassy Attacked in Beirut". Retrieved from CIA. https://www.cia.gov/news-information/featured-story-archive/2014-featured-story-archive/flashback-april-18-1983-u-s-embassy-bombed-in-beirut.html

Choucair, Chafic (2016), "Hezbollah in Syria: Gains, Losses and Changes," Al-Jazeera Centre for Studies. Retrieved from http://studies.aljazeera.net/en/reports/2016/06/hezbollah-syria-gains-losses-160601093443171.html

Clarity, James F. (1982), "Israelis Killed in Blast in Southern Lebanon," *The New York Times*, 12 November. Retrieved from: https://www.nytimes.com/1982/11/12/world/israelis-killed-in-blast-in-southern-lebanon.html

CNN (2017), "Beirut Marine Barracks Bombing Fast Facts," CNN, 18 October. Retrieved from https://edition.cnn.com/2013/06/13/world/meast/beirut-marine-barracks-bombing-fast-facts/index.html

Daher, Aurelie (2015), "Hezbollah and the Syrian Conflict," Middle East Institute, 4 November. Retrieved from http://www.mei.edu/content/map/hezbollah-and-syrian-conflict

Economic Cooperation Foundation (ECF) (1983), "Israel-Lebanon Treaty (1983)," The Israeli-Palestinian Conflict: An Interactive Database, Retrieved from http://ecf.org.il/issues/issue/183

Fildis, Ayse Tekdal (2011), "The Troubles in Syria: Spawned by French Divide and Rule," Middle East Policy Council, 8 December. Retrieved from https://doi.org/10.1111/j.1475-4967.2011.00515.x

Gagliardini, Federica (2015), "The Role of Hezbollah in the Syrian Crisis," *Mediterranean Affairs*, 13 July. Retrieved from: http://mediterraneanaffairs.com/the-role-of-hezbollah-in-the-syrian-crisis/

Global Security Organisation (2018), "Syria's Involvement in Lebanon," *Global Security*, 20 September. Retrieved from https://www.globalsecurity.org/military/world/syria/forrel-lebanon.htm

Goldenberg, Suzanne (2000), "Chaos and Humiliation as Israel Pulls Out of Lebanon," *The Guardian*, 24 May. Retrieved from https://www.theguardian.com/world/2000/may/24/israelandthepalestinians.lebanon

Grace, Robert & Mandelbaum, Andrew (2006), "Understanding the Iran-Hezbollah Connection," United States Institute of Peace, 22 September. Retrieved from https://www.usip.org/publications/2006/09/understanding-iran-hezbollah-connection

Haaretz (2019), "Outgoing Army Chief: Israel Attacked Thousands of Iranian Targets in Syria," *Haaretz*, 13 January. Retrieved from www.haaretz.com/israel-news/outgoing-army-chief-israel-attacked-thousands-of-iranian-targets-in-syria-1.6829836.

Haberman, Clyde (1992), "Israelis Kill Chief of Pro-Iran Shiites in South Lebanon," *The New York Times*, 17 February, p. 1. Retrieved from https://www.nytimes.com/1992/02/17/world/israelis-kill-chief-of-pro-iran-shiites-in-south-lebanon.html

Haran, V. P. (2016), *Roots of the Syrian Crisis* (New Delhi: Institute of Peace and Conflict Studies). Retrieved from https://reliefweb.int/sites/reliefweb.int/files/resources/RootsoftheSyrianCrisis_VPHaran.pdf

Harb, Ali (2017), "'A Regional Power': How Fighting Assad's War Transformed Hezbollah," *Middle East Eye*, 12 October. Retrieved from https://www.middleeasteye.net/news/regional-power-how-syria-civil-war-changed-hezbollah-lebanon-israel-1187885930

Harris, William (2018), "Syria in Lebanon," Middle East Research and Information Project. Retrieved from http://www.merip.org/mer/mer134/syria-lebanon

Hashem, Al (2018), "Hezbollah's Journey from Syria's Battlefield to Lebanon's Political Minefield," Carnegie Middle East Centre, 28 August. Retrieved from carnegie-mec.org/2018/08/28/hezbollah-s-journey-from-syria-s-battlefield-to-lebanon-s-political-minefield-pub-77115.

Hijazi, Ihsan A. (1989), "Group in Beirut Says it Hanged U.S. Colonel; 2D Threat Issued; Bush Convenes Security Panel; Videotape Released," *The New York Times*, 1 August, p. 1. Retrieved from https://www.nytimes.com/1989/08/01/world/group-beirut-says-it-hanged-us-colonel-2d-threat-issued-bush-convenes-security.html

Israel Ministry of Foreign Affairs (1996), "Cease-Fire Understanding in Lebanon- and Remarks by Prime Minister Peres and Secretary of State Christopher," Israel Ministry of Foreign Affairs, 26 April. Retrieved from https://web.archive.org/web/20070310234701/http://www.israel-mfa.gov.il/MFA/Foreign%20Relations/Israels%20Foreign%20Relations%20since%201947/1995-1996/Cease-fire%20understanding%20in%20Lebanon-%20and%20remarks%20b

Jewish Telegraphic Agency (1996), "Germany Mediates Exchange Between Hezbollah and Israel," JTA, 22 July. Retrieved from https://www.jta.org/1996/07/22/archive/germany-mediates-exchange-between-hezbollah-and-israel

Joffe, Lawrence (2003), "Shlomo Argov: Israeli Diplomat Whose Shooting Triggered the Invasion of Lebanon," *The Guardian*, 25 February. Retrieved from https://www.theguardian.com/world/2003/feb/25/israelandthepalestinians.lebanon

Jones, Seth G.; Markusen, Maxwell B. (2018), "The Escalating Conflict with Hezbollah in Syria," Centre for Strategic and International Studies, 20 June . Retrieved from https://www.csis.org/analysis/escalating-conflict-hezbollah-syria

Khoury, Jack, and Reuters (2018), "Iranian Forces Pulling Back From Israel Border, Says Russia," *Haaretz*, 1 August. Retrieved from www.haaretz.com/middleeast-news/iran/iranian-forces-withdraw-to-a-distance-of-85-km-from-golan-heights-1.6337360.

Khraiche, Dana (2014), "Suicide Bomber Kills Three in e. Lebanon," *The Daily* Star-Lebanon, 22 February. Retrieved from www.dailystar.com.lb/News/Lebanon-News/2014/Feb-22/248183-suicide-bomber-kills-two-soldiers-in-e-Lebanon.ashx.

Los Angeles Times (2000), "Israel Leaves South Lebanon After 22 Years," *Los Angeles Times*, 24 May. Retrieved from http://articles.latimes.com/2000/may/24/news/mn-33497

Lebanon National Assembly (2018), "Lebanon Majlis Al-Nuwwab (National Assembly)," Inter-Parliamentary Union, 10 May. Retrieved from archive.ipu.org/parline/reports/2179_E.htm.

Levitt, Matthew (2013), *Hezbollah: The Global Footprint of Lebanon's Party of God* (Georgetown University Press). Retrieved from http://www.washingtoninstitute.org/policy-analysis/view/hezbollah-the-global-footprint-of-lebanons-party-of-god

Levitt, Matthew (2013), "The Hezbollah Connection in Syria and Iran," Council on Foreign Relations, 15 February. Retrieved from https://www.cfr.org/interview/hezbollah-connection-syria-and-iran

Levitt, Matthew (2014), "Hezbollah's Syrian Quagmire," PRISM: 101-115. Retrieved from www.washingtoninstitute.org/uploads/Documents/opeds/Levitt20140911-PRISM.pdf

Macaron, Joe (2016), "What Municipal Elections Mean for Lebanon," Arab Centre Washington D.C., 17 May. Retrieved from arabcenterdc.org/policy_analyses/what-municipal-elections-mean-for-lebanon/.

Masters, Jonathan, & Laub, Zachary (2014), "Hezbollah," Council on Foreign Relations, January. Retrieved from https://www.cfr.org/backgrounder/hezbollah

Michaels, Jim (2013), "Recalling the Deadly 1983 Attack on the Marine Barracks," *USA Today*, 23 October. Retrieved from https://www.usatoday.com/story/nation/2013/10/23/marines-beirut-lebanon-hezbollah/3171593/

International Crisis Group (2014), "Hezbollah's Syria Conundrum,", Middle East Report N°175. Retrieved from https://www.crisisgroup.org/middle-east-north-africa/eastern-mediterranean/lebanon/175-hizbollah-s-syria-conundrum

Miller, Marjorie, Daniszewki, John; Wilkinson, Tracy (2000), "Israel Leaves South Lebanon After 22 Years," *Los Angeles Times*, 24 May. Retrieved from http://articles.latimes.com/2000/may/24/news/mn-33497

Mishra, Anant (2018), "Understanding Hezbollah's Military Engagement in Syria: Achieving Political Goal or a Religious Drift"? *Modern Diplomacy,* 10 March. Retrieved from https://moderndiplomacy.eu/2018/03/10/understanding-hezbollahs-military-engagement-in-syria-achieving-political-goal-or-a-religious-drift/.

Mounir, Al Rabih (2017), "Hezbollah and Iran in Syria," *Fikra Forum*, 13 November. Retrieved from http://www.washingtoninstitute.org/fikraforum/view/hezbollah-and-iran-in-syria.

Moussawi, Ibrahim (2010), "The Making of Lebanon's Hezbollah", in Khaled Hroub (eds.), *Political Islam: Context versus Ideology* (London: SAQI and London Middle East Institute SOAS), pp. 210-230.

The New York Times (1989) "2 Warring Shiite Muslim Militias Sign Truce Agreement in Lebanon," *New York Times*, 31 January: 1. Retrieved from https://www.nytimes.com/1989/01/31/world/2-warring-shiite-muslim-militias-sign-truce-agreement-in-lebanon.html.

The Times of India (2019), "Nasrallah Says Iran, Hezbollah May Begin Responding to Syria Strikes," *The Times of Israel*, 27 January. Retrieved from www.timesofisrael.com/nasrallah-says-iran-hezbollah-may-begin-responding-to-syria-strikes/.

Osnos, Peter (1983), "3 Arabs Sentenced for London Attack on Israeli Envoy," The *Washington Post*, 6 March. Retrieved from https://www.washingtonpost.com/archive/politics/1983/03/06/3-arabs-sentenced-for-london-attack-on-israeli-envoy/8b4d05dd-fff9-475b-9803-87778e44541a/?utm_term=.4297a27cdc53.

Pan, Esther (2005), "Middle East: Syria and Lebanon," Council on Foreign Relations, 22 February. Retrieved from https://www.cfr.org/backgrounder/middle-east-syria-and-lebanon.

_______ (2006), "Syria, Iran, and the Mideast Conflict," Council on Foreign Relations, 18 July. Retrieved from https://www.cfr.org/backgrounder/syria-iran-and-mideast-conflict#chapter-title-0-7.

Peace Accords Matrix (2015), "Paramilitary Groups: Taif Accord," University of Notre Dame. Retrieved from: https://peaceaccords.nd.edu/provision/paramilitary-groups-taif-accord.

Perry, Tom; Bassam, Laila (2018), "Hezbollah Role in Syrian South Exposes Limits of U.S. Policy," Reuters, 5 July. Retrieved from https://www.reuters.com/article/us-mideast-crisis-syria-iran/hezbollah-role-in-syrian-south-exposes-limits-of-u-s-policy-idUSKBN1JV19U.

Pollack, Nadav (2016), "The Transformation of Hezbollah by its Involvement in Syria," The Washington Institute for Near East Policy, pp. 1-21. Retrieved from www.washingtoninstitute.org/uploads/Documents/pubs/ResearchNote35-Pollak-2.pdf.

Porter, Lizzie (2018), "Analysis: What's Next for Hezbollah in Syria?," Al-Jazeera, 19 May. Retrieved from https://www.aljazeera.com/news/2018/05/analysis-hezbollah-syria-180519141604977.html.

Rasmussen, Sune Engel, and Nazih Osseiran (2018), "Hezbollah Faces Rising Discontent in Heartland Ahead of Election," *The Wall Street Journal*, 3 May.

Retrieved from www.wsj.com/articles/hezbollah-faces-rising-discontent-in-heartland-ahead-of-election-1525348801.

Reuters (2013), "Insight: Battered by War, Syrian Army Creates its Own Replacement," Reuters, 21 April. Retrieved from https://www.reuters.com/article/us-syria-crisis-paramilitary-insight/insight-battered-by-war-syrian-army-creates-its-own-replacement-idUSBRE93K02R20130421

Reuters (2014), "Bomb Explodes at Hezbollah Checkpoint in Eastern Lebanon," Reuters, 21 September. Retrieved from www.reuters.com/article/us-lebanon-security/bomb-explodes-at-hezbollah-checkpoint-in-eastern-lebanon-idUSKBN0HF0LT20140920.

Rosenfeld, Jesse (2017), "How the Syrian Civil War Has Transformed Hezbollah," *The Nation*, 30 March. Retrieved from https://www.thenation.com/article/how-the-syrian-civil-war-has-transformed-hezbollah/

Rossi, Rachel (2018), "Escalating Tensions Between Israel and Hezbollah in Syria," Atlantic Council, 4 October. Retrieved from www.atlanticcouncil.org/blogs/syriasource/escalating-tensions-between-israel-and-hezbollah-in-syria.

Salloukh, Bassel F. (2005), "Syria and Lebanon: A Brotherhood Transformed," Middle East Report, doi:10.2307/30042457

Shabak (1983), "The Tyre HQ Bombing – First Suicide Attack against Israel (1983)," *Shabak*, 3 March. Retrieved from https://www.shabak.gov.il/english/heritage/affairs/Pages/TheTyreHQBombing.aspx

Stanford University (2016), "Mapping Militant Organizations: Hezbollah", 5 August. Retrieved from http://web.stanford.edu/group/mappingmilitants/cgi-bin/groups/view/81?highlight=hezbollah

Sullivan, Marisa (2014), "Hezbollah in Syria," Washington DC: Institute for the Study of War. Retrieved from http://www.understandingwar.org/sites/default/files/Hezbollah_Sullivan_FINAL.pdf

The Associated Press (1987), "A Beirut Hostage is Reported Free," *The New York Times*, 18 August: 1. Retrieved from https://www.nytimes.com/1987/08/18/world/a-beirut-hostage-is-reported-free.html

The Telegraph (2003), "Lebanon: A Brief History," *The Telegraph*, 24 February. Retrieved from https://www.telegraph.co.uk/news/1400004/Lebanon-A-brief-history.html

Tokmajyan, Armenak (2014), "Hezbollah's Military Intervention in Syria: Political Choice or Religious Obligation?" *Approaching Religion:* 105-112. Retrieved from https://ojs.abo.fi/ojs/index.php/ar/article/view/822

United Nations (1989), "The Taif Agreement," United Nations, 4 November. Retrieved from: https://peaceaccords.nd.edu/provision/paramilitary-groups-taif-accord

United Nations (1992), "Treaty' of Brotherhood, Cooperation and Coordination between the Syrian Arab Republic and the Lebanese Republic," United Nations-

Treaty Series. Retrieved from https://peacemaker.un.org/sites/peacemaker.un.org/files/LB-SY_910522_TreatyBrotherhoodCooperationCoordination.pdf.

Voltaire Network (2013), "Hezbollah Leader Hassan Nasrallah's Speech on Syria," Voltaire Network, 25 May. Retrieved from http://www.voltairenet.org/article178691.html.

Ward, S. (2016), "Axis of Resistance: The Hezbollah-Iran-Syria Relationship," *The Cipher Brief*, 14 July. Retrieved from https://www.thecipherbrief.com/axis-of-resistance-the-hezbollah-iran-syria-relationship.

White, Jeffrey (2014), "Hizb Allah at War in Syria: Forces, Operations, Effects and Implications," Combating Terrorism Centre, 3 (1).

Yacoubian, Mona (2006), "Syria's Role in Lebanon," United States Institute of Peace, 9 November. Retrieved from https://www.usip.org/publications/2006/11/syrias-role-lebanon.

Ynet News (2006), "Operation Grapes of Wrath (1996)," *Ynet News*, 8 January. Retrieved from https://www.ynetnews.com/articles/0,7340,L-3284744,00.html.

Zisser, Eyal (2017), "A Decade of Decisions: Lebanon and Syria, from the Second Lebanon War to the Syrian Civil War", in U. Dekel, G. Siboni, & O. Einav (eds.) *Decade: In the Aftermath of the Second Lebanon War, 2006-2016* (Tel Aviv: The Institute for National Security Studies), pp. 97-106, Retrieved from www.css.ethz.ch/content/dam/ethz/special-interest/gess/cis/center-for-securities-studies/resources/docs/INSS-Memorandum%20167.pdf.

8. Jihadi Terrorism: A Case Study of AQAP

Jatin Kumar

Abstract

The *jihadi* terror threat has become a major security challenge since the end of the Afghan War in 1989. To mobilise the larger Muslim community against the Western countries, Al-Qaeda used the concept of *jihad* in two stages: first, it established the base of Al-Qaeda in the late 1980s, and then it developed a group of affiliates that were not directly under its control but shared its objectives. In this process, the establishment of Al-Qaeda in the Arabian Peninsula (AQAP) in 2009 was a great success. This chapter is an attempt to understand the establishment, tactics, strategies and status of the AQAP in Yemen.

Key Words: Terrorism; *Jihad*; AQAP; Franchise Terrorism; Yemen

In the aftermath of the September 11 terror attacks, Al-Qaeda moved terrorism away from the anti-Soviet *jihadist* movement to a vibrant global *jihadist* one (Byman, 2015). It has confronted the world with new and lethal kinds of threats, and functions at two levels: at the upper level, the centralised Al-Qaeda takes vital decisions related to its worldwide operations, and, at the ground level, it has a loose network of affiliates which operate on their own, away from the Al-Qaeda core. Among these decentralised affiliates, Al-Qaeda in the Arabian Peninsula (AQAP) is the most prominent and threatening. The AQAP is Al-Qaeda's first success story in founding a major branch outside the Afghanistan-Pakistan region (BBC, 2015). The group largely operates from Yemen and targets the Western interests around the globe.

The intensified civil war in Yemen, widespread sectarianism, an atmosphere of state collapse and rising security vacuum have provided the AQAP with the best available conditions to expand its foothold in the Arabian Peninsula (Byman & Williams, 2015). According to Bruce Riedel (2015), the unlawful nature of Yemen made it an attractive place for Al-Qaeda. In the long history of Yemen, there has not been a single government which was able to enforce its jurisdiction over the entire country (Riedel, 2015). Large ungoverned places have proved to be an asset for Al-Qaeda to thrive. The growth of the AQAP in Yemen has convinced security experts that Yemen can be turned into a stronghold and training and operational hub for the AQAP (ADL, 2013).

On the ideological side, the AQAP finds itself close to the central Al-Qaeda and, like the latter, it challenges the Saudi monarchy. This critical stand against Saudi Arabia led Riyadh to take strict action against AQAP elements within the kingdom, forcing its members to take refuge in Yemen (Novak, 2009). Since its formation in 2009, the AQAP had tried to launch various attacks against the Western countries and the US, including three major foiled attempts, when it targeted the US-bound aircraft in 2012 (Joscelyn, 2017). Its terror attacks are not limited to foreign targets but also focus on regional ones (BBC, 2015).

The AQAP has intelligently utilised even its failed attempts by garnering substantial media attention. The key aim of its operational tactics outside the Arab world is to attract, as much as possible, the English-speaking audience through its propaganda material (Harris, 2010). The literature provided by AQAP motivates the like-minded Western individuals to adopt its ideology and launch lone wolf strikes against the West, within and outside the Arabian Peninsula. In two messages released in 2015, it urged the carrying out of lone wolf attacks on Western targets and exhorted its followers to carry out more such attacks, insisting "America is first" (Louisa, 2015). In the same year, its operatives launched a major terror strike in France on the *Charlie Hebdo* office (Al-Jazeera, 2015). In 2015, the Saudi-led military involvement in the Yemeni civil war gave space to the AQAP to strengthen itself. In April, it captured the strategically important port city of Mukalla and operated in the largest province of Yemen until April 2016 when, in a joint operation, Saudi and UAE forces recaptured the strategically located port city (Edroos & Al Batati, 2018).

Origin

Since the end of the Soviet-Afghan War in 1989, Yemen has been a safe haven for the *jihadists* (Ryan, 2015). However, Yemen's ties with Al-Qaeda began with the Islamic *jihad* against the Soviet Union in Afghanistan in the 1980s. In the 1990s, President of North Yemen Ali Abdullah Saleh welcomed the Mujahideen who had fought against the Soviet Union in Afghanistan: they were basically of Yemeni origin but also comprised a sizeable number of other nationals (Edwards, 2010). For the resettlement of these Mujahideen, Yemen received US$20 million from Osama bin Laden (Burns, 2000). According to some experts, Saleh allegedly employed these Mujahideen to fight against his domestic rivals (Council on Foreign Relations, 2015). Due to the changed geo-political situation, many of these Mujahedeen were not allowed to resettle in their own countries such as Saudi Arabia, and Iraq and Yemen emerged as their refuge. Osama Bin Laden was also among the Mujahideen who were thrown out from their home countries; initially, he left for Yemen and later settled in Sudan, where he remained until 1996 (ibid.).

In the early 1990s, Yemen emerged as a safe haven for the Afghan Mujahideen (Rollins, 2011). In this regard, the country's powerful tribal system, fragile economy, chaotic political environment and difficult mountainous terrain proved a boon (Al-Dawsari, 2018). These Mujahideen formed the Islamic Jihad in Yemen (IJY). Though it was disbanded in 1994, it was a forerunner of the AQAP. It was followed by other groups as well, such as the Army of Aden Abyan (1994), and, finally, Al-Qaeda in Yemen (AQY) in 2003 (Council on Foreign Relations, 2015).

In 1998, Al-Qaeda in Yemen (AQY) was formed. In 2000, the AQY carried out a major strike against the US on 12 October by targeting the US missile destroyer *USS Cole* (Perl & O'Rourke, 2001). Simultaneously, during this time, Bin Laden, under his personal supervision, trained Nasir al-Wuhayshi, Qasim al-Raymi, Said al-Shihri, and Mohamed al-Wafi, who eventually created the AQAP in 2009. Responding to the September 11 attacks, the US Administration declared a global "War on Terror" and started a military operation against Al-Qaeda and its affiliates. The AQY was a comparatively small local branch of Al-Qaeda, under the direct control of Bin Laden. The AQAP is not under the direct control of Al-Qaeda, it freely selects its targets and largely comprises the remnants of local Al-Qaeda supporting groups. These are mainly the Mujahideen who left Saudi Arabia amidst of the massive crackdown by the government (Johnsen et al., 2009; BBC, 2015).

In November 2001, Yemen's President Saleh visited the US and met President George W. Bush, Secretary of State Colin Powell and Central Intelligence Agency (CIA) Director George Tenet to discuss a "US$400 million aid package" for his country (CNN, 2017). During the visit, he also underlined his support to the US plan of action (Chakravortty, 2017). From 2002 onwards, the Yemen government, along with the US Special Forces, launched a crackdown on the AQY operatives. In November 2002, a US drone strike killed AQY leader Salim Sinan al-Harethi along with several other operatives. Afraid of a massive crackdown, most of the members of Al-Qaeda left Yemen and joined other local branches of Al-Qaeda (ibid.: 113).

During 2002-03 the US and Yemeni governments worked closely to fight Al-Qaeda. Khaled Ali Hajj, one of the top leaders, was executed by the Saudi forces in 2004 (BBC, 2015). The group soon recovered from and launched a chain of attacks under the leadership of Abdul Aziz al Muqarin who was killed in June 2004. The group was devastated as the US and Yemeni forces launched the joint operation in which most of its operatives were either killed or exposed (McGregor, 2004; BBC, 2015).

By the end of that period, Al-Qaeda seemed to be considerably damaged and, therefore, both the US and Saudi Arabia shifted their attention to the other issues in Yemen such as the political stability, Houthi insurgency and growing Iranian influence, and this gave another chance to the Al-Qaeda to strengthen their foothold (BBC, 2015; McGregor, 2004: 4). Gregory Johnsen noted,

> The interlude of a little over two years in which it appeared as though al-Qaeda in Yemen had been largely defeated was the biggest mistake of the US in its 'war against al-Qaeda'. Instead of securing the win, both the US and Yemeni governments treated victory as an absolute. They failed to realize that in this case, a defeated enemy was not a vanquished

> one. Al-Qaeda was crossed off the list of priorities of both the countries and was replaced by other, seemingly more pressing, concerns. While the threat from al-Qaeda was certainly not forgotten in 2004 and 2005, I argue that it was largely ignored. This lapse of vigilance by both the US and Yemen, I believe, was largely responsible for the relative ease with which one of Osama Bin Laden's former secretaries [began] rebuilding al-Qaeda in the wake of his escape from Yemen in 2006. (Johnsen, 2013: 116)

On 3 February 2006, a massive prison break in Yemen fuelled the rebirth of the AQY. In the incident, around 23 militants escaped, including "convicted al-Qaeda terrorists, some of whom were involved in attacks on the US and French ships in 2000 and 2002" (CNN, 2006). The escape was notable because the escapees included Jamal Ahmed Badawi, the alleged architect of the *USS Cole* attack, Abdullah Al-Raymi (the current Emir of the AQAP) and Nasir al-Wuhayshi, who later became the founding father of the AQAP (Counter Extremism Project, 2018).

The escape of key operatives of Al-Qaeda created a base for the formation of the AQAP. In March 2007, Al-Qaeda officially affirmed its return and declared Al-Wuhayshi as its commander (Sajjan, 2017). With this declaration, it also started a chain of suicide attacks in Saudi Arabia and Yemen and these ended in September 2008 when the US Embassy in Riyadh was targeted by Al-Qaeda, leading to the killing of 18 people (Hedberg, 2005). It led the US and Saudi Arabia start joint-fight against Al-Qaeda severely. The Saudi crackdown pushed Al-Qaeda operatives to leave the area and again take refuge in Southern Yemen. The arrival of Al-Qaeda members provided the necessary impetus for the formation of the AQAP (Counter Extremism Project, 2018).

In January 2009, Al-Qaeda in Saudi Arabia and Yemen merged and formed the AQAP. The unification was recognised by Bin Laden's deputy, Ayman al-Zawahiri (Al-Jazeera, 2009). The declaration of unification of both the Al-Qaeda affiliates was made through a video in which Nasir al-Wuhayshi declared the amalgamation (Counter Extremism Project, 2018). The video was recorded by Wuhayshi, Raymi and Said Ali al-Shihri. The video also underlined its objective, *modus-operandi* and intention to set up an Islamic Caliphate based on *Sharia* law (*Wall Street Journal*, 2014). It clarified that the AQAP was planning to establish an Islamic Caliphate in its areas of influence. On 19 January 2010, the UN Security Council listed AQAP as a terror outfit (UNSC, 2008), for the first time, in 2011, due to its association with Al-Qaeda. The group captured territories in Yemen and started ruling the area on the basis of "strict interpretation of the *Sharia* and declaring an Emirate" (Fanusie and Entz, 2017). This was the time when the entire region was facing a series of protests, and Yemen was no exception. Due to the protests, President Saleh stepped down, and this resulted in the Yemeni civil war (BBC, 2012). The AQAP's successful control over a large number of territories was an outcome of this political chaos. The unstable political situation provided space to the group to expand its reach in Yemen. However, after a few months, the US-supported forces pushed it out from the land it controlled but it remained a critical threat to the Western countries (Fanusie & Entz, 2017).

Since 2009, it has launched multiple attacks on various Western targets. On 21 May 2012, a suicide bomber from the AQAP attacked the rehearsal of the unity day military parade at Sana'a and killed more than 120 people (BBC, 2012). In December 2013, it raided a hospital situated in a Defence Ministry compound and killed 56 people (CNN, 2017). In January 2015, it claimed responsibility for the lethal strike on the office of "*Charlie Hebdo*, which had published caricatures of the Prophet Muhammad" (BBC, 2015). On 2 April 2015, the AQAP launched a major offensive on the coastal city of Mukalla and after successfully capturing the city, it handed over the control to a civilian council. According to the Central Bank of Yemen, it looted around the US$ 120 million from the bank (International Crisis Group, 2017). To provide local services in the city, the AQAP also allocated a budget of more than US$ 4 million (ibid.). On 2 December 2015, Zinjibar and areas of Jaār were seized by AQAP operatives. Similar to Mukalla, in both places, AQAP handed over the control to a civilian council (Horton, 2017).

Aims, Objectives and Structure

The aims and ideology of AQAP are very similar to those of Al-Qaeda. The key objective of the organisation is to establish an Islamic Caliphate based on a strict interpretation of the *Sharia* law (Government of Australia,

2018). Its ideology was well captured in its inaugural video, in which its founder Al-Wuhayshi confirmed the outfit's intentions to take revenge on its enemy "with blood and destruction" and establish the Islamic Caliphate based on *Sharia* law (Chakravortty, 2017: 115). A 19-minute video that was released on 20 January 2009 by AQAP titled *We Start from Here and We will Meet at al-Aqsa*, broadly underlined the guiding ideology of the organisation. In the video, Al-Wuhayshi says, "O Allah! Bring conquest over the Holy Mosque and the Haramain by our hands! O Allah! Give us the honour by establishing the Islamic State with our hands!" (Leibrock, 2017: 24).

The video also warned the Muslim leaders of the region, especially Yemeni President Saleh, the royal family of Saudi Arabia and the Egyptian President Hosni Mubarak (Calamur, 2017). The message made it clear that AQAP's operations were not limited to the Western targets, but would also target the Islamic countries working with the Western countries (Chakravortty, 2017). In another video with Al-Jazeera on 27 January 2009, Al-Wuhayshi made the case of the Israeli presence in Palestine, the US war against Iraq, Afghanistan and Somalia (Burton & Stewart, 2009). He also said that since the Crusaders had used the Arabian Peninsula to launch a war against the Islamic countries, "all Crusader interests" in the peninsula "should be struck" (Burton & Stewart, 2009).

These objectives were further expanded in 2012 when the AQAP published another paper which highlighted that the main objectives of the group are to "expel the Jews and Christians from the Arabian Peninsula" and to "establish the Islamic Caliphate and *Sharia* rule which the apostate governments have suspended" (Herring, 2017). According to Fred Burton and Scott Stewart, the main objective of the AQAP is associated with the ideology of radical *jihad*, which urges Muslim majority states to replace "apostate" governments with Islamic regimes (Burton & Scott, 2008). Regarding Yemen, its aims comprise removing the government from power; killing Westerners and their collaborators, including members of the Saudi royal family; and attacking the US homeland (ibid.).

The strongholds of the AQAP are the areas of al-Mahfad, which is a part of the Abyan province. However, its training camps are also situated in Shabwa, Hadramawt, and Marib (O'Driscoll, 2017). The organisational structure of AQAP is hierarchical and decentralised. The decentralised nature of the organisation allows it to withstand attacks and arrests (START, 2015). According to Johnsen, the early organisational structure of the AQAP was based on the ideas and personalities of the leaders, particularly Al-Wuhayshi (cited in Chakravortty, 2017: 119). According to Joshua Koontz, the AQAP's source of success lies in its "formalized mid-level leadership structure with three components: a chain of command, a training and education program, and a consistent promotion process" (Koontz, 2015).

The leadership structure of the organisation is divided into two levels, District Commanders and Governorate Commanders, and it is administered by a military committee (ibid.). To enhance the striking capabilities of these Commanders, the Al-Qaeda affiliate trains them to learn from previous errors and "adapt to changing circumstances with a series of classes, videos, and textbooks. The AQAP's promotion process also bolsters its internal cohesion by retaining fighters via a sense of inclusion and opportunities for advancement" (ibid.). According to Barak Barfi, the AQAP is a hierarchical organisation wherein the job responsibility is divided among the operatives. It has political leaders for overall guidance, a military chief to plan operational issues, a propaganda wing which mobilises the recruits, and a religious unit which justifies its military operations from the theological point of view (Barfi, 2010: p.1).

Key of Success in the Arabian Peninsula

Soft Power Tactics

The key to the success of the AQAP in the peninsula is not its military leadership but its tactics to involve itself with the societal issues in Yemen (Green, 2015; Osman, 2012). The kind of support it has received from tribal leaders in the remote areas demonstrate its success in winning the hearts and minds of the locals. Its leaders knew that the control in the remote areas was in the hands of the local tribal leaders, with limited meddling by the military (Barfi, 2010). These areas were vital from the AQAP's point of view for two reasons: first, the Mujahedeen could easily run their training camps without military intervention; and two, it was easy for Al-Qaeda to introduce alternative social and political systems and gain the people's support (ibid.). Thus, close and cordial relations with the tribal leaders and the locals comprised the key to the AQAP's strategy. It was authenticated in the statements of Al-Wuhayshi and Zawahiri as well:

> I call on the noble and the defiant tribes of Yemen and tell them: don't be less than your brothers in the defiant Pushtun and Baluch tribes who aided Allah and his messenger and made America and Crusaders dizzy in Afghanistan and Pakistan, noble and defiant tribes of Yemen ...don't be helpers of Ali Abdullah Saleh, the agent of Crusaders ... be a help and support to your brothers, the Mujahedeen. (Phillips, 2010: 78)

The AQAP exploited the societal void which was generated in the absence of civic services in the tribal areas. Furthermore, it collaborated with the Quranic schools and charities to implement an alternative system and to hide its financial flow (Osman, 2012). Some of the important charitable institutions which were closely associated with the group were Al-Haramein, Dar al-Hikma al-Yemenia and Al-Islah (Startfor, 2012). According to Startfor, Dar al-Hikma al-Yemenia and Dar al-Islah were reportedly two charities working for the AQAP. Dar al-Hikma al-Yemenia has been charged for providing funds and technical assistance to Al-Qaeda operatives in Yemen and Saudi Arabia (ibid.).

On the other hand, academic institutions such as the Al Eman University provided a fertile ground for radical preaching of the AQAP. This university was established by the "Sheik Abdul Majid al-Zindani a theological adviser to Osama Bin Laden and founder of the Yemeni opposition party, Islah" (Erlangerjan, 2010). During 2004-05, the American-born internet preacher, Anwar al Awlaki, served as a teacher at the university (Johnsen, 2006). The role of this university in radicalising young minds was authenticated with the assassination attack on the opposition leader of Yemen, Jarallah Omar in 2002 (ibid.).

The AQAP has also used social media platforms as a vital tool in its soft power strategy. In this context, *Inspire* magazine and *Sada al-Malahim* channel played an important role (Zimmerman, 2010). Both the AQAP magazine and channel respectively, were aimed at communicating the outfit's agenda to the wider population and to mobilise them to attack

Western targets. *Inspire* magazine, published in the English language focussed on the Western audience (Boucek, 2009). The magazine provides information on how to make a bomb in a kitchen and how to launch lone wolf attacks by using a variety of easily available weapons. The first issue of *Inspire,* which was published in July 2010, carried an article entitled "Make a Bomb in the Kitchen of Your Mom", with illustrations to develop a home-made bomb using day-to-day things (*Inspire,* 2010). In 2012, the AQAP published an article by Samir Khan as a recruitment guide, entitled "Expectations Full". The article urged West-based operatives to target the US rather than coming to the West Asian region (Cruickshank & Levine, 2016). It advised that "attacking the enemy in their backyard" would be more useful than joining the AQAP in Yemen (ibid.).

The August 2014 issue carried a story on how to launch car bomb attacks on Western targets, and the December issue published the blueprints for developing a high-intensity car bomb that could breach airport security (Counter Extremism Project, 2018). According to Johnsen, *Inspire* facilitates a channel for the AQAP to contact and manipulate like-minded individuals in the Western countries (Johnsen, 2013). It enables individuals who do not know the Arabic language nor have visited Yemen, to receive instruction and basic training from the AQAP.

Apart from the print media, AQAP has also utilised the electronic media platform through video messages. In 2014, it started a concerted active media effort to report on, and take responsibility for, its military operations on a regular basis. This change in strategy was different from its past pattern, where it only took responsibility for a major attack (Zelin & Hoover, 2015). This may have been a media strategy to compete with the IS which was getting almost all the media mileage at that time. In addition, the AQAP created a Twitter account to upload its various contents. One of its news feed accounts was *Akhbar Ansar al-Sharia fi Jazira al-Arab*[1] (ibid.). Since August 2014, this feed was the key platform to convey information about the AQAP's military operation. Till April 2015, it had taken responsibility for 374 attacks, mostly against Houthi (224) and government forces (147) (ibid.).

---

1. The name of the feed is inspired from Ansar al-Sharia, another affiliate of Al-Qaeda in Yemen, largely known for its social welfare activities.

Hard Power Tactics

The AQAP follows a remarkable *modus operandi*. Its target selection, tactics, and geographic concentration are different from those of other outfits (Osman, 2012; Zelin & Hoover, 2015). In its operations, most of the targets have been government positions, military convoys, and specific important individuals. Its fighting strategies highlight the evolution in its "style from a guerrilla warfare-style to organised army-style warfare" (Osman, 2012: 5). It was reflected in the two-week-long battle of Mukalla when AQAP terrorist attacked the coastal city on 2 April 2015 and successfully captured it.

In 2014, *Al-Malahem* made public eight video lectures on military tactics and fighting techniques. These lectures were designed and delivered by a top-level *jihadist* in the AQAP, Nasr bin Ali al-Ansi. These recorded lectures were later compiled and documented by the Jihadist Military Academy (IDC Herzliya, 2016). These highlighted the AQAP's orientation towards developing a well trained *jihadi* force. These videos also revealed that in its approach, the AQAP was systematic and professional. According to the International Institute for Counter-Terrorism (IDC Herzliya), in November 2014, an additional 26 documents were published to summarise the key points of the lectures (ibid.). According to IDC Herzliya,

> The introduction to the lectures indicates that 'military strategy' is only one of many (33) topics covered in over 60 lessons, about a wide variety of military issues—in the areas of history, tactics, training, naval warfare, military engineering, and more—which the AQAP transmits to its students in lectures at the 'Jihadist Military Academy'. (Ibid.: 16)

Along with this, lone wolf attacks have also received significant attention in the AQAP's hard power strategy. It has been promoting lone wolfs as an effective strategy to attack Western targets. This was also captured in the 16th issue of its propaganda magazine which was published on 12 November 2016. To encourage lone wolf attacks, the magazine lauded the lone wolf *jihadist* as a hero and asked others to target America (Reaves, 2016). Similarly, in 2017, AQAP Emir, Qasim Al Raymi appeared in a video broadcast on the internet by the organisation's propaganda machine, *Al Malahem,* which asked its operatives to launch "simple lone wolf attacks in the West" (Agnon, 2017).

Economic Status

The AQAP has generated a substantial amount of revenue from oil and gas, taxation and extortion, trafficking, looting, kidnapping and ransom donation and external assistance (David, 2017). According to *The New York Times,* the AQAP received two major ransom payments: first, the "French Government paid US$9 million in 2011 for three French nationals"; and, second, "US$20.4 million in 2012-13, paid by Oman and Qatar, for four Europeans" (Callimachi, 2014).

In 2016, a sharp decrease in the AQAP's revenue had been registered but it remained well funded. The reduction in the revenue was mainly because of losing control over the Yemeni port city of Mukalla (Fanusie & Entz, 2017). At present, the AQAP is expected to make US$5-10 million per year, with the most of this coming from criminal acts and donations. Furthermore, when it controls the major cities, taxation becomes an important source of funds (ibid.). For example, in Mukalla (2015-16), it received a huge amount of money from taxes.

In Mukalla, it also successfully ransacked Rial 13 billion and looted another "US$1.5 million from the Central Bank and Rial 20 million from an agricultural bank" (UNSC, 2016). The AQAP's control over the key financial city of Mukalla and its coastline allowed it to earn income from taxation on shipments and traders; this amount was estimated by the UN to be nearly US$2 million per day (UNSC, 2014). It continued to get funds from external donations, kidnapping and ransom. This income was sufficient for the group to stay active in the peninsula. According to Yemeni officials, an estimated US$10 million per year is enough for the AQAP to remain functional in the region (Bayoumy & Browning et al., 2016). The revenue which was gathered during the capture of Mukalla highlights that the group retains substantial cash reserves.

Post-Arab Spring Period (2011-17)

The year 2011 was a year of change in the Middle East. This also affected Yemen and a series of protest against President Ali Abdullah Saleh surfaced

(Al-Jazeera, 2017). These protests were a game changer for the AQAP. Before the Arab Spring, it was a minor yet deadly franchise of Al-Qaeda, largely focussing on attacking Western targets (International Crises Group, 2017). However, since 2011, it started taking an interest in the domestic politics of Yemen. Due to the turmoil, President Saleh, who came to power in 1978, handed over power to Abd Rabbuh Mansour al–Hadi, under an initiative led by the Gulf Cooperation Council (GCC) on 23 November 2011 (Boone & Raghavan, 2011).

The transition of power was followed by a chain of protests that soon turned into a civil war kind of situation. The protestors who were sympathetic to the Saleh family turned violent and attacked the government institutions (Chakravortty, 2017). The supporters of Saleh launched a massive crackdown on the protestors. In the northern part of the country, the Houthis set up a parallel government in the three provinces of Al-Jawf, Hajjah and Sa'ada. In this regard, the power vacuum which was created by the uprising in 2011 played an important role (Ibid).

The separatist of Southern Yemen made use of this political chaos. The secessionist movement in the south boycotted the electoral process and demanded freedom (Wells, 2012). This political chaos and failed military control in Yemen created a fertile ground for the AQAP and it started a gradual expansion in Southern Yemen (Watson, 2018). Soon, AQAP members started establishing training camps in Sana'a and a series of clashes began between AQAP operatives and Houthi tribesmen.

Under such a situation in 2012, Mansour al Hadi started an army offensive against the AQAP in South Yemen with the support of the UN. The military offensive was also supported by the US through its constant drone attacks authorised by President Barak Obama. However, these military actions did not stop the AQAP terror strikes. In May 2012, it attacked the military parade in Sana'a, killing more than 120 people (*The Telegraph*, 2016). After some time, the security forces intercepted the communications of an AQAP operative which highlighted that two AQAP operatives had planned to target the US Embassies in the Middle East as well as Africa.

On 24 December 2012, *Al-Malahim* released a video message of the AQAP which lacked some of the important portions and these were later released on 27 December (*IntelCenter*, 2016). These seven missing portions entitled, "Jihad of an Ummah", were released on 27 December. The video also highlighted the same threat that was captured in the intercepts gathered by the US forces.

The video said:

> We, al-Qaeda in the Arabian Peninsula (AQAP), to inspire to do jihad and to encourage our Muslim Ummah.... 3,000 grams of gold to whoever kills the Jewish US ambassador in Sana'a. Five million Yemeni Riyals to whoever kills any American soldier in Yemen. Do not consult anyone in killing the Americans. (*IntelCenter*, 2016)

These indicators forced the US policy-makers to shut or scale down the US Embassies in the Middle East region in 2013, for a long time. It was almost around the same time when Wuhayshi became the leader of the AQAP.

The year 2014 registered an increase in the AQAP's terror activities. On 24 April, the group's operative tried to abduct two employees of the US Embassy in Sana'a (Leibrock, 2017). During the attempt, one of the gunmen was killed by the security forces. In November, the AQAP took responsibility for a failed assassination attempt on the US Ambassador in Sana'a. On 3 December, it assumed responsibility for an elimination attempt of "the Iranian Ambassador by detonating a Vehicle-Borne Improvised Explosive Device (VBIED) at his residence in Sana'a, Yemen" (Government of Australia, 2018).

On a parallel track, other actors tried to find a solution to the chaotic situation. On 23 January 2014, the National Dialogue Conference (NDC) was concluded (BBC, 2014). The NDC was mainly a transitional dialogue process which was based on UN Security Council (UNSC) Resolution 2051 and the GCC agreement signed on 23 November 2011 (Chakravortty, 2017). The Houthis and the southern leaders boycotted the NDC. They rejected the idea of a coalition government and forcefully demanded a division in the country (Schmitz, 2014; Chakravortty, 2017). This led to a grave civil war situation in which many people lost their lives and thousands were internally displaced. During April-December 2014, the AQAP carried out 28 terror attacks in which more than 86 soldiers and 150 Houthis were killed (UNSC, 2014).

In 2015, the AQAP successfully targeted the French satirical newspaper *Charlie Hebdo* on 7 January 2015 (*Independent,* 2015). This attack was important for two reasons: one, it was the first attack launched by a European citizen in a European country on behalf of the AQAP (Fanusie & Entz, 2017). Two, it broadly highlighted that the AQAP could launch attacks on considerably safe targets outside its area of occupation.

On the other hand, in Yemen, the domestic situation worsened severely. In 2015, the Houthis expanded their power in Sana'a which forced Mansour Hadi to flee to Aden in February (Al-Batati, 2015). Under such a situation, the AQAP expanded its reach in the southern provinces of Yemen. It formed a mini-state in the areas it controlled. Though a US drone attack eliminated its leader Wuhayshi, the organisation continued to flourish under a new leader, Raymi (BBC, 2015).

In March 2015, Saudi Arabia led a military campaign "Operation Decisive Storm", in support of the government of Mansur Hadi (*Alabrabiya,* 2015). As a result, most of the Yemeni forces left the southern part of Yemen and moved towards, the north. The forces even left the city of Mukalla defenceless, thereby allowing AQAP operatives to exploit the situation (Chakravortty, 2017: 125). On 2 April, its fighters attacked the coastal city of Mukalla and captured it. The city of Mukalla was strategically important for the AQAP as it provided it with a sea trade route and strong geographical defence (Al-Batati & Fahim, 2015). On 2 December, the Abyan governorate, Zinjibar, and Jaār also came under the control of the AQAP (Mukhashaf, 2015). In all these areas, the group's forces soon handed over the controls of the city to the civilian council, which highlighted the intentions of the AQAP to establish a proper, functional state. Though the organisation lost control of Mukalla in April 2016, it had,by then, managed to gain enormous wealth from the city (Joscelyn, 2016).

The AQAP has also challenged the supremacy of the IS. Unlike other Al-Qaeda affiliates, it refused to pledge allegiance to the IS because it wanted to show that its understanding of an Islamic Caliphate was different from that of the IS (Chakravortty, 2017, p. 125). Many security experts believe that the weakening of the IS had positively favoured the AQAP in the peninsula. This was authenticated in the strategic assessment of the new US administration as well; therefore, the Trump administration soon after coming to power, started strikes against the AQAP. On 29 January 2017, it launched its military operation against the group and killed 41 suspected operatives and 16 civilians (Windrem & Arkin, 2018). The intensity of attacks was increased in the first week of March when the US military launched 45 air strikes against the AQAP (Phil & Mukhashaf, 2017).

Conclusion

The military operations in Yemen have weakened the AQAP, yet it is far from being defeated. It may have lost territory, but its ideology and operatives are still thriving. Despite the chaotic situation in Yemen, it is financially stable and well-funded. This gives the outfit the ability to come out of setbacks. On the other hand, currently, the focus of the international community is on Syria and Iran and under such a situation, a strong military campaign against the AQAP is not expected. The stronghold of the organisation among the tribal lords of Yemeni society is still unbroken. In many areas, it has received support from the local population, hence, to break the spine of the organisation, it is mandatory to crush this link. The war against the AQAP cannot reach its end till an assertive strategy is developed to deal with its soft power approach.

Since President Donald Trump came to office, the drone strikes against the AQAP have escalated. These drone strikes have the potential to weaken the organisation but not destroy it. As the war in Syria against the IS is coming to an end, Al-Qaeda and its other franchise in the region have started rising again as powerful actors. It was evident in the rising influence of the AQAP in the peninsula. It was also reflected in Syria where the destruction of the IS has strengthened the Al-Qaeda stronghold.

References

ADL (2013), "Al Qaeda in the Arabian Peninsula". Retrieved from https://www.adl.org/education/resources/reports/al-qaeda-in-the-arabian-peninsula?_ga=1.200620334.1876467819.1484870400.

Agnon, Shmuel Yosef (2017), "AQAP Emir, Qasim Al Raymi Calls For Simple-Lone Wolf Attacks in the West, *Strategic Intelligence*, 10 May. Retrieved from https://intelligencebriefs.com/aqap-emir-qasim-al-raymi-calls-for-simple-lone-wolf-attacks-in-the-west/.

Alarabiya (2015), "Your Guide to 'Operation Decisive Storm". Retrieved from http://english.alarabiya.net/en/perspective/features/2015/03/26/Allies-back-Saudi-led-Decisive-Storm-op-in-Yemen-with-fighter-jets-.html.

Al-Batati, Saeed (2015), "Yemen's Houthi Rebels say Former President has Fled Capital", *The Guardian*, 21 February. Retrieved From https://www.theguardian.com/world/2015/feb/21/yemen-houthi-rebels-president-hadi-fled-capital.

Al-Batati, Saeed & Kareem Fahim, (2015), "Affiliate of Al Qaeda Seizes Major Yemeni City, Driving Out the Military" , 3 April, Retrieved from https://www.nytimes.com/2015/04/04/world/middleeast/al-qaeda-al-mukalla-yemen.html.

Al-Jazeera (2015), "Al-Qaeda in Yemen Claims Charlie Hebdo Attack," 15 January. Retrieved from https://www.aljazeera.com/news/middleeast/2015/01/al-qaeda-yemen-charlie-hebdo-paris-attacks-201511410323361511.html.

Al-Jazeera (2017), "Yemen: Who was Ali Abdullah Saleh?", 5 December. Retrieved from https://www.aljazeera.com/indepth/spotlight/yemen/2011/02/201122812118938648.html.

Al-Jazeera (2009), "Al-Qaeda in the Arabian Peninsula," 29 December 2009. Retrieved from https://www.aljazeera.com/news/middleeast/ 2009/12/ 2009122935812371810.html.

Almasmari, Hakim (2013), "Militants Attack Hospital at Yemen's Defense Ministry, Killing 52", 16 December. Retrieved from https://edition.cnn.com/2013/12/05/world/meast/yemen-violence/index.html.

Barfi, Barak (2010), "Yemen on the Brink?: The Resurgence of al Qaeda in Yemen," New America Foundation. Retrieved from https://www.academia.edu/28865984/Yemen_on_the_Brink.

Bayoumy, Yara & Noah Browning et al. (2016), "How Saudi Arabia's War in Yemen has Made Al Qaeda Stronger - and Richer," Reuters, 8 April. Retrieved from http://www.reuters.com/investigates/special-report/yemen-aqap/.

BBC (2012), "Yemen's President Ali Abdullah Saleh Cedes Power", 27 February. Retrieved from https://www.bbc.com/news/world-middle-east-17177720.

BBC (2014), "Yemen's National Dialogue Conference Concludes with Agreement," 21 January. Retrieved from https://www.bbc.com/news/world-middle-east-25835721.

BBC (2015), "Profile: Al-Qaeda in the Arabian Peninsula", 16 June. Retrieved from https://www.bbc.com/news/world-middle-east-11483095.

Boone, Jeb & Raghavan, Sudarsan (2011), "Yemen's President Saleh Agrees to Step Down in Return for Immunity," 23 April. Retrieved from https://www.washingtonpost.com/world/yemens-president-saleh-agrees-to-step-down-in-return-for-immunity/2011/04/23/AFu59SWE_story.html?noredirect=on&utm_term=.b5848145655e.

Boucek, Christopher (2009), "Yemen: Avoiding a Downward Spiral," Carnegieendowment.org. Retrieved from http://carnegieendowment.org/files/yemen_downward_spiral.pdf.

Burns, John F. (2000), "Yemen Links to bin Laden Gnaw at F.B.I. in Cole Inquiry," *The New York Times*, 26 November. Retrieved from http://www.nytimes.com/2000/11/26/world/yemen-links-to-bin-ladengnaw-at-fbi-in-cole-inquiry.html?pagewanted=all.

Burton, Fred & Stewart, Scott (2009), "Al Qaeda in the Arabian Peninsula: Desperation or New Life?" Stratfor, 28 January, https://worldview.stratfor.com/article/al-qaeda-arabian-peninsula-desperation-or-new-life.

Burton, Fred & Stewart, Scott (2008), "The 'Lone Wolf' Disconnect," Stratfor, January 30. Retrieved from https://worldview.stratfor.com/article/lone-wolf-disconnect.

Byman, Daniel L. & Williams, Jennifer R. (2015), "Will al Qaeda be the Great Winner of Yemen's Collapse?". Retrieved from https://www.brookings.edu/articles/will-al-qaeda-be-the-great-winner-of-yemens-collapse/.

Byman, Daniel L. (2015), "Comparing Al Qaeda and ISIS: Different Goals, Different Targets," Brookings, April 29. Retrieved from https://www.brookings.edu/testimonies/comparing-al-qaeda-and-isis-different-goals-different-targets/.

Calamur, Krishnadev (2017), "Saleh's Death in Yemen Sends a Message to Other Dictators", 4 December. Retrieved from: https://www.theatlantic.com/international/archive/2017/12/yemen-saleh-dead/547385/.

Callimachi, Rukmini (2014), "Paying Ransoms, Europe Bankrolls Qaeda Terror", *New York Times*, 30 September. Retrieved from https://www.nytimes.com/2014/07/30/world/africa/ransoming-citizenseurope-becomes-al-qaedas-patron.html.

Chakravortty , Dipanwita (2017), "Al-Qaeda in Arabian Peninsula." in Sanjay Singh (eds.) *West Asia in Transition II* (New Delhi: Pentagon Press, 2018), pp. 113-129.

CNN (2006), "USS *Cole* Plotter Escapes Prison," CNN, 5 February. Retrieved from http://edition.cnn.com/2006/WORLD/meast/02/05/cole.escape/index.html.

CNN (2017), "Ali Abdullah Saleh Fast Facts," CNN, 7 December. Retrieved from https://edition.cnn.com/2013/07/08/world/meast/ali-abdullah-saleh-fast-facts/index.html.

Cordesman, Anthony H., Robert M. Shelala II, & Omar Mohamed (2013), "The Gulf Military Balance, Volume III: The Gulf and the Arabian Peninsula". Retrieved From https://csis-prod.s3.amazonaws.com/s3fs-public/legacy_files/files/publication/120228_Iran_Ch_VI_Gulf_State.pdf.

Council on Foreign Relation (2015), "Al-Qaeda in the Arabian Peninsula (AQAP)". Retrieved from https://www.cfr.org/backgrounder/al-qaeda-arabian-peninsula-aqap.

Counter Extremism Project (2018)., "Al-Qaeda in the Arabian Peninsula (AQAP)". Retrieved from https://www.counterextremism.com/threat/al-qaeda-arabian-peninsula-aqap.

Cruickshank, Paul & Levine, Adam Levine (2016),"Wage Jihad at Home, Not in Yemen, Al Qaeda Urges Recruits", CNN, May 2016. Retrieved from http://security.blogs.cnn.com/2012/05/16/wage-jihad-at-home-not-in-yemen-al-qaeda-urges-recruits/.

DW (2013), "Al Qaeda says Attack on Yemen Military Hospital was a 'Mistake'", 22 December. Retrieved from https://www.dw.com/en/al-qaeda-says-attack-on-yemen-military-hospital-was-a-mistake/a-17316190.

Edroos, Faisal & Saleh Al Batati, Saleh (2018), "After al-Qaeda: No Signs of Recovery in Yemen's Mukalla", Al-Jazeera, 11 January. Retrieved from https://www.aljazeera.com/indepth/features/al-qaeda-signs-recovery-yemen-mukalla-180111135554851.html.

Edwards, Haley Sweetland (2010), "Uncle Ali". Retrieved from, https://pulitzercenter.org/reporting/uncle-ali.

Elizabeth Grimm Arsenault & Tricia Bacon (2015), "Disaggregating and Defeating Terrorist Safe Havens", *Studies in Conflict & Terrorism*, 38(2): 85-112.

Erlangerjan, Steven (2010), "At Yemen College, Scholarship and Jihadist Ideas," *The New York Times,* 29 January 2018. Retrieved from URL: http://www.nytimes.com/2010/01/19/world/middleeast/19yemen.html.

Fanusie, Yaya J. & Entz, Alex Entz (2017), "Al-Qaeda in the Arabian Peninsula: Financial Assessment". Retrieved from http://www.defenddemocracy.org/content/uploads/documents/CSIF_TFBB_AQAP_web.pdf.

Gohel, Sajjan M. (2017), "Deciphering Ayman Al-Zawahiri and Al-Qaeda's Strategic and Ideological Imperatives", *Perspectives on Terrorism*, 11 (1): 54-67.

Government of Australia (2018), "Al-Qa'ida in the Arabian Peninsula". Retrieved from https://www.nationalsecurity.gov.au/Listedterroristorganisations/Pages/Al-QaidaintheArabianPeninsulaAQAP.aspx.

Green, Daniel (2013), "Al-Qaeda's Soft-Power Strategy in Yemen," The Washington Institute, 23 January. Retrieved from http://www.washingtoninstitute.org/policy-analysis/view/al-qaedas-soft-power-strategy-in-yemen.

Gunaratna, Rohan. (2002). *Inside Al-Qaeda Global Network of Terror* (New York: Columbia University Press).

Hedberg, Nicholas J. (2010), "The Exploitation of a Weak State: Al-Qaeda in the Arabian Peninsula in Yemen". Retrieved from http://www.dtic.mil/dtic/tr/fulltext/u2/a524655.pdf.

Herring, Steven (2017), "What You Need to Know about Al-Qaeda in the Arabian Peninsula". Retrieved from https://www.theodysseyonline.com/al-qaeda-arabian-peninsula.

Hill, Evan & Laura Kasinof (2015), "Playing a Double Game in the Fight against AQAP," *Foreign Policy*, 21 January. Retrieved from http:// foreignpolicy.com/2015/01/21/playing-a-double-game-in-thefight-against-aqap-yemen-saleh-al-qaeda.

Hodali, Diana (2013), "Al Qaeda Finds Safe Haven to Plot in Yemen," DW, 9 August. Retrieved from http://www.dw.com/en/al-qaeda-finds-safe-haven-to-plot-in-yemen/a-17009355.

Horton, Michael (2017). "Fighting the Long War: The Evolution of al-Qa`ida in the Arabian Peninsula," *Combating Terrorism Centre*,10(1): 1-34. Retrieved from https://ctc.usma.edu/fighting-the-long-war-the-evolution-of-al-qaida-in-the-arabian-peninsula/.

IDC Herzliya (2016), "Modus Operandi of Al-Qaeda in the Arabian Peninsula". Retrieved from file:///C:/Users/Jatin/Downloads/JWMG-Ins-Modus-Operandi-AQAP-Mar-16.pdf.

Inspire (2010), "Make a Bomb in the Kitchen of Your Mom". Retrieved from https://azelin.files.wordpress.com/2010/06/aqap-inspire-magazine-volume-1-uncorrupted.pdf https://ctc.usma.edu/aqaps-soft-power-strategy-in-yemen/.

IntelCenter (2016), "Al-Qaeda Arabian Peninsula (AQAP) on Attacking Embassies and Diplomatic Personnel". Retrieved from https://intelcenter.com/reports/AQAP-EmbassyThreats-6Aug2013.html#gs.lD01ZDA.

Javier E. David (2017), "Al-Qaeda in the Arabian Peninsula said to be Flush with Cash and Positioned to Launch New Attacks", 31 July. Retrieved from https://www.cnbc.com/2017/07/31/al-qaeda-in-arabian-peninsula-said-to-be-flush-with-cash-and-positioned-to-launch-new-attacks.html.

Johnsen, Gregory D. & Boucek, Christopher, Shari Villarosa (2009), "Al-Qaeda in Yemen". Retrieved from http://carnegieendowment.org/2009/07/07/al-qaeda-in-yemen-event-1372.

Johnsen, Gregory D. (2013), *The Last Refuge: Yemen, al-Qaeda and America's War in Arabia* (New York: WW Norton).

Joscelyn, Thomas (2016), "Arab Coalition Enters AQAP Stronghold in Port City of Mukalla, Yemen", 25 April, https://www.longwarjournal.org/archives/2016/04/arab-coalition-enters-aqap-stronghold-in-port-city-of-mukalla-yemen.php.

Joscelyn, Thomas (2017), "AQAP Leader Calls for 'Simple' Attacks in the West". Retrieved from https://www.longwarjournal.org/archives/2017/05/aqap-leader-calls-for-simple-attacks-in-the-west.php.

Koontz, Joshua (2015), "Al Qaeda in the Arabian Peninsula Mid-Level Leadership". Retrieved from https://www.criticalthreats.org/analysis/al-qaeda-in-the-arabian-peninsula-mid-level-leadership.

Leibrock, Larry (2017), "The Case of Yemen, AQAP, and the War". Retrieved from https://www.researchgate.net/publication/317126354_Yemen_The_case_of_New_War_and_AQAP.

Lippold, Kirk S. (2012). *Front Burner: Al Qaeda's Attack on the USS Cole* (New York: Blackstone Audio, Inc.).

Loveluck, Louisa (2015), "Al Qaeda in Yemen Urges Followers to Carry out Lone Wolf Attacks in West," *The Telegraph*, 5 August. Retrieved from, https://www.telegraph.co.uk/news/worldnews/middleeast/yemen/11785109/Al-Qaeda-in-Yemen-urges-followers-to-carry-out-lone-wolf-attacks-in-West.html.

McGregor, Andrew (2005), "Shi'ite Insurgency in Yemen: Iranian Intervention or Mountain Revolt?". Retrieved from https://jamestown.org/program/shiite-insurgency-in-yemen-iranian-intervention-or-mountain-revolt/.

Miller, Greg & DeYoung, Karen (2012), "Al-Qaeda Airline Bomb Plot Disrupted, U.S. says," *The Washington Post*, 7 May. Retrieved from https://www.washingtonpost.com/world/national-security/cia-disrupts-airline-bomb-plot/2012/05/07/gIQA9qE08T_story.html?noredirect=on&utm_term=.41cc5f526b93.

Mukhashaf, Mohammed (2015), "Al Qaeda Militants Quit South Yemen Town of Jaar, Still in Zinjibar: Residents", https://www.reuters.com/article/us-yemen-security/al-qaeda-militants-quit-south-yemen-town-of-jaar-still-in-zinjibar-residents-idUSKBN0TM1L020151203.

Novak, Jane (2009), "Arabian Peninsula Al Qaeda Groups Merge". Retrieved from https://web.archive.org/web/20100211172638/http://www.longwarjournal.org/archives/2009/01/arabian_peninsula_al.php.

O'Driscoll, D. (2017), "Violent Extremism and Terrorism in Yemen", K4D Helpdesk Report (Brighton, UK: Institute of Development Studies). Retrieved from https://assets.publishing.service.gov.uk/media/59ad50b540f0b6616a1cbd68/154-156-Violent-Extremism-and-Terrorism-in-Yemen.pdf.

Osman, Awo Abdi (2012), "Al Qaeda in the Arabian Peninsula and Counterterrorism Strategies in Yemen," *Journal of Political Inquiry*, (5)5: 1-14.

Perl, Raphael & O'Rourke, Ronald (2001), "Terrorist Attack on USS Cole: Background and Issues for Congress," Congressional Research Service. Retrieved from http://www.au.af.mil/au/awc/awcgate/crs/rs20721.pdf.

Phillips, Sarah (2010), "What Comes Next in Yemen?: Al-Qaeda, the Tribes, and State-Building". Retrieved from http://www.jstor.org/stable/resrep12736.

Reaves, Jessica (2016), "Practical Weaponry Inspired by Foreign Terrorist Organizations," ADL, 21 September. Retrieved from https://www.adl.org/blog/practical-weaponry-inspired-by-foreign-terrorist-organizations?_ga=2.241944002.1303733348.1518075831-1412288644.1516423525.

Riedel, Bruce (2015), "Al-Qaeda Gains Ground in Yemen War," *Al-Monitor*. Retrieved from https://www.al-monitor.com/pulse/fr/content/articles/orignals/2015/04/al-qaeda-benifits-yemen-war.html

Rollins, John (2011), "Al-Qaeda and its Affiliates: Historical Perspective," Global Presence and Imprecation for US Policy". Retrieved from https://fas.org/sgp/crs/terror/R41070.pdf.

Ryan, Michael W. S. (2015), "Al-Qaeda's Purpose in Yemen Described in Works of Jihad Strategists." Retrieved from https://jamestown.org/program/al-qaedas-purpose-in-yemen-described-in-works-of-jihad-strategists/.

Schmitz, Charles (2014), "Yemen's National Dialogue,"The Middle East Institute, 10 March, http://www.mei.edu/content/yemens-national-dialogue.

START (2015), "Al-Qa'ida in the Arabian Peninsula (AQAP)". Retrieved from http://www.start.umd.edu/baad/narratives/al-qaida-arabian-peninsula-aqap.

Startfor (2012), "Al Qaeda in the Arabian Peninsula: Yemen's Ambitious Jihadists, Part 1", 4 June. Retrieved from, https://worldview.stratfor.com/article/al-qaeda-arabian-peninsula-yemens-ambitious-jihadists-part-1.

Startfor (2012), "Al Qaeda in the Arabian Peninsula: Yemen's Ambitious Jihadists," June 4. Retrieved from https://worldview.stratfor.com/article/al-qaeda-arabian-peninsula-yemens-ambitious-jihadists-part-1.

Stewart, Phil & Mukhashaf, Mohammed (2017), "U.S. Wages Second Day of Strikes on al Qaeda in Yemen", 2 March. Retrieved from, https://www.reuters.com/article/us-yemen-security-idUSKBN16A0K0.

The Government of Australia (2018), "Statement of Reasons For Al-Qa'ida in the Arabian Peninsula". Retrieved from https://www.nationalsecurity.gov.au/.Listedterroristorganisations/Pages/Al-QaidaintheArabianPeninsulaAQAP.aspx

The International Crisis Group (2017), "Yemen's al-Qaeda: Expanding the Base," Retrieved from http://www.refworld.org/pdfid/58933e434.pdf.

The Telegraph (2016), "Yemen Cancels Military Parade after 100 Soldiers Killed in Suicide Bombing," 22 May. Retrieved from http://www.telegraph.co.uk/news/worldnews/middleeast/yemen/9281502/Yemen-cancels-military-parade-after-100-soldiers-killed-in-suicide-bombing.html.

The Wall Street Journal (2014), "Al Qaeda's Number Two Rallies Jihadis in New Video,". Retrieved from https://www.youtube.com/watch?v=rI1L9_S2Phs.

Transfeld, Mareike (2016), "Political Bargaining and Violent Conflict: Shifting Elite Alliances as the Decisive Factor in Yemen's Transformation," *Mediterranean Politics*, 21: 1, 150-169.

UNSC (2016), "Al-Qaida and Associated Individuals. Groups. Undertakings and Entities Addressed to the President of the Security Council". Retrieved 29 January 2018, from http://www.un.org/en/ga/search/view_doc.asp?symbol=S/2016/629. pp. 11.

UNSC (2008), "Security Council Committee Pursuant To Resolutions 1267 (1999) 1989 (2011) And 2253 (2015) Concerning ISIL (Da'esh) Al-Qaida and Associated Individuals Groups Undertakings And Entities". Retrieved from https://www.un.org/sc/suborg/en/sanctions/1267/aq_sanctions_list/summaries/entity/al-qaida-in-the-arabian-peninsula-%28aqap%29.

UNSC (2014) "Letter dated 22 January 2014 from the Chair of the Security Council Committee Pursuant to Resolutions 1267 (1999) and 1989 (2011) Concerning Al-Qaida and Associated Individuals and Entities Addressed to the President of the Security Council". Retrieved from http://undocs.org/S/2014/41.

UNSC (2014), "Report on Yemen December 2014". Retrieved from www.securitycoucilreport.orgmonthly-forcast/2014-12yemen_12.php.

UNSC (2014),"Letter dated 19 July 2016 from the Chair of the Security Council Committee Pursuant to Resolutions 1267 (1999), 1989 (2011) and 2253 (2015) Concerning Islamic State in Iraq and the Levant (Da'esh), Al-Qaida and Associated Individuals, Groups, Undertakings and Entities Addressed to the President of the Security Council". Retrieved from https://www.un.org/sc/ctc/wp-content/uploads/2016/09/MT-18th-report.pdf.

Watson, Ben (2018), "The War in Yemen and the Making of a Chaos State: What Future is There for the Devastated Country?," 3 February. Retrieved from, https:wwwtheatlantic.com/international/archive/2018/02/the-war-in-yemen-and-the-making-of-chaos-state/551987.

Whitaker, Brian (2011), "Yemen's Ali Abdullah Saleh Resigns – but it Changes Little", *The Guardian*, 24 November. Retrieved from https://www.theguardian.com/commentisfree/2011/nov/24/yemen-ali-abdullah-saleh-resigns.

Windrem, Robert & Arkin, William M. (2018), "U.S. Airstrikes in Yemen have Increased Sixfold under Trump", 2 February 2018, https://www.nbcnews.com/news/mideast/u-s-airstrikes-yemen-have-increased-sixfold-under-trump-n843886.

Zelin, Aaron Y. & Patrick Hoover (2015), "What Aqap's Operations Reveal About Its Strategy in Yemen". Retrieved from https://warontherocks.com/2015/04/what-aqaps-operations-reveal-about-its-strategy-in-yemen/.

9. Trajectory of the Sadrist Movement in Iraq

Yasir Ali Mirza

Abstract

The Sadrist Movement in Iraq is a popular Islamist movement. Under the leadership of firebrand Shia cleric Moqtada al-Sadr, it gained popularity after the fall of the Ba'thist regime and was involved in insurgency against the US forces in Najaf in 2004. The movement has a long history of confrontation and struggle with Ba'thist Iraq. Sadr, who professes to carry on the legacies of his father and uncle, Ayatollahs Sadiq al-Sadr and Baqir al-Sadr respectively, wields unprecedented clout among the urban poor in Iraq. Unlike other Islamist groups, the Sadrist Movement boasts of having opposed Saddam's regime, and bore the brunt of his ruthless repression. The movement played an important role in Iraq's campaign against the Islamic State in Iraq and Syria (ISIS) along with the *Al-Hashd al-Sha'bi* (Popular Mobilisation Units). Sadr, as the leader of the movement, has the potential to give direction to the Iraqi political landscape. This chapter outlines the rise of the movement since its inception and how it became a formidable force in post-Saddam Iraq.

Key Words: Moqtada al-Sadr, Iraq, Shia Islamism, Shia Revivalism, Iraqi Nationalism, Ba'ath, Arab Shia, *Al-Hashd al-Sha'bi*

The US-led invasion of Iraq and the defeat of the dictatorial Ba'athist regime of Saddam Hussein in 2003 provided enormous opportunities to many underground and even exiled opposition organisations to emerge as formidable political actors in Iraq. The scion of a prominent family, the Najaf-based Shia cleric, Hojjat al-Islam Sayyid Moqtada al-Sadr, was one of the leaders who capitalised on the post-Saddam political vacuum and emerged on the horizon with his anti-US rhetoric in early 2004. Moqtada al-Sadr is the only surviving son of Ayatollah Sayyid Sadiq al-Sadr and the nephew of Ayatollah Sayyid Mohammad Baqir al-Sadr, the stalwarts of the Sadrist Movement in Iraq. The origin of the Sadrist Movement lies in the dynamic of a triangular relationship among the Iraqi regime, the urbanised Shia tribes and the political activism of Ayatollah Sayyid Mohammad Sadiq al-Sadr. In a class analysis, the Sadrist Movement remains a deeply entrenched, popular mass movement of the young, poor and disenfranchised Shias, reflecting the aspirations of a significant chunk of the Iraqi people.[1] The emergence of Moqtada al-Sadr and his Sadrist Movement, after confronting trials and tribulations, has opened a new chapter in the history and politics of Iraq and in general, what Vali Nasr (2007) has called, a "Shia revival" in the region.

The Sadrists had largely borne the brunt of Saddam's political repression and survived in the most difficult circumstances. The movement's gradual rise to prominence since the political activism of Ayatollah Sadiq al-Sadr, following the First Gulf War, gave it numerous nomenclatures such as Harkat al-Sadr or Sadriyyun. It was also known as Al-Taiyyar al-Sadri, Sadrist Current or Trend and Al-Jamat al-Sadr al-Thani or Association of Sadr-II. As a popular movement blended with Shia Islamism and Iraqi nationalism, the Sadrist Movement has a strong network of grassroots organisations across the country. It draws support mainly from the poor strata of the urban society and is primarily a youth movement (Cole, 2003: 544). In northern Baghdad, the sprawling quarter of Madinat al-Sadr or Sadr City (earlier known as Saddam City and Revolution City) is the main bastion of Moqtada al-Sadr's movement. It is an impoverished area to which tribal Shias migrated *en masse* from the southern region, and settled down in the ghetto during the 1960s. The poorer Shias in the cities were an underprivileged class in relation to both the Sunnis and the affluent Shias and they were, therefore, doubly disadvantaged in their opportunities for integration into society (Fuller & Francke, 1999: 92).The movement also made inroads across southern Iraq (International Crisis Group, 2003). Basra is another stronghold of

1. During the author's three visits to Iraq in 2012, 2014 and 2018, he had the opportunity to witness the large following Sadr enjoys and the respect he had earned among his followers due to his ability to take up the issues of the underclass. One could see large portraits and banners depicting pictures of Moqtada al-Sadr along with Baqir al-Sadr and Sadeq al-Sadr inside and outside the Mustansiriya University campus situated close to Sadr City in Baghdad

the Sadrist Movement where they fought a battle with the government security forces in 2008.

Progenitor of Sadr Movement

The genesis of the Sadrist Movement lies in the Islamic political activism of Ayatollah Sayyid Mohammad Baqir al-Sadr who was known as "Khomeini of Iraq" (Aziz, 1993: 207) and Ayatollah Sayyid Mohammad Sadiq al-Sadr. Baqir al-Sadr was an erudite scholar of Shia theology who established himself as a leading *mujtahid* with a reputation in *fiqh* and *usul al-fiqh* and other modern Islamic thought among the scholarly circle of the *hawza al-ilmiyya* of Najaf. In the words of Fouad Ajami (2007), "The Shia had their own great clerical figure: Ayatollah Muhammad Baqir al Sadr, a luminary of the Shia world, an intellectual in his own right, a prolific author" (p. 90). In the history of Iraq's Islamic Movement, Baqir al-Sadr has been considered an outstanding leader who commanded enormous respect among the Iraqi people. He was born in the early 1930s[2] in the reputed clerical family of Kadhimiya in Baghdad whose ancestor Sayyid Sadroddin came from the Jabal al-Amil region of southern Lebanon in the 8th century.

Gertrude Bell, Oriental Secretary to the British High Commissioner in Baghdad, describing the Shias of Kadhimiya, particularly the Sadr family, in her diary of 14 March 1920, wrote:

> There is a group of these worthies in Kadhmain, the holy city, eight miles from Baghdad, bitterly pan-Islamic, anti-British ... chief among them a family called Sadr possibly more distinguished for religious learnings than any other family in the whole Shia world. (Cited in Ajami, 2007: 89)

Ayatollah Sadr became famous when he published his first seminal work on Islamic philosophy *Falasafatuna* (*Our Philosophy*) in 1959. It was a critique of European philosophy and Communism, the materialist school of thought and dialectic materialism and class struggle, in

2. According to Hanna Batatu (1982), Joyce N. Wiley (1992) and Hizb' al-Da'wa al-Islamiyya's official website, the year of his birth is mentioned as 1930, 1931 and 1935 respectively.

which he explained that it had too many flaws and shortcomings to be considered the final truth for mankind. It was an exposition of Islamic philosophy in which he argued that Islam can give the alternatives to these fallacies. His magnum opus *Iqtisaduna* (*Our Economy*) was published in 1961 wherein the discourse is characterised by a strong emphasis on the refutation of Marxist economic theory by rational rather than religious arguments.

These two works prompted a debate on the independence of Islamic theory and on its capacity to answer the challenges of the modern world (Mallat, 1998: 706). A third scholarly work in the series that is titled *Mujtamauna* (*Our Society*) was never published. Though several of his articles on social issues that were published in *Al-Adwa* (*The Light*), the journal was later compiled as a book under the title of *Risalatuna* (*Our Message*) (Aziz, 1993: 210).

Two other major works on Islamic finance, *Al-Bank al-la-Ribawi fil-Islam* (*The Non-Usurious Bank in Islam*) and *Al-Usus al-Mantiqiyya lil-Istiqra* (The Logical Base of Induction) were published in 1969 and 1972 respectively. Soon, he became rallying point for the Islamist opposition in Iraq until his execution by the Ba'athist regime on 9 April 1980. Charles Tripp (2001: 229) underlines that this was the first time in Iraq that such a senior cleric had been killed and was an ominous indicator of the regime's determination to force the Shia leaders into obedience. He was an ideologue of the *Hizb al-Da'wa al-Islamiyya* whose aura spread far beyond the borders of Iraq. After his execution, he was referred to as *Shahid al-Khamis,* the fifth martyr.[3]

3. In modern Shia history, there are five recognised martyrs who were executed by the 'state' in their defence of Shiism. Ayatollah Sadr is considered the fifth; the preceding four are: (i) Ibn Makki al-Amuli (*Shahid al-Awwal,* First Martyr) who was killed in Jabal al-Amil region of Lebanon on the order of Mamluk Sultan in Damascus in 1384 AD (Momen 1987: 92); (ii) Zayn al-Din al-Amuli (*Shahid al-Thani,* Second Martyr) who was killed in Balbek region of Lebanon in 1558 AD on the order of the Ottomans (Ibid.: 320); (iii) Qazi Nurullah ibn Sharif Shustari (*Shahid al-Thalith,* Third Martyr) an Iranian-descent scholar who was executed by Mughal Emperor Jahangir in Agra, then the capital of the Mughal Empire in India in 1600 AD (Rizvi,1986: 342-387); and (iv) Mirza Mohammad Kamil (*Shahid al-Rabi',* Fourth Martyr) who was killed by the Nawab of Jhajjar

Avant-Garde of Shia Activism

The Iraqi Shia political movement remained muted in the 1980s and witnessed a revival only after the emergence of Ayatollah Sadiq al-Sadr in the early 1990s. Sadiq al-Sadr is also known as *Al-Shahid al-Sayyid al-Sadr al-Thani* (Martyr Sayyid Sadr-II).[4] He was one of the Shia Islamist leaders and activists from Hawza who remained grounded in Iraq and took a defiant stand against the Ba'athist regime's onslaught when all the movements had been ruthlessly crushed in Iraq. Whereas the Da'wa and its offshoots, as well as the Supreme Council for the Islamic Revolution in Iraq (SCIRI), became the largest Islamist groups in exile, the movement of Muhammad Sadiq al-Sadr (a cousin of Baqir al-Sadr known among Shias as Sadr-II) evolved into a most organised Shia opposition within Iraq in the period leading up to the US invasion (Nakash, 2006: 95). Like his cousin Baqir al-Sadr, he was also inspired by the Iranian revolution and its system of *Velayat-e-Faqih*. One of the strongest advocates of this concept was Ayatollah Muhammad Sadiq al-Sadr, the nephew of Muhammad Baqir al-Sadr, whose activism led the Ba'athist regime to first attempt to coopt him, and then to his assassination when he refused to cooperate with the regime (Davis, 2008: 14).

Although Sadiq al-Sadr grew to be an outspoken figure in Iraq, he kept a low profile in his earlier years. During the 1990s, after the humiliating defeat of the Ba'athist Army in the US-led Operation Desert Storm, the harsh economic sanctions imposed by the UN Security Council weakened the position of the government in Baghdad. Consequently, it loosened its iron grip on political activities and promoted religious symbolism to gain mass support.

At the same time, the Saddam regime continued to pursue a carrot-and-stick policy to contain Shia political activism. Many of the Shia tribal leaders in the south were coopted and given special favours. The regime implemented harsh policies such as intimidation and assassination of the

---

on the instruction of the Mughal King Akbar II in 1777 AD. He is buried in the present day Dargah Panja Sharif, an Imambada located in Kashmere Gate locality, near the Old Delhi Railway Station in Old Delhi (Ibid.: 97).

4. Ayatollah Baqir al-Sadr has been termed as the first one of this duo. He is the cousin of Ayatollah Sadiq al-Sadr and Moqtada al-Sadr is his son-in-law.

Shia clergy and other leaders. However, in view of the vulnerability of the regime after the Kuwait crisis, the Shias, mostly in the south, revolted against Saddam Hussein in 1991. In response, the regime implemented harsh measures under the garb of the "Plan of Action for the Marshes" to depopulate the inhabitants of the southern marshes. An estimated 500,000 Shia inhabitants of the area were forced to flee to Iran or to other parts of Iraq, while thousands were killed by the government forces (Cockburn, 2008). The environmental damage rendered the region inhabitable (Fuller and Francke, 1999: 104). This catastrophe instilled a sense of sectarian identity and dispossession among the Iraqi Shias. The insurrection of March 1991 has had a profound impact in shaping the national identity of the Iraqi Shias and their collective memory as the stories and episodes connected with the insurrection are transmitted to the younger generations (Nakash, 2003: 276).

After the death of the leading Najaf-based *marja' al-taqlid,* Grand Ayatollah Sayyid Abul Qasim al-Khoei who died in 1992, Ayatollah Sadiq al-Sadr, father of Moqtada al-Sadr, began to mobilise the marginalised Shia majority in the country. He took to the pulpits of mosque and through Friday sermons started urging the people to change the status quo. He targeted the economically poor who were living in desperate conditions. Through speeches, he familiarised the masses with Islamic values and how the teachings of the *Ahlulbayt* (the family of Prophet Muhammad) could bring happiness and dignity to ordinary Iraqis. Sadiq al-Sadr enthused them with new hope and a sense of dignity. He got a massive response from the Shia masses, who had faced social and political marginalisation (Cockburn 2008: 14).

Over time, Sadiq al-Sadr became more vocal against the government which ultimately cost him his life. He was killed, along with his two sons, Muammal and Mustafa, by the Ba'athist security service agents on 19 February 1999 after leading the Friday prayers in the historic Kufa mosque. He had sensed his impending elimination and had entrusted his long-time friend and colleague and *Hizb al-Da'wa Islamiyya* activist Ayatollah Sayyid Kazim al-Husseini al-Ha'eri, the Qom-based Iranian-descent Iraqi cleric, who was deported to Iran in the 1980s, to guide the movement (Cockburn, 2008: 113).

A group of young clerics who had been close deputies and students of Sadiq al-Sadr led the movement after his death until the rise of Moqtada al-Sadr in 2003. They were Riyad al-Nouri, Mohammed Tabatabai, Mustafa al-Yaqoubi, Qais Khazali, and Jaber al-Khafaji (Shadid, 2005). In later years, Qais al-Khazali became the leader of a powerful group called *Asa'ib Ahl al-Haq* (League of Righteous) that was active in anti-Islamic State of Iraq and Syria (ISIS) operations under the *Al-Hashd al-Sha'bi* (Popular Mobilisation Forces) umbrella. His representatives were tightly networked and had the reputation of being young, upright and highly competent (Cole, 2003: 553).

Ayatollahs Baqir al-Sadr and Sadiq al-Sadr created the Sadrist Movement to awaken the people and help lead the *ummah* into the Islamic fold, as "both wanted an Islamic society that would prepare the way for the return of the Imam Mehdi, the twelfth Shi'i Imam, the redeemer who would end the rule of tyrants and establish justice in the world" (Cockburn, 2008: 114). Accordingly, the intent of the Sadrist Movement was to propagate a way of life that would allow Iraqi Shias to promote Islamic values. The ideology was rooted in the belief of the *ulema's* active socio-political participation in public affairs with the sole mission of welfare of the *ummah*. The clerical establishment of the traditional Najaf *hawza* became politically active. First, they came out from the aloofness and 'passive tendency' called *Al-Madrasa al-Hawza al-Samita* or the quietist school of thought. Consequently, due to the political activism they were termed as members of the *Al-Madrasa al-Hawza al-Natiqa*, or vocal school of thought who often advocated the notion of *marja'iyya al-maydan*, or "field based *marja'iyya*" (International Crisis Group, 2006)

Cultural framing plays a pivotal role in any political or social movement, especially in the Middle Eastern Islamic movements where Islam is a part and parcel of daily life of the Muslims. It is so intertwined with the social and political fabric that it cannot be ignored. The Sadrist leadership managed to mobilise the Shias by invoking Shiite symbols and narratives. Indeed, framing the symbolism of the *Ashura* has always been a characteristic of the Shia revolt throughout the Islamic history and is a key factor of Shia rejection of any sense of injustice imposed by regimes. The Sadrist movement, during the 1990s and after the 2003 invasion of Iraq, utilised this episode: (a) to bring to the subjugated a sense of sorrow by comparing their situation with that of Imam Hussein; and (b) to channelise this religious-cultural connect for political mobilisation (Abood, 2013: 89).

Sadr's Collective Action and Social Networks

The Sadrist Movement witnessed upheavals in the tumultuous years of political repression and dispossession but survived, defying all odds. In the 1990s, the movement was not interested in violence despite severe Ba'athist repression (Abood, 2013: 95). The movement consolidated itself by disseminating its political and social messages to the masses through peaceful means and evaded some of the regime's brutality by creating substantial informal social networks. The main factors behind its survival were its close ties with the masses and its charitable work, as the Ba'athist regime had failed to provide even basic amenities to the disgruntled Iraqis. Kenneth Pollack (2006) notes that Sadr developed a social services network that could provide the average Iraqis with the protection, medicines, supplies, and financial assistance that they so desperately needed.

Ayatollah Sadiq al-Sadr took upon himself the responsibility to fulfill the basic needs of the people through informal social networks such as religious schools, hospitals, charities, etc. These informal social networks contributed to the poor people in many ways. Besides the distribution of funds to needy people, these networks played an important role in connecting the base and the super-structure (leadership) of the movement, socially and politically, during the 1990s and after 2003 (Abood, 2013: 82). Moqtada al-Sadr was able to reorganise the movement after the fall of the Saddam regime based on these social networks and welfare activities. He established the *Maktab al-Shaheed al-Sadr* (Office of Martyr Sadr) and reinstated the Friday prayers in the historic Kufa mosque, imitating his father's style, including putting a white shroud on his shoulders while delivering the sermons (International Crisis Group Report, 2006).

Rise of Moqtada al-Sadr

Within weeks of the April 2003 downfall of the Saddam regime, Ayatollah Ha'eri, the Iranian-based Iraqi cleric who had been Sadiq al-Sadr's close aide, issued a *fatwa* urging the Iraqi Shias to seize power. At the time, Moqtada al-Sadr was a low ranking cleric, holding the title of *Hojjat al-Islam*. Ayatollah Ha'eri appointed him his deputy and representative in Iraq, a tactical move that gave legitimacy to Moqtada in the eyes of the Iraqi Shias. As Ha'eri's representative in Iraq, Sadr was authorised to collect the *khums* (an Islamic tax which Shias give to their *marja' al-taqlid*) on his behalf. On 4 June 2003, after performing his first *hajj*, Moqtada al-Sadr travelled to Iran to participate in Imam Khomeini's fourteenth death anniversary commemoration programmes and supposedly to consult his mentor, Ayatollah Hae'ri. He reportedly also met the top Iranian leadership. Apparently, he spent a week there, meeting Iranian leaders, including Khamenei, Mahmud Hashemi Shahrudi, the leader of the Iranian judicial institutions, and Qasem Soleymani, the commander of the Quds Force (Luizard, 2010: 267).

It was during this visit that Sadr and Ha'eri developed a proposal for the creation of an armed militia, and this led to the formation of the *Jaysh al-Mahdi* (Mahdi Army) on the birth anniversary of the 12th and last Imam in the Twelver Shia tradition (Cockburn, 2008: 134). In the early years, the Mahdi Army was a loosely organised band of impoverished youths but within three years, it developed into a well-organised militia. A 2006 report assessed that the Mahdi Army could number as many as 60,000 fighters and was following the Hezbollah model of building a political party that controlled the basic services within the government and an armed militia outside of the government (Baker & Hamilton, 2006: 115). Cordesman and Ramos (2008: 14), on the other hand, claim that the Mahdi Army and its affiliated special groups had a combined nationwide strength of approximately 25,000 to 40,000 active members, supported by a large body of non-active supporters.

When Sadr sensed that the US-backed Coalition Provisional Authority (CPA) wanted to maintain the status quo and was not interested in redressing the legitimate grievances of the Shias, he began to tap the underground network of his father's followers to mobilise the Sadrist cadres to reemerge as a mass movement. He targeted the young, poor and marginalised Shia population and invoked a sense of Iraqi nationalism to bolster his objectives. He called for resistance, denounced the CPA and US forces as 'occupiers,' and demanded their immediate withdrawal (Cordesman & Ramos, 2008: 11). As a result, the CPA started to target the Sadrist Movement and its rank and file. Sadr and two of his close aides, Mustafa al-Yaqoubi and Riad al-Nouri, were accused of the murder of Hojjat al-Islam Abd al-Majid al-Khoei, son of the revered *marja' al-taqlid* Grand Ayatollah Sayyid Abul Qasim al-Khoei, who had returned to the country from exile in 2003. However, some argue that the murder was not directly linked to Sadr and was caused by fighting among the followers of various clerics, including the Sadrist (Patel, 2005: 26).

The situation escalated when the US shut down the main Sadrist newspaper, *Al Hawza*, on 28 March 2004 and arrested prominent Sadrist aide, Mustafa al-Yaqoubi. It was the first direct and violent face-off between the CPA and the Sadrist Movement. In a swift reaction, the newly-formed Mahdi Army began to mobilise and launched uprisings (*intifada*) in Baghdad, Karbala, Najaf, Kufa and Basra. In response, the US forces initiated military operations against the Mahdi Army, which took tactical positions in and around the holy shrines in Karbala, Kufa and Najaf. The fighting lasted for nearly two months. Ultimately, the Sadrist fighters were no match for the US air power, artillery, and armour. However, the "heroic" resistance of the militiamen of the Mahdi Army to the combined American and Iraqi forces lent Muqtada an amount of prestige that transcended the Shia community (Luizard, 2010: 266). The shrines suffered minimal damage, but the Mahdi Army suffered heavy losses in the fighting (Cockburn, 2008: 147-149).

The conflict ended in late May 2004 but the ceasefire between the CPA, Iraqi politicians and Sadrist leaders proved to the short-lived. A second uprising broke out in Najaf in August after Mahdi Army fighters attacked a US Marine patrol in Najaf, which they believed was coming to arrest Sadr. The conflict escalated and again clashes broke out across Najaf. Militia fighters operated in and around the holy shrines and the Wadi al-Salam necropolis—some of the most sacred places in the Shia tradition—which they used as sanctuaries. A truce was brokered after the direct intervention of the most revered *marja' al-taqlid* Grand Ayatollah Sayyid Ali Hosseini al-Sistani. The ceasefire enhanced the stature of Grand Ayatollah Sistani and the traditional Iraqi Shia clergy, or Najaf *hawza* (Rahimi, 2007: 15).

Fragmentation and Political Transformation

After the showdown with the US-led coalition forces, differences emerged among the ranks of the Sadrist Movement. First of all, Sadr's ideological mentor, Ayatollah Ha'eri, broke relations with him and announced that he was no longer his representative in Iraq. He was critical of his actions during the uprising. In the initial years during the US occupation, Sadiq al-Sadr's former student and close aide Mohammad al-Yaqoubi parted ways with him, and established his own *Hizb al-Fadhila al-Islamiyya* (Islamic Fadhila Party) which later contested the elections. Many top Sadrist leaders, such as Sheikh Qais al-Khazali, Sheikh Akram al-Ka'bi and Abd al-Hadi al-Darraji disagreed over strategy during the US onslaught and distanced themselves from the Sadr. After Khazali broke away from Sadrist Movement, he nurtured his own network, known as the 'Khazali Network' (of both Qais and his brother Laith) or 'Khazali Faction' which later transformed into another Sadrist splinter group, *Asa'ib Ahl al-Haq* (Watts, 2012: 40). Ka'bi became the leader of the powerful *Harkat Hezbollah al-Nojaba*, which cut its teeth in fighting against the ISIS in the Syrian civil war.

The mainstream Sadrist faction became known as the Golden Brigade of the Mahdi Army or Golden JAM and followed the Najaf-based clerical leadership and Baghdad-based political leadership. It called for strict discipline and a purge of rogue elements among the rank and file. Sadr's decision to stand down and his subsequent departure revealed at least five major divisions within the militia (Cochrane, 2009: 25).

Moqtada reemerged during the parliamentary elections held in January 2006 when he joined the *Al-Itilaf al-Iraqi al-Muwahed* or United Iraqi Alliance (UIA, a coalition of Shia parties led by SCIRI and *Hizb al-Dawa*). This grouping also came to be known as the *Bayt al-Shia* or House of Shia. He decided to enter electoral politics to achieve the movement's objectives and to impose more discipline among the rank and file. The Sadrists garnered 30 seats in the 275-member Iraqi Parliament and got the Ministries of Health, Transportation, and Agriculture under the Nouri al-Maliki government (Cochrane, 2009: 18). Becoming part of the government provided them a powerful political voice and enabled them to expand their network in the country.

The Sadrists' involvement in the Bayt al-Shia paved the way for Maliki's ascendence as Prime Minister. In the 2010 general elections, Shia political parties fought the elections under a coalition *named Al-Itilaf al-Watani al-Iraqi* or Iraqi National Alliance (INA, the successor to the UIA). Another main component of Maliki's Islamic Da'wa Party broke away from its allies and formed its own bloc, called the *Dawlat al-Qanoon* or State of Law. After differences emerged with Maliki, the Sadrist Movement broke away from the Shia grouping in 2014 elections and formed its own coalition called the *Kotlat al-Ahrar* or Al-Ahrar Bloc under the leadership of Dia Najem Abdallah al-Assadi.

However, Sadr again retreated from politics in February 2014 prior to the 30 April polls and announced his retirement from active politics to resume his higher studies in Iran. It is important to note that in both the 2006 and 2010 elections, Sadr's bloc played the role of king-maker, effectively deciding who would form a government (Al-Abbasi, 2018). He went back to the *hawza al-ilmiyya* of the holy city of Qom in Iran to pursue his *bahath al-kharij*, or higher jurisprudential studies under Ayatollah Mahmoud al-Hashemi Shahroudi and Ayatollah Ha'eri.

Sectarian Strife

In Sadr's absence, the Mahdi Army became involved in sectarian strife with the residual Ba'thist elements and Al-Qaeda's *'takfiri'* groups during 2006-07. Sectarian violence became rampant throughout much of Iraq and the Mahdi Army often provided the security to Shia population (Cordesman, 2008: 23). The bombing and destruction of the Al-Askariyya shrine[5] situated in Samarrah in Salahadin province on 22 February 2006 by the Abu Musab al-Zarqawi-led *Jama'at al Tawheed wal-Jihad* (later known as *Tanzim Qaidat al-Jihad fi Bilad al-Rafidayn* or al-Qaeda in Iraq) further escalated the sectarian violence. Although emotions were running

5. It has been considered as one of the holiest places in the Shia tradition as the graves of the tenth and eleventh Imams, that is, Imam Ali al-Naqi al-Hadi and Imam al-Hassan al-Askari are situated here. It was also related to the site where the last and twelfth Imam Mohammad al-Mahdi is believed to have gone into occultation. The Mahdi Army was named after him. Moqtada al-Sadr announced the formation of his armed wing in Najaf in 2004 on his birth anniversary which falls on 15 Shaban of the Islamic year (Tabatabai, 1975).

high, the backlash against the Sunnis was mitigated after the *fatwas* given against bloodshed by the responsible leadership of the *maraji'* (plural of *marja'*) (Mamouri, 2013). The Mahdi Army gained legitimacy after the 2006 bombing in Samarra, by fighting against Sunni radicals when the Iraqi government was unable to contain the situation (Cordesman, 2008: 14).

The Sadrist movement was sucked into the sectarian strife raging in Iraq at the time. The movement is inherently sectarian, rather, its ideological roots are based in Shia theology and Iraqi nationalism. It blends nationalism with homegrown clerical authority from the Sadr family name and is now portraying Muqtada as a theological authority rather than a political leader (Mansour & Jabar, 2017: 15). On numerous occasions, the Sadrists had called for unity among the various groups in Iraq, including the Sunnis and Christians. As part of the reconciliation process, in 2013, Sadr had joined the Assyrian Christians to express solidarity after the bombing at the community's Our Lady of Salvation Church in Baghdad. In reaching out to the Sunnis, he also visited the Imam Abu Hanifa Mosque in Baghdad's Adhamiyya district and sent his representatives to the Umm al-Qura mosque to meet the members of the Association of Muslim Scholars or *Haya al-Ulama al-Muslimeen* during the siege of Fallujah in 2005 (Meijer, 2005). During the coalition's operation in Falluja in 2004, the Sadrist Movement organised assistance to the Sunni-Islamist fighters in that city (Schmidt, 2008: 30).

Proximity with Iran

Sadr came closer to Iran in 2007 after the US forces attacked the Mahdi Army fighters in 2006 in the holy city of Najaf. In February 2008, at the height of excessive violence, the government security forces started purging the 'rogue' Shia groups as well as extremist Al-Qaeda groups in Baghdad and Basra in an operation called *Fardh al-Qanoon* (Enforcing the Law). However, the Sadrist leadership in Najaf ordered the Mahdi Army fighters not to resist the crackdown. To avoid any fissure in the UIA government, Iran intervened and succeeded in stopping the fighting. Notably, the Iraqi government enlisted the help of the Islamic Revolutionary Guard Corps (IRGC) Commander Qasim Suleimani, to mediate in talks between Sadr and the Iraqi government (Cochrane, 2009: 32).

Despite their differences, Iran succeeded in convincing them to form a unity government under Maliki. One report suggested that Sadr's decision resulted from an agreement made between Maliki and Ha'eri during the former's visit to Tehran on 7 June 2008. Maliki reportedly warned that the Sadrists would be barred from participating in the provincial elections unless Sadr issued a clear order to disband the Mahdi Army and end violence against the Iraqi government forces (Cochrane, 2009: 37). Although the report was not substantiated, it does underscore that Sadr's moves were likely to have been made with some kind of Iranian endorsement as Iran's position in the Iraqi politics became prominent (Salamey & Othman, 2011: 208).

In a surprise move in 2008, at the height of the military showdown with the Iraqi security forces, the leadership sought to restructure the movement in the wake of its political and military losses. The internal strife and disagreement led to the disbanding of the Mahdi Army because it was no longer under the total command of Sadr. Many factions broke away from the movement and started acting on their own, without any clerical sanctions in Najaf (Cochrane, 2009: 21).

On 13 June 2008, Sheikh Salah al-Obaidi, chief spokesman of the Sadrist Movement, read out Sadr's statement and announced the reorganisation of the Mahdi Army which was split into two wings: *Al-Mumahidoun* (those who pave the way), or 'The Trailblazers' and *Al-Munasiroun* (The Supporters) – and announced that the Sadrist Movement has ceased all armed resistance. It transformed into an unarmed group that would support social services and Iraqi reconstruction. The first group, *Al-Mumahidoun* is a kind of socio-cultural wing and its primary role is that of "leading an intellectual *jihad*" (Cochrane, 2009: 37). This wing primarily involves the centralisation of the command structure into a small, tight units of loyalists, coupled with vigorous religious training for the militiamen who will prepare the way for the coming of the Hidden Imam Mahdi, as believed by the Shias, to culminate in the establishment of divine justice on earth (Rahimi, 2008a). Hazem al-Araji became the leader of this new Sadrist reform movement, with other nine clerics.

The Munasiroun is a kind of support organisation which intends to assist the Mumahidoun in its endeavour in social services. Soon after the demobilisation of the Mahdi Army, the formation of the *Liwa' Youm al-Mawoud* or (Promised Day Brigade—PDB) was announced. The PDB cooperated closely with the Special Groups that were under the influence and indirect command of Iran's IRGC's expeditionary arm, the Quds Force (IRGC-QF) (Heras, 2017). However, Sadr also announced that the movement would not demobilise totally and armed resistance by a small cadre of well-trained and tightly controlled militiamen would continue as long as the US coalition forces were stationed in Iraq (MusingsonIraq, 2011).

ISIS Phenomenon

In June 2014, the Islamic State of Iraq and Syria or Islamic State of Iraq and Levant (*Dawlat al-Islamiyya al-Iraq wa' Sham*) (ISIS), also known by its acronym Daesh, took over large swathes of the Iraqi territory in a *blitzkrieg* offensive. Iraq's second largest city, Mosul, fell into the hands of the terrorist group which advanced rapidly into the provinces of Nineveh and Salahaddin, stunning the transitional central authorities in Baghdad. Soon, it emerged as the biggest threat to the integrity of Iraq. It compelled various political actors to play a pragmatic role in repulsing the ISIS onslaught. However, the ISIS threat of razing the revered Shia shrines located in the *atabat al-aaliyat,* the religious circuit of Najaf, Karbala, Samarrah and Kadhmain in Baghdad, emboldened the Shias and compelled them to take up arms against the threat (based on the author's interaction with Shias in Iraq).

The spectre of violence and political fallout forced Sadr to respond to the call of Ayatollah Sistani to take up arms in order to save the Iraqi nation from the ISIS. When Ayatollah Sistani issued a *wajib al-kifai fatwa*[6] to all Iraqis to mobilise against ISIS attacks, which resulted in the formation of the *Al-Hashd al-Sha'bi* (Popular Mobilisation Units or PMU), Sadr also joined in the counter-offensive campaign and again formed an armed resistance group.

6. The sermon from Sistani's representative Abd al-Mahdi al-Karbalai, on 13 June 2014, declared: "Citizens who are able to bear arms and fight terrorists, defending their country and their people and their holy places should volunteer and join the security forces to achieve this holy purpose" (Morris, 2014).

Soon after the promulgation of Ayatollah Sistani's call, on 26 November 2016, the Iraqi Parliament voted into law the Al-Hashd al-Sha'bi Commission Law, and a month later, President Fuad Masum ratified it, which formally institutionalised the Al-Hashd as a legalised entity of the Iraqi government. Under this new law, the Al-Hashd militias "shall be a part of the Iraqi armed forces, subordinate to the commander-in-chief of the armed forces" (Frentzel, 2017: 13). The militias themselves, however, prefer to call themselves, somewhat ominously, the *Al-Muqawama al-Islamiya* ("the Islamic resistance") (Spyer & Tamimi, 2014).

The Sadrist Movement joined the ranks of the newly formed umbrella organisation of Al-Hashd. Sadr called on his supporters to mobilise into an armed group called *Saraya al-Salam* (Peace Brigade or Peace Companies). In a swift move, around 10,000 Sadrist cadres mobilised in a short span of time (Frentzel, 2017: 8). Shaykh Kazim al-Issawi, a close aide of Sadr, who had risen through the ranks of the Sadrist Movement's Mahdi Army and Promised Day Brigade, was name its commander (Heras, 2017). After the ISIS counter-offensive came to an end and with the next parliamentary elections scheduled for May 2018, many pro-Iran factions of Al-Hashd or PMU announced their willingness to contest in the poll under a unified coalition called 'Mujahideen Alliance' or 'Al-Fatah Alliance'. But, Sadr began to change his overtures as he was against the PMU's participation in the 2018 national elections. He demanded that PMU officials not take part in the elections, and hand over their weapons to the state forces (MacDonald, 2017). He argued that not doing would lead to political rivalry and corruption.

On the domestic front, the Sadrist Movement protested against the reforms stalled by the Abadi government as Sadr made a demand for a "technocratic Cabinet" and ousting of the corrupt officials (Thanassis Cambanis, 2018). The supporters marched into the Green Zone and stormed the Parliament to get their demands accepted, but were unsuccessful. He had previously announced his support for Prime Minister Haider al-Abadi and pledged to back his candidacy for a second term in the 2018 elections, believing that he could tackle the rampant corruption. In the next parliamentary elections, held in May 2018, Sadr stayed away from the mainstream political alliances—the PMU's Al-Fatah alliance led by Hadi al-Amiri and the Nasr al-Iraq coalition of Haider al-

Abadi, and formed his own alliance called the Sairoon Coalition with the Iraqi Communist Party led by Raed Fahmi (Sattar, 2018b). However, this was an unusual occurrence as it was the first instance of convergence of interests for both political streams since the Sadrist philosophy had emerged out of the antagonism to Communism, way back in the 1950s. He had also been instrumental in the ascension of Adel Abd al-Mahdi for the prime ministerial post as a replacement for Abadi in November 2018. For his pivotal role in government formations, he earned the title of 'King-maker of Iraq' (Dehghanpisheh, 2010).

Conclusion

The transformation of the Sadrist Movement from a grassroots social organisation into a formidable political force is an important phenomenon in the history of Iraq. Though the movement was severely oppressed by the Saddam regime and suffered heavy losses due to the violent clashes with the US coalition forces, it survived the tumultuous phases and rebuilt itself. The Sadrist Movement comprises a phenomenon with deep roots in contemporary Iraqi history and has provided a voice to a large number of dispossessed Iraqi Shias. It has utilised the network initially built by Sadr's father to build a strong and mass-based movement. Sadr's pedigree played a crucial role in preventing the major fragmentation of the movement, as well as his survival. The movement has established itself as the most popular socio-political organisation in Iraq today, with a strong base among the young and poor and aggressive advocacy of the legitimate rights and demands of Iraqi Shias.

References

Abedin, Maha (2005), "The Sadrist Movement (Al-Sadriyuun)," *The Middle East Intelligence Bulletin*. Accessed 20 May 2019.

Abood, Aqeel (Spring 2013), "The Sadrist Movement: Success in Mobilizing People in Iraq" *Kufa Review*: 2 (2): 89.

Ajami, Fouad (2007), *The Arab Predicament, Arab Political Thought and Practice Since 1967* (New York: Cambridge University Press), p. 237.

Alabbasi, Mamoon (2014), "Soaring Expectations for Iraq's Sadrists After Vote", *Al-Monitor*. Accessed on 30 January, 2018. http://www.middleeasteye.net/news/soaring-expectations-iraqs-sadrists-after-vote-1074912437

Aziz, Talib Mohammad (1993), "The Role of Muhammad Baqir al-Sadr in Shii

Political Activism in Iraq from 1958 to 1980," *International Journal of Middle East*, 25 (4): 207-222.

Baker, III, James A & Hamilton, Lee H. (2006), *The Iraq Study Group Report* (New York: Vintage Books).

Batatu, Hanna (1982), "Iraq's Underground Shi'i Movements", *Middle East Research and Information Project*, No. 102: 578-594.

Cambanis, Thanassis (2018), "Can Militant Cleric Moqtada al-Sadr Reform Iraq?," The Century Foundation. Accessed on 23 May 2019.

Cochrane, Marisa (January 2009), "The Fragmentation of the Sadrist Movement," Iraq Report No.: 12. (Washington DC: Institute for the Study of War).

Cockburn, Patrick (2008), *Muqtada: Muqtada Al Sadr, the Shi'a Revival and the Struggle for Iraq* (New York: Scribner, Simon & Schuster).

Cockburn, Patrick (2008), *Muqtada Al-Sadr and the Battle for the Future of Iraq* (New York: Scribner, Simon & Schuster).

Cole, Juan R.I. (2003). "The United States and Shi'ite Religious Factions in Post-Ba'thist Iraq," *The Middle East Journal*, 57 (4): 543-566.

Cordesman, Anthony H. & Ramos, Jose (2008), *Sadr and the Mahdi Army: Evolution, Capabilities and a New Direction* (Washington, DC: Centre for Strategic and International Studies).

Davis, Eric (Spring 2008), "Reflections on Religion and Politics in Post-Ba'thist Iraq," *Newsletter of The American Academic Research Institute in Iraq (TAARII)*, Washington DC.

Dehghanpisheh, Babak (2010), "The King of Iraq," *Foreign Policy*. Accessed on 24 May 2019.

Fouad Ajami, *The Foreigner's Gift: The Americans, the Arabs and the Iraqis in Iraq* (New York: Free Press).

Frentzel, Kari (2017), "The Future Role of the Hashd al-Shaabi in Iraq- Key Influencers of Post-ISIS Politics?" Konrad Adenauer Stiftung, Policy Paper No.: 11, May 2017.

Fuller, Graham E. & Francke, Rend Rahim (1999), *The Arab Shi'a: The Forgotten Muslims* (New York: Palgrave).

Heras, Nicholas A. (2017), "Shia Popular Mobilization Units in a Post-Islamic State Iraq: A Look at Peace Brigade Commander Shaykh Kazim al-Issawi, "*Militant Leadership Monitor*. Accessed 30 January 2018, https://jamestown.org/brief/shia-popular-mobilization-units-post-islamic-state-iraq-look-peace-brigade-commander-shaykh-kazim-al-issawi/.

Hizb' al-Da'wa al-Islamiyya's (Islamic Da'wa Party) official website. Accessed on 8 April 2018. URL: www.islamicdawaparty.com.

Hunter, Shireen (2017). "Muqtada al-Sadr's Saudi Visit and Iraq's Shifting Shia Politics," *Lobelog*, Accessed 1 February, 2018. https://lobelog.com/muqtada-al-sadrs-saudi-visit-and-iraqs-shifting-shia-politics/.

International Crisis Group (2006), "Iraq's Muqtada Al-Sadr: Spoiler or Stabiliser?" Crisis Group Middle East Report No. 55, Brussels.

International Crisis Group, "Iraq's Shiites Under Occupation," ICG Middle East Briefing, 9 September 2003, p. 16.

Kadhim, Kadhim and al-Khatteeb, Luay, "What Do You Know About Sistani's Fatwa?," *Huffington Post*. Accessed on 11 February 2018, https://www.huffingtonpost.com/luay-al-khatteeb/what-do-you-know-about-si_b_5576244.html.

Loveday Morris 2014), "Shiite Cleric Sistani Backs Iraqi Government's Call for Volunteers to Fight Advancing Militants," *The Washington Post*, 13 June, https://www.washingtonpost.com/world/middle_east/volunteers-flock-to-defend-baghdad-as-insurgents-seize-more-iraqi-territory/2014/06/13/10d46f9c-f2c8-11e3-914c-1fbd0614e2d4_story.html?utm_term=.bddca5ef964e.

Luizard, Pierre-Jean (2010), "The Sadrists in Iraq: Challenging the United States, Marja'iyya and Iran," in Mervin, Sabrina (ed.), *The Shi'a World and Iran* (London: Saqi).

MacDonald, Alex (2017). "Sadr Calls for Hashd al-Shaabi to Disarm and not Stand in Elections," *Middle East Eye*. Accessed on 30 January 2018. URL: http://www.middleeasteye.net/news/muqtada-hashd-861713142.

Mallat, Chibli (1988), "Religious Militancy in Contemporary Iraq: Muhammad Baqer as-Sadr and the Sunni-Shia Paradigm", *Third World Quarterly*, 10 (2): 699-729.

Mamouri, Ali (2013), "Clerics Play Crucial Role in Iraq's Sectarian Conflict," *Al-Monitor* [Online Web]. Accessed on 6 December 2013. http://www.al-monitor.com/pulse/originals/2013/09/iraq-role-preachers-sectarian-conflict.html.

Mansour, Renad and Jabar, Faleh A. (2017), *The Popular Mobilization Forces And Iraq's Future* (Washington DC: Carnegie Middle East Centre).

Meijer, Roel (Winter 2005), "The Association of Muslim Scholars in Iraq," *Middle East Research and Information Project,* Report No. 237: 12-19.

MOI (2009), Musings of Iraq, "A Divided Sadr Trend" [Online Web]. Accessed on 20 May 2019.

Momen, Moojan (1987), *An Introduction to Shi'a Islam: The History and Doctrines of Twelver Shi'ism* (New Haven: Yale University Press).

Nakash, Yitzhak (2006), *Reaching for Power: The Shi'a in the Modern Arab World* (Princeton University Press).

Nakash, Yitzhak (2003), *The Shi'is of Iraq* (New Jersey: Princeton University Press).

Patel, David Siddhartha (2005). "Ayatollahs on the Pareto Frontiers: The Institutional Basis of Religious Authority in Iraq," Stanford University, 18 November 2005, p. 26.

Pollack, Kenneth M (2006), "Muqtada al-Sadr: Iraq's Shadowy Power Broker", Brookings. Accessed on 17 May 2019.

Rahimi, Babak (2008), "Muqtada Reinvents Himself," *Asia Times*, Accessed on 28 January 2018, http://www.atimes.com/atimes/Middle_East/JI19Ak01.html.

Rahimi, Babak (2018), "The Rise of Ayatollah Moqtada al-Sadr", July 27, 2009, *Foreign Policy*. Accessed on 25 January 2018. http://foreignpolicy.com/2009/07/27/the-rise-of-ayatollah-moqtada-al-sadr/.

Rizvi, Sayyid Athar Abbas (1986), *Socio-Intellectual History of Isna Ash'ari Shi'is in India* (New Delhi: Munshiram Manoharlal Publishers).

Robertson, John (2016), *Iraq: A History* (London: Oneworld Publications).

Salamey, Imad and Othman, Zanoubia (2011), "Shi'a Revival and Welayat Al-Faqih in the Making of Iranian Foreign Policy," *Politics, Religion & Ideology*, 12 (2): 197-212.

Sattar, Omar (2018), "Meet Iraq's Plentiful Parliamentary Alliances", *Al Monitor*. Accessed on 30 January 2018, https://www.al-monitor.com/pulse/originals/2018/01/iraq-election-shiite-alliance-sectarianism.html.

Schmidt, Søren (2008), "Shi'a -Islamist Political Actors in Iraq," *DIIS Report 2008:3*.

Shadid, Anthony (2005), "Sadr's Disciples Rise Again to Play Pivotal Role in Iraq," *The Washington Post*, 30 August 2005.

Tabatabai, Allamah Sayyed Muhammad Husayn (1975), *Shi'ite Islam*, trans., Seyyed Hossein Nasr (Albany: State University of New York Press).

Watts, James N. (2012), "Iranian Influence in Iraqi Shi'a Groups", Naval Postgraduate School, California.

Wiley, Joyce N (1992), *The Islamic Movement of Iraqi Shi'as* (Boulder, Colorado: Lynne Reinner).

10. Houthi Uprising and Normalisation of Violence in Yemen

Parnika Praleya

Abstract

Despite the unfolding humanitarian crisis, the violence in Yemen did not receive the international attention it deserved, until recently. Sectarian tension and political instability have plagued Yemen since the civil wars of the 1960s. The conflict today has become increasingly confessional and tribal, due to the demographic divisions, political rhetoric and nature of alliance-making. Additionally, the impoverished nation, relying predominantly on oil revenues, marred by corruption and conflict, was ill-equipped for the food price shock of 2007-08, which pushed vulnerable Yemenis below the breadline. During the Arab Spring protests, thousands of Yemenis came onto the streets, demanding better economic conditions from a more responsive regime. A purely economic movement was soon coopted by entrenched political forces. Yemen's location and the nature of the sectarian strife made it a battleground for Iran's and Saudi Arabia's quest for regional hegemony. Looked upon as a proxy war between the two regional powers, the conflict has taken on a logic and momentum of its own, transcending the initial regime or Houthi motives. While 2018 saw progress in negotiations, any lasting solution will have to take the complex interplay of political, economic and regional factors into account in devising a framework for a post-conflict peace economy in Yemen.

Key Words: Humanitarian Crisis, Houthis, Iran-Saudi Arabia Proxy Conflict, Zaidi Revivalism, Arab Spring in Yemen, Saudi Arabia-Yemen Relations, Stockholm Agreement

The civil war in Yemen has exacted a huge toll on its citizens, raising questions regarding the ability of the country to remain stable and united. In what was until recently an "obscure war," a population of over 22 million has been affected and forced to depend on humanitarian assistance. Referred to as the "world's largest humanitarian crisis" (UN News, 2018), the war in Yemen has resulted in the internal displacement of 2.2 million people. The death of five children in an attack on the Tahita district, south of Hudeida, on 28 February 2019 is a stark reminder of the humanitarian crisis that the conflict is creating (Fore, 2019). According to the United Nations (UN), the total number of people facing pre-famine conditions (entirely reliant on external aid for survival) could soon reach 14 million (more than half of the total population) (United Nations Security Council [UNSC], 2018b), with 8.4 million people severely food insecure in September 2018. More than 1.1 million cases of acute diarrhoea or cholera have been reported since April 2017 in what is the largest and fastest-spreading outbreak of the disease in modern history (Lyons, 2017).

Despite the unfolding humanitarian crisis and the resurgence of Al-Qaeda in the Arabian Peninsula (AQAP), the conflict in Yemen did not receive the international attention it deserved until recently. A host of regional conflicts, including in Syria, Iraq, Libya and the menace of the Islamic State of Iraq and Syria (ISIS) could be the reason that the world did not take notice of Yemen. In fact, one of the reasons why Yemen finally came into the international spotlight was the execution of journalist Jamal Khashoggi in the Saudi Consulate in Istanbul. It was this brazen act which made the world in general, and the United States in particular, question the recent Saudi policies, including its intervention in Yemen in March 2015.

To understand how Yemen found itself in its present crisis, one needs to appreciate the multiple dimensions which are behind the emergence of the fault lines that are evident in Yemeni society. Beginning the narrative with the Arab Spring of 2011 misses the fact that this movement, with its focus on economic demands, was coopted by tribal and sectarian politics that have ruled the roost in Yemen for decades. Thus, focussing exclusively on the political roots of the conflict overlooks the role that Yemen's impoverished economy played in fomenting the violence. Consequently, this essay analyses the causes of the current conflict from multiple dimensions while separating the different contextual roots. The first section gives an overview of the current conflict, focussing on recent progress and the humanitarian crisis. The next section elucidates the multiple dimensions of the conflict, beginning with the roots of the conflict in the vicissitudes of Yemen's history, entangled as it is with Zaidism. This political context is followed by the economic context. The regional dimension looks primarily at the history of Yemen's relations with its northern neighbour, Saudi Arabia. Finally, the concluding section discusses the possible steps ahead and out of the conflict.

"The World's Largest Humanitarian Crisis"

The Arab Spring started off as youth protests against dire economic conditions, extreme unemployment and rampant corruption in 2010-11 in Tunisia. The spread of political unrest through the Arab world soon reached Yemen. A movement demanding economic reforms was coopted by political forces wanting to end the rule of long-time authoritarian President Ali Abdullah Saleh, who belonged to the Zaidi Shia community. The political unrest and resulting security vacuum strengthened the terrorist elements. A case in point is the declaration of an Emirate in the Abyan Governorate in March 2011 by militias associated with Al-Qaeda in Arabian Peninsula (AQAP). The United States, Saudi Arabia and other members of the international community, alarmed by the ramifications of the security vacuum, attempted to broker a political compromise. After receiving assurances of immunity from prosecution, President Saleh stepped down in 2012, handing over power to his Vice-President, Abdrabbuh Mansour Hadi, as interim President.

The transition, brokered by the Gulf Cooperation Council (GCC) and backed by the United States, marked a short-lived period of hope. It was during this period that a UN-sponsored National Dialogue Conference (NDC) comprising 565 delegates convened and deliberated throughout 2013 to formulate a new Constitution acceptable to all factions. In January 2014, the NDC ended without resolving the disputes over the distribution of power. The entire process was marred by infighting among the centres of political power, further eroding governmental authority amidst the prevailing political turmoil.

Any hope for reforms proved elusive amidst the militant attacks, corruption and food insecurity. Within weeks of the conclusion of the unsuccessful NDC, the Houthis, a dominant faction of the Zaidi Shias, concentrated in northern Yemen and opposed to President Hadi's government, resorted to violent protests to reshape the political order. The Houthis were joined in an alliance of convenience by a faction of the General People's Congress (GPC) loyal to former President Saleh, despite the two having fought each other in a prolonged conflict between 2004 and 2010. Together, they launched a military offensive, seizing control of Northern Saada province and neighbouring areas, violating several power-sharing agreements arrived at during the transition period. The Houthis took over the capital, Sana'a, in September 2014, forcing President Hadi to flee to Saudi Arabia. The United Nations Security Council placed two Houthi leaders and former President Saleh on a sanctions list for their role in derailing Yemen's transition. In February 2015, the Houthis dissolved the Parliament and announced a five-member 'Presidential Council' with the purpose of forming a technocrat government (Al-Jazeera, 2015). This 'unilateral' announcement was rejected by a cross-section of the Yemeni population, the political forces as well as the international actors, including the United Nations.

In March 2015, President Hadi appealed for international intervention. Saudi Arabia and eight other Sunni Arab states—backed by the US, UK, and France—launched a military offensive aimed at restoring President Hadi's rule and evicting the Houthi fighters from the capital and other major cities. This marked a dramatic escalation in the conflict. While the Houthi-Saleh forces remained ensconced in the capital and the mountainous highlands of northern Yemen (their traditional stronghold), the Saudi-led coalition retook the port city of Aden and the lowland areas of southern Yemen (traditionally Sunni). The coalition forces have controlled Yemen's air space ever since. Given the nature of alliances on different sides of the conflict, they have been beset by infighting. On the anti-Houthi side, the militias include the separatists, seeking independence for South Yemen and factions who oppose the idea. Their suspicions notwithstanding, the separatists allied with President Hadi, a Southerner who supports unification with the North, in an attempt to prevent the Houthis from capturing Aden. In late 2017, the alliance of convenience between former President Saleh and the Houthis crumbled as the former indicated his willingness to break away from the latter in favour of reconciling with his erstwhile benefactor, Saudi Arabia. He was killed by Houthi fighters on 4 December 2017. There exist uneasy fault lines within the Saudi-led coalition. Saudi Arabia supports President Hadi while the UAE, a key player in the coalition, is closely aligned with the separatists. Consequently, the lines of control in 2018 loosely resemble the boundaries which existed up to 1990, prior to Yemen's unification.

Progress in 2018

In January 2018, Southern Yemeni separatists seized control of Aden (BBC News, 2018) in what Prime Minister Ahmed bin Dagher called a coup. The spotlight in 2018 was on the battle for Hodeida and the peace negotiations. Beginning on 13 June, Saudi Arabia and UAE-backed government forces began an assault on the rebel-held port of Hodeida, an alarming development with grave consequences for Yemen's human catastrophe. Hodeida port is the entry point for roughly 80 per cent of commercial goods, aid, food, medicines and fuel going into Yemen (UN Office for the Coordination of Humanitarian Affairs, 2017). Consequently, the Hodeida truce became a priority agenda during the peace talks later in the year.

The first attempt, after two years at the UN-mediated consultation in Geneva, collapsed after the Houthis failed to show up. With Western involvement in Yemen coming under increased international scrutiny following the killing of Saudi journalist Jamal Khashoggi at Saudi Arabia's Consulate in Istanbul in October last year, and a mounting civilian toll from the coalition's air campaign, the United States called for a ceasefire and peace talks.[1] The joint efforts resulted in UN-sponsored peace consultations between the warring parties, held in Sweden from 6 December to 13 December, the first official negotiations since talks were held between the Yemeni parties in Kuwait in 2016. The Houthi rebels and Yemen's internationally recognised government of President Hadi

1. On 20 October, US Secretary of Defence James Mattis and the US State Department called on the participants in the Yemen conflict to agree to a ceasefire "in the next 30 days." He also said he expected to see the warring parties at the peace talks.

agreed to a deal in Sweden, the Stockholm Agreement (UNSC, 2018a), with the following provisions:

- Agreement on the city of Hodeida and the ports of Hodeida, Salif and Ra's Isa which called for an immediate ceasefire and redeployment of forces to create a demilitarised zone around the country's vital Red Sea trade corridor;
- Executive mechanism on activating the prisoner exchange agreement;
- Statement of understanding on Ta'iz and the formation of a committee to discuss the future of the contested city; and
- Continuation of unconditional consultations in January 2019 in a location to be agreed upon by the parties.

This was accompanied with the unanimous adoption (after fraught talks and a United States veto threat) on 21 December of the Security Council Resolution 2451 (2018) in which the UN endorsed the Stockholm Agreement, calling for a ceasefire in Yemen (Borger, 2018). The resolution became the first UN Resolution on Yemen in more than three years. It called for implementation of a ceasefire in Hodeida and authorised the Secretary-General to establish and deploy, for an initial period of 30 days from the date of adoption of the resolution, an advance team to monitor, support and facilitate the immediate implementation of the Stockholm Agreement. Interestingly, on 20 November, a day after the UK introduced a draft resolution on Yemen in the Security Council, Riyadh and Abu Dhabi pledged US$500 million in aid which was designed to ward off a declaration of famine in Yemen by the UN.

As of May 2019, the peace deal was only beginning to be implemented after a five-month lull since the agreement was adopted (TRT World, 2019). According to the UN, both parties were to withdraw from the city within 21 days and international monitors were to be deployed. A prisoner swap involving about 16,000 inmates was to be completed before 20 January 2019 (Al-Jazeera, 2018a). In an environment of mutual distrust between the warring parties, these targets became a casualty of opposing fighters, locked in combat for years. After months of a tenuous ceasefire in Hodeida, the Houthis finally began withdrawing from the city in May 2019, handing over the Hodeida port to the Coast Guards.

Viewed by some as a first step in a broader redeployment process, others considered the withdrawal to be a Houthi ploy. It is argued that under the Stockholm Agreement, the port was to be handed over to a mutually agreed entity or the UN, a provision that was violated considering that the Coast Guards are under Houthi control. Complicating the matters further is the regional dimension of the conflict, with many viewing it as a proxy war between Saudi Arabia and Iran in their pursuit for regional hegemony (Bewley, 2019). Questions have been raised regarding the absence of regional players from the peace process (Munassar, 2019).

Humanitarian Crisis

The scourge of a prolonged civil war in an already impoverished nation has resulted in what has been referred to by the UN as the "world's largest humanitarian crisis". According to the Armed Conflict Location and Event Data Project, the conflict has resulted in 91,600 deaths since 2015 (Magdy, 2019). The displacement of over two million people, looking for shelter from disease and violence, has deepened economic and humanitarian woes. Since 2015, the Gross Domestic Product (GDP) of Yemen has shrunk by 50 per cent (World Bank, 2018a). Yemen is almost entirely reliant on imports of food, fuel and medicine. According to the World Bank, soaring prices, along with a depreciating currency (the Yemeni rial has lost more than half its value against the dollar since the start of the civil war) have put basic commodities out of the reach of many Yemenis. With more than 80 per cent Yemenis (24 million) living below the poverty line, the conflict has made them extremely vulnerable, with 14.3 million in acute need of assistance (World Bank, 2019).

Approximately 3.2 million people, including two million children below the age of five require treatment for acute malnutrition. At the end of 2017, one aid agency estimated that 130 children under the age of five were dying daily from extreme hunger and disease (United Nations Security Council Report, 2018) and only 15 per cent of children were eating the minimum acceptable diet for survival, growth and development (UNICEF, 2019). Assessments in 2017 had identified 107 out of Yemen's 333 districts to be at risk of famine (United Nations Security Council Report, 2018). In its overview of Yemen, the World Bank estimated that 17.8 million people do not have access to clean water and sanitation.

Many Yemenis are too poor to access what remains of the crumbling health infrastructure, resulting in 19.7 million lacking access to adequate healthcare. Outbreaks of preventable epidemics like cholera, diphtheria, measles and dengue fever, with only half of the health facilities functioning, have made the Yemeni conflict a human catastrophe unseen in decades.

According to the World Health Organisation (WHO), 21 out of the 22 governorates (305 out of 333 districts) have been affected by the cholera epidemic, the worst in history (Lyons, 2017). The cumulative total number of suspected cases between January 2018 and April 2019 is 668,891, with 1,081 associated deaths. Children below five years of age represent 22.7 per cent of total suspected cases during 2019. The outbreak has affected 22 of 23 governorates and 294 of 333 districts in Yemen (WHO, 2019).

More than 570,000 people were forced to flee from their homes (United Nations Security Council Report, 2018) in the battle of Al-Hodeida. According to the UN, Hodeida has the largest number of sick people in Yemen and more than 70 per cent of its population (especially children) are at risk of malnutrition (Al-Jazeera, 2018b). In this context, the tenuous ceasefire around Hodeida port, the lifeline of the aid operations and commercial imports, is a remarkable achievement in averting an unprecedented humanitarian catastrophe.

How did the crisis in Yemen reach this point?

Roots of the Conflict

Conflict is not new to Yemen. Its geo-strategic location, straddling important trade routes on the southwestern tip of the Arabian Peninsula, overlooking the vital Bab-el-Mandeb Strait connecting the Red Sea with the Gulf of Aden, made it a coveted piece of territory through history. In the past century alone, there have been close to a dozen conflicts, involving over half a dozen countries (*The Economist*, 2017). The roots of the present conflict are entwined with older conflicts. Involving many groups with their own vested interests, the conflict has sucked in Yemen's powerful neighbours. Consequently, to make sense of the present conflict, this section looks at the political, economic and regional contexts which have culminated in this seemingly intractable war.

Political Context

Prior to the emergence of a unified Yemen in 1990, there existed two distinct Yemeni states: Yemeni Arab Republic (YAR or North Yemen) and the People's Democratic Republic of Yemen (PDRY or South Yemen). From the civil war of the 1960s emerged the US and Saudi supported YAR, with a predominantly Zaidi population. The North derived its legitimacy from religion, enlisting the support of Islamic clerics. An insurgency in the South against the British colonial forces led to the withdrawal of British troops from Southern Yemen, resulting in the creation of the Soviet Union aligned Marxist PDRY in 1967. Political feuding culminated in clashes between North and South Yemen along their border in 1972 and again in 1979. Amidst this fighting, Saleh, a Zaidi Shia military officer, became the ruler of North Yemen in 1978, continuing to remain the leader of unified Yemen post-1990.

Unification notwithstanding, the central government never had absolute control beyond the capital Sana'a. In the absence of substantive control, sovereignty was maintained through patronage and by playing factions against each other. The policies targeted the capital Sana'a or areas endowed with economic resources, resulting in the marginalisation of other regions, especially the Saada-'Amran-Hajja belt. Poor infrastructure, lack of social welfare, dismal education and inadequate security presence in this region were proof of the state's neglect. Saleh relied on material cooptation of local tribal leaders in establishing a patron-client relationship, typical of rentier economies (Laub, 2015). This enabled the continuation of the relative historic autonomy of the northern peripheries in matters of economic exchange, political activity and conflict mediation.

Autonomy from interference by the republican government at the Centre is also (albeit only partially) explained by the geographical context. Scarce resources scattered across a harsh terrain meant that population concentrations were also scattered and relatively small. The presence of natural obstacles like deserts and mountains to movement resulted in physical isolation of communities, strengthening local identities based on place and kin networks. A social value system based in tribalism in which individual autonomy and collective honour took precedence over other ideas of law and legitimacy, emerged. Honour was associated with solidarity with kinsmen, protection of a kin group's women and other subordinate allies, and the inviolability of an individual's or a group's territory and possessions. Local leaders at each level of the social structure of nested tribes drew legitimacy by providing access to material goods, common defence of collective property and territory, and mediation of conflicts. This group cohesion made collective action relatively easy, rendering the state irrelevant to local concerns, particularly in the North (RAND, 2010).

Despite being a chequered terrain, communities were able to coexist without engaging in conflict due to the mediating role of the tribal leaders and religion. Religion provided a basis for commonality of beliefs and practices in this region. Northern Yemen is the historical heartland of Zaidi Islam, the branch of Shia Islam that provided the doctrinal underpinning for the Yemeni Imamate. The Zaidis, also known as the "Fivers", comprise one of the three main surviving branches of Shia Islam. While the Shias believed that the Imamate was to remain within a certain bloodline (descendants of the Prophet), the fulfilment of certain conditions, rather than direct appointment, became the criterion for the Zaidi Imamate. According to Lucas Winter (2011), Yemeni Zaidism was first formulated by Al-Qassim al-Rassi, a *Sayyid* (a Muslim claiming descent from Prophet Mohammad through his daughter Fatima and son-in-law Ali) in mid-ninth century, whose grandson, Yahya bin al-Hussein, declared himself Imam under the title *Al-Hadi ila'l-Haqq* (Guide to Righteous Path) in AD 897, with his base in the current Saada province. The rise and fall in its fortunes notwithstanding, the Imamate ruled over most of present-day Yemen for over 1,000 years, with Saada as the seat of power for Yemen's first Imamate and its capital (RAND, 2010).

Decline in the political fortunes of the region did not prevent it from continuing to be a centre of scholarship for Zaidism until 1962, when the Imamate was overthrown by republican forces inspired by Egyptian President Gamal Abdul Nasser. After 1962, the YAR republican leaders, despite a tribal background from among Zaidis, resorted to denigrating "Zaidi communalism and tribalism as atavistic and backwards" in their search for legitimacy (RAND, 2010). Two other factors were responsible for the decline of Zaidism over time (Winter, 2011). The first was the increased political and jurisprudential influence of non-*Sayyid* Zaidi scholars, beginning in the 1800s. This shift was associated with a reformulation of some stringent *hadawi* concepts. Chronologically, the next was the 1962 overthrow of the Imamate which ended the *Sayyid* monopoly over political power. Finally, the spread of Salafism in Yemen in general, and traditionally Zaidi areas in particular, proved to be a formidable threat to Zaidism. According to Winter (2011), Salafist espousal of political quietism and its egalitarianism, juxtaposed against the Zaidi principle of revolting against an unjust ruler and *Sayyid* exceptionalism respectively, appealed to young men from tribal families. Salifist principles fomented a hitherto dormant resentment of the key tenets of Zaidism. Supported by official encouragement from the Saudi Arabia, Salafism became increasingly popular. Additionally, the nearly one million Yemenis expelled from Saudi Arabia in the aftermath of the Gulf War of the 1990s brought back with them Salafi/Wahhabi ideas (Winter, 2011). Apprehending their faith to be under assault, there emerged a Zaidi revivalist movement in response to these threats._

Northern Yemen rose up against the republican government that overthrew the Imamate in 1962. Through the tumultuous decades ever since, government presence in Saada province has been weak and mostly military. An ebb in its fortunes in the 1990s was again met with the forces of Zaidi revivalism. The opposition to the republican state was based on the argument that the institutions of the state strip the world of greater meaning. Identifying the decline of Zaidism as the cause of the people's suffering, the revivalists accused the state of actively seeking the extermination and denigration of the Zaidis, while supporting Salafism. This revivalist movement of the 1990s eventually manifested in the Houthis.

The Zaidi revivalism of the 1990s was aided by multiple factors. Widespread poverty and comparative deprivation became a significant feeling during the 1980s when the first generation of post-Imamate Zaidis reached maturity. Their exposure to the world around them at a time when they were seeing unprecedented wealth due to the oil price hikes of the 1970s engendered rising material expectations. Literacy, travelling abroad and the resultant exposure to peoples and ideas (for instance, the Iranian Revolution of 1979) enabled them to locate common problems afflicting their region or people as a whole (RAND, 2010). The disappointment with secular political rulers and revival of various expressions of Islam through the Middle East found expression in Zaidi revivalism in Yemen.

After Yemen's unification in 1990, the state allowed greater freedom of association. This allowed the Hashimi elite to establish the Hizb al-Haqq, a political party to protect Zaidi interests in the light of Yemen's unification with the socialist South and the spread of Wahhabism. The Believing Youth (BY), a grassroots youth movement for the reassertion of Zaidi identity and learning, came into existence in 1991 under the patronage of Houthi family members. They established a strong support base among the social classes and tribes which had been excluded from the government's patronage network. Internal differences regarding the revivalist message led to organisations parting ways and mutating through the years to finally culminate in the Houthis in their present form (Winter, 2011). These dynamics, along with problematic regime approaches, built the scaffolding for the current discord.

In 1994, Yemen faced the first major challenge to its unity when the Al-Hirak, a movement of Southern Yemenis who felt marginalised post-unification, rebelled (Laub, 2015). In the ensuing confrontation, Saleh's Northern forces emerged victorious, his General People's Congress (GPC) dominated Parliament and the victors set about consolidating power. After 1994, there was an occlusion of Yemen's democratic opening, in line with predictions of the theories which view electoral politics and violence as strategic substitutes (Dunning 2011). Hegre et al. (2001) and Fearon and Laitin (2003) contend that "semi-democracies" (or "anocracies") are more likely to experience political violence than either democracies or autocracies. Their argument is that the former generate exclusion by not having representative governments elected through free and fair elections while not repressing enough to impede the organisation of insurgent violence. Pure democracy allows for peaceful collective action, allowing people to vent disapproval or anger through electoral politics. Pure dictatorship does not give the space for the organisation and perpetration of dissatisfaction into political violence and, therefore, eliminates the chances of violent conflict (Hegre et al, 2001, Fearon and Laitin, 2003, Vreeland, 2008). Semi-democracies, like Yemen, are caught in between. They allow dissidents to organise, but they realise that non-violent collective action is ineffective.

Violence, therefore, becomes the most effective recourse for dissidents, and the state reacts with violence accordingly.

In Yemen, after 1994, violence erupted once again in 2004. Yemen's fledgling relationship with the United States in the post-11 September world was a cause of concern for the Houthis, already wary of foreign influence in Yemen. The Houthis began making their grievances known. In January 2003, then President Saleh was confronted with anti-US and anti-Israeli chants in Saada. The subsequent government crackdown caused resentment among the Zaidis. Attempts at reconciliation failed. When troops were sent to arrest their leader Husayn al-Houthi in 2004, three soldiers were killed outside Saada city. In response, the government retaliated with a heavy military and bombing campaign which marked the beginning of armed conflict in 2004. Al-Houthi was killed in September 2004 but the conflict, which had developed a logic of its own, continued until 2010.

In addition to the Southern discontent and Al-Qaeda-inspired terrorism, the Houthi conflict emerged as an enduring threat to the regime of Saleh. At its origin, the Houthi rebellion might have been inspired by Zaidi revivalism led by charismatic Zaidi elites, but it evolved into "a conflict in which local material discontent and Zaidi identity claims have intersected with the state centre's methods of rule and self-legitimation" (RAND, 2010). The government portrayed the conflict as an ideological and political battle wherein the Houthis intended to seize control and impose their extremist political programme, including reestablishing the Imamate in Yemen (Boucek, 2010). Government suppression (for instance, its stand on Eid al-Ghadir, viewing it as a rallying point for Zaidi revivalism, endangering state security) served to reinforce feelings of religious discrimination. Consequently, the Houthis claimed to be fighting in self-defence and for the protection of their constitutional and human rights. Economic and political marginalisation apart, the growth in the Saudi influence and Yemen's alliance with the US in its war on terror, bolstered group solidarity further (RAND, 2010). Today, after decades of conflict and with regional influences, the differences between the warring factions have developed tribal and confessional contours.

Clashes between the Houthis and the government forces since 2004 resulted in President Saleh resorting to measures that sustained the initial drivers of the conflict: historical grievances, competing sectarian identities, perceived socio-economic injustices, tensions between the Zaidi-Shia and Salafist-Sunni populations, and regional underdevelopment. Tribal rivalries complicated matters due to the regime recruiting tribal fighters as combatants. In response to the government's repressive measures, the Houthis relied on the social bonds of kin networks and religion (RAND, 2010). Additionally, the war against the Houthis had absorbed the government's political attention and coercive resources, weakening the state's ability to deal with other challenges, especially the AQAP. Amidst this turmoil, the 2008 food price shock made economic conditions dire in a progressively contracting Yemeni economy. To this firewood, the Arab Spring provided the spark that was needed for a nation-wide revolt against President Saleh's regime.

Economic Context

It has been argued that with the end of the Cold War, under the burden of economic hardships and the prospect for exploiting the oil resources discovered in 1989, North and South Yemen finally agreed on unification under a new Constitution in 1990 (*The Economist*, 2017). After the unification, for a brief period, foreign investments did flow into Yemen, aiding the extraction and export of oil, and boosting the economy. But the economy failed to meet the needs of the population on account of domestic policies and socio-economic and political turmoil.

From its early years, unified Yemen was rocked by crises—political and economic—often playing out together. Yemen had to pay a heavy price for its support to Iraq during the first Gulf War. Within a few weeks, close to 800,000 people were forced to return to Yemen from the GCC countries (Schmitz, 2012). Within three months, Yemen experienced a 7 per cent increase in its population and a 15 per cent increase in its workforce (Whitaker, 2015), severely exacerbating unemployment. Not only did this entail a sudden loss of remittances, it also created the problem of absorbing this huge influx of returnees. Things came to head with the conflict of 1994. Yemen was staring at a fiscal crisis which led the country to knock on the doors of the International Monetary Fund (IMF). It accepted the IMF's advice and agreed to implement a structural reform programme starting in 1995. The programme included the removal of food subsidies and resulted in a roll back of public services (International Monetary Fund, 1999). These developments put a strain on the already stretched health and other basic social services infrastructure, culminating in the slowing down of the pace of improvement in social indicators in the period since 1997, compared to the first seven years of Yemen as a unified country (Pournik & Abu-Ismail, 2013).

Decades of corruption, crises and the logic of a rentier economy culminated in the absence of the necessary infrastructure to tap the potential of a low dependency ratio and extremely high working age population (Pournik & Abu-Ismail, 2013). Yemen, like many of its neighbours, adopted a rentier political economy defined by distinct tribal identities that are reinforced through patron-client relationships facilitated by revenues from resource-based activities. The inability of a rule and merit-based public policy decision-making process to emerge enabled the use of public investments as tools in perpetuating the patron-client relationship, contributing to Yemen's dismal performance on corruption indicators. With a score of 14 on 100, Transparency International ranked Yemen 176 out of 180 countries on the Corruption Perceptions Index, 2018 (Transparency International, 2018)

The result is abysmal socio-economic indicators. As per the United Nations Development Programme (UNDP) estimates, the headcount of the population in the multi-dimensional poverty is 47.8 per cent with 18.8 per cent of the population living below the income poverty line of US$1.90 a day. Yemen's per capita GDP in 2017 was US$ 2,600 in Purchasing Power Parity (PPP) terms (World Bank, 2018b). The Human Development Index of 0.452 made Yemen rank 178 out of 189 countries (Human Development Index, 2018). Only a marginal improvement in Yemen's Human Development Index goes to prove the inability of the Yemeni government since 1990 to create the basic socio-economic infrastructure. As of 2017, Yemen has an estimated population of 28.3 million people with the median age being 19.2 years (implying that over half of the Yemeni population is under 20 years of age); yet the average expected number of years of schooling is 9 (with 7.6 for females, 10.3 for males). The skilled population in Yemen is just 30 per cent of the total labour force, despite

16 million of the 28 million Yemenis belonging to the age group of 15-64 years. Few employment opportunities, along with a burgeoning labour force, made workers resort to low paying and irregular informal-sector jobs, the reason behind the high incidence of the working poor in Yemen. They constitute 81.2 per cent of total employment (working poor defined as those with incomes less than US$ 3.10 a day) (UNDP, 2019).

The Yemeni economy has been in the grips of a jobless, slow growth cycle, leading to stagnant per capita incomes and rising levels of unemployment, particularly amongst the youth, ever since the unification in 1990. The structure of Yemen's economy underwent fundamental changes from the 1990s to the mid-2000s. According to a United Nations Development Programme (UNDP) report (Pournik & Abu-Ismail, 2013) while the share of agriculture and manufacturing declined from over 24 per cent to 10.5 per cent and from 19 per cent to 7.1 per cent respectively between 1990 and 2005, and the share of oil and gas increased from 11.8 per cent to 35.6 per cent over the same period. The service sector remained the most important one in the economy, with its share rising slightly from 40.2 per cent to 41.4 per cent. This hides the changes that took place in the nature of the services—from those supporting agriculture and manufacturing in 1990 by the mid-2000s, services revolved around the distribution of oil revenues. The main components of the services sector like trade, transport, and government services were dependent on, and fuelled by, the oil income. Yemen's reliance on oil-led growth was, however, associated with little direct employment. The services sector it created could not generate enough jobs to absorb the increase in the labour supply. The agricultural sector, employing more than 50 per cent of Yemen's population, is already stretched to capacity given the technological and environmental constraints. Public sector employment has also been insufficient to absorb the excess labour. As per UNDP estimates for 2019, 44.8 per cent of the youth between 15 to 24 years of age were neither employed nor in school (UNDP, 2019). A huge population of unemployed youth is a cause of concern because of the potential for latent frustration to be transformed into aggression with very little incitement.

To make matters worse, violence in Yemen had made self-preservation and perpetuation the primary objective of the regime.

Health and education have failed to become priority areas of public policy. Public spending on health and education as a share of GDP increased from a combined total of 5.5 per cent of GDP in 1991 to a mere 5.8 per cent by 2008. Their share in total government expenditure showed a decrease from 18.7 per cent in 1991 to only 16.1 per cent by 2008 and, in total, public expenditures peaked at 25.7 per cent in 1994 (Pournik & Abu-Ismail, 2013), the year when Yemen experienced major political violence for the first time after unification (and subsequently, approached the IMF).

The scenario of widespread corruption, high youth unemployment, and the regime's focus on self-preservation in a rentier economy was exacerbated by Yemen's population growth, which, at over 3 per cent (before the political unrest began in 2011), was twice the regional average (World Bank, 2012) and one of the highest in the world. The increased demand for educational and health services, drinking water, and employment opportunities that this created was not met due to the factors highlighted above. A consequence of this was (and still is) that the young population of Yemen, which could have been a potential asset, became a pool of disenchanted and disgruntled youth.

Widespread corruption in Yemen has been associated with the emergence of inequality in socio-economic and political conditions. Yemen has a relatively unequal distribution of income and expenditure, confirmed by its Gini coefficient of 36.7. The urban areas exhibit larger inequality compared to the rural areas, with inequality in expenditure distribution in the wealthier governorates being more pronounced than in the poorer governorates. For instance, as per the UNDP report cited earlier, Sana'a had the second largest Gini index (42.1) while the rural areas in Amran, the lowest (21.9). However, the issue with these inequality figures is that they do not go far in helping explain the political violence in Yemen. This is because these figures measure vertical inequality, or normal inequality which measures economic (income) inequality among individuals only. They are silent on the horizontal and perceived inequalities, which according to scholars working on the links between inequalities in society and political violence, are more relevant. In his seminal work, Horowitz (1985) explains that the distribution of economic and political power between ethnic groups is crucial to understand ethnic conflict, thereby shifting the emphasis from the individual level of analysis to the group level.

Multiple theories have tried to link political violence with structural inequality. The causal mechanism can potentially be traced as inequality being associated with frustration, and psychological studies have shown the link between frustration and aggression. The literature initially focussed primarily on vertical inequality causing political violence. However, a plethora of inconsistent findings in statistical studies trying to establish the relation between inequality and collective violence led to the emergence of case-based literature with the seminal work of Frances Stewart (2000). She shifted the focus to the role of "Horizontal Inequalities" (HIs), or systematic economic and political inequalities between ethnic, religious or regional groups, in affecting conflict likelihood and conflict dynamics (Stewart, 2000, 2002).

The concept of horizontal inequality differs from vertical inequality, in that, the latter measures inequality over a range of individuals rather than groups. Furthermore, HIs are conceived of as inherently multi-dimensional, encompassing economic, social and political dimensions. According to the horizontal inequality argument, when inequalities coincide with cultural cleavages, they can enhance group grievances, which, in turn, may facilitate mobilisation for conflict. The political context plays an important role in the relationship between horizontal inequalities. Recent research is focussing on perceived inequalities. According to a report of the Peace Research Institute, Oslo (Peace Research Institute, Oslo, 2017),

> Prominent authors within the horizontal inequality literature (Stewart, 2000, 2002; Cederman et al., 2013) have emphasized the central importance of how inequality is experienced, or perceived... perceived and objective horizontal inequality do not necessarily overlap... The relationship between perceived horizontal inequality and attitudes to violent conflict is thus not an artefact or proxy for the relationship found between objective horizontal inequality and conflict. More and better-quality data to measure perceived inequality, as well as a deeper knowledge about how these perceptions are triggered, are crucial for assessing more fully how inequalities affects conflict.

Amidst rampant corruption, dismal public services, widespread inequality, secessionist sentiments in the South and the on-going clashes between the Houthis and the Yemeni government, came the food price shock of 2008. In *Conflict in Yemen: From Ethnic Fighting to Food Riots,* the authors have argued that the socio-economic origins of violence in Yemen changed after 2008 (Gros, 2012). While the pre-2008 violence could have been attributed to inter-group conflict between ethnically and religiously distinct groups, restricted mostly to the ethnically patchy North, after 2008, violence spread to the endemically poor Southern areas which began demanding government change and economic concessions.

Implementation of IMF advice in 1995 had already resulted in the removal of food subsidies, but this happened in an environment of relative stability of international food prices (between 1995 to 2006-07, FAO Food Price Index). The 2007-08 surge in global food prices was, therefore, the first such price shock in the period after the removal of food subsidies. That it would cause widespread impoverishment and resentment seems likely, evident in the protests which met the government's decision to slash the fuel subsidies in 2014. Threatening to plunge thousands below the breadline in an already impoverished nation, the decision to slash the fuel subsidy was met with widespread discontent and protests in the capital Sana'a (*The Guardian*, 2014). In 2007, without a food subsidy cushion, the deeply impoverished Yemeni population was left vulnerable. Horizontal inequalities (actual and perceived) exacerbated the impact of this purely exogenous economic shock, creating conditions for collective violence.

The socio-economic and political landscape was rife for opposition to the government to emerge. The spark that would ignite this latent resentment came from the series of protests demanding greater political rights and better economic governance which began in Tunisia and spread throughout the region. Thousands of Yemenis took to the streets in opposition to President Saleh's rule, demanding change. In its origin, the Arab Spring was a movement with economic demands, which subsequently got coopted by sectarian politics that have plagued Yemen since the 1960s.

Regional Context

The conflict in Yemen has broad geopolitical dynamics. What started off as a clash between Zaidi revivalist forces (Houthis) and the regime in 2004, metamorphosed into a broader conflict with the 2008 food price shock. The ceasefire between the Houthis and the government in February 2010 did not bring any lasting stability, rocked as it was with the Arab Spring protests demanding better economic conditions from a more responsive regime. During the ensuing period of political transition, the Houthis continued to distrust the government. Deposed President Saleh, who sought to undermine the transition in the hope of retaining political power within his family, joined forces with the Houthis. Mutual resentment towards President Hadi and opposition to the growing power of Al-Islah (an Islamist party linked to the Muslim Brotherhood) brought the Houthis and Saleh into an alliance of convenience in 2014. In September of that year, their forces entered Sana'a, marking the beginning of the current civil war. Their advent led to President Hadi's exile in Riyadh. Saudi Arabia assembled an international coalition in response to the conflict, beginning its military campaign in March 2015. This was the second occasion within a decade that Saudi Arabia intervened in Yemen, 2009 being the last occasion (Boucek, 2010). Understanding Saudi Arabia's involvement in Yemen is critical to gain a perspective on the current conflict.

The reason Yemen became a battleground for conflicting Saudi-Iranian interests can be traced to the nature of the sectarian strife in Yemen. As Zaidi Muslims, the Houthis have had a religious affinity with Iran and have received help from Tehran, given Iran's foreign policy stance adopted after the revolution in 1979, namely, of exporting the revolution (Ansari and Aarabi, 2019; Rabinovich, 2019). Historically, though, Iran's involvement in Yemen has been limited when compared to Saudi Arabia's. The latter's involvement has been continuous, extensive and tumultuous, beginning with the Treaty of Ta'if (at the end of the Saudi-Yemeni War), 1934, which formally demarcated the westernmost section of the border adjacent to the Red Sea and led Saudi Arabia to claim the ethnically Yemeni provinces of Asir and Najran (Treaty of Ta'if, 1934). During the protracted civil war between 1962 and 1970, Saudi Arabia, Iran, under the Shah, and Jordan supported the royalist cause, while Nasser's Egypt threw its weight behind the republican side. The civil war ended with North Yemen becoming a republic (Paul et al., 2013).

The varying interpretations of the provisions of the Treaty of Ta'if by Yemen and Saudi Arabia created differences time and again between the two neighbours. Yemen interpreted the provisions of the Treaty of Ta'if as providing relatively unrestricted entry of Yemenis to Saudi Arabia. Saudi Arabia viewed the entrance of Northern Yemenis into its territory as preferential terms allowed to Yemen. For instance, the Yemenis did not need a Saudi sponsor to work in that country. North Yemen viewed this not as a privilege but a legal right. Aided by a porous border, the oil boom of the 1960s and 1970s saw a substantial number of Yemenis migrating in search of work to Saudi Arabia. Up to two million Yemenis were working in the kingdom at the peak of this migration (Whitaker, 2015).

The end of the 1980s saw relations between Saudi Arabia and Yemen headed south. Yemeni unification in 1990 created ripples in the region's geo-politics (Dunbar, 1992). With roughly 15 million citizens, Yemen espousing democratisation engendered fear concerning the spread of similar demands within Saudi Arabia (Katz, 1992). Additionally, the discovery of modest but useful quantities of oil and natural gas in Northern Yemen, starting from the mid-1980s, became a bone of contention between the two neighbours. Renewed interest in the border question, partly a result of the discovery of oil, was another issue in the litany of complaints between Yemen and Saudi Arabia (Whitaker, 2015).

By 1989, Yemen's oil fields were producing 200,000 barrels a day. Proven reserves at the time were estimated at 4 billion barrels (Whitaker, 2015). Compared to Saudi Arabia's 260 billion barrels of proven reserves in 1990 (Rapier, 2019), Yemen's endowment, though meagre, provided Yemen the prospect of weaning itself off remittances and aid from Saudi Arabia. Discovery of oil was also associated with increasing clamour on the Yemeni side for settlement of the largely undefined border. The oil reserves in the disputed areas were marginal in relation to the Saudi reserves but hugely important to Yemen. Saudi prevarication over the border issue and belligerence over the oil fields with their miniscule reserves compared to its own endowment suggested that Saudi Arabia was less interested in acquiring the oil for itself than in depriving Yemen the benefit of economic development and self-reliance (Whitaker, 2015). The border question was finally resolved in the Treaty of Jeddah on 12 June 2000 (International Border Treaty between the Republic of Yemen and the Kingdom of Saudi Arabia, 2000).

Yemen's attitude towards the Iraqi invasion of Kuwait in 1990, soon after its unification, brought a rapid deterioration in its relations with Saudi Arabia. When Saddam Hussein invaded Kuwait, Yemen found itself facing the first major challenge in its foreign policy: trying to balance its relations with Iraq with its economic interests in Saudi Arabia (Whitaker, 2015). Yemen tried to take a middle path by condemning the invasion of Kuwait while opposing Western military intervention, in favour of a regional Arab solution. Observing a neutral stance or maintaining distance from the conflict became difficult for Yemen as it was the only Arab member of the UN Security Council at the time. The Security Council vote imposing trade sanctions against Iraq saw Yemen abstaining, along with Cuba (the resolution was adopted by 13 votes to nil). The same voting pattern continued in a second vote seeking military enforcement of the blockade. Yemen voted against United Nations Security Council Resolution 678, which authorised UN member states to "use all necessary means to uphold and implement resolution 660 (1990) and all subsequent relevant resolutions and to restore international peace and security in the area" (UNSCR 678, 1990).Yemen's action was interpreted as evidence of secret support for Saddam. The United States, deeply dissatisfied with Yemen's decision, cut off its US$70 million annual aid to Yemen in response (Eldar, 2008). The UN sanctions cut off Yemen's trade with Iraq, and Saudi Arabia ended all economic assistance to the country. In addition, Yemenis working in the kingdom now needed to find a Saudi sponsor or business partner or leave the country before a set deadline. As a consequence of its opposition to the UN Resolution, Yemen suffered, so much so that the vote was declared the most expensive one in history (Whitaker, 2015). The Mass expulsions of Yemeni workers happened again in 2013 when the Saudi authorities began a crackdown on undocumented migrant workers. Once again, large numbers of Yemenis were herded across the border.

The most recent instance of Saudi involvement in Yemen was in March 2015. Saudi Arabia, along with the United Arab Emirates, assembled an international coalition and intervened in Yemen's civil war. At the time, Yemen's warring political factions were on the verge of a power-sharing deal between twelve rival political and tribal groups. According to the United Nations envoy Jamal Benomar, who mediated in the talks, a fact that was significant but went unnoticed was that the Saudi-led coalition's intervention derailed the negotiations at a time when the Yemenis were close to a deal that would institute power-sharing with all sides, including the Houthis (Lauria and Coker, 2015). The reasons for the Saudi intervention have been traced to Iran's relations with the Houthis and a long history of involvement. An obscure aspect is Yemen's "untapped potential to provide an alternative set of oil and gas trans-shipment routes for the export of Saudi oil, bypassing Iran and the Strait of Hormuz" (Ahmed, 2016). Saudi Arabia's desire to get a corridor across Yemen connecting it to the Arabian Sea and, hence, the Indian Ocean, by-passing the choke points of the Strait of Hormuz and Bab-el Mandeb, was the subject of a secret 2008 State Department cable from the US Embassy in Yemen to the US Secretary of State, obtained by Wikileaks:

> A British diplomat based in Yemen told PolOff [US embassy political officer] that Saudi Arabia had an interest to build a pipeline, wholly owned, operated and protected by Saudi Arabia, through Hadramawt to a port on the Gulf of Aden, thereby bypassing the Arabian Gulf/Persian Gulf and the straits of Hormuz (Ahmed, 2016).

The cable also discusses the then President Saleh's opposition to the project and Saudi Arabia's attempts at influencing the Yemeni policy "through supporting the Yemeni military leadership, paying for the loyalty of sheikhs and other means...positioning itself to ensure it would, for the right price, obtain the rights for this pipeline from Saleh's successor" (Ahmed, 2016).

As the dominant power in the Arabian Peninsula, and Yemen's northern neighbour, Saudi Arabia views with consternation a stable and democratic Yemen (Ahmed, 2016). The Saudi support for the secessionist South in the 1994 War in Yemen is a case in point. It has been argued that Saudi Arabia's "strategy of breaking down Yemen without allowing it to collapse entirely...provides the kingdom with more opportunities to lead its reconstruction", granting the kingdom greater leverage in Yemen (Karasik and Depretto, 2019). Saudi Arabia's role as a warring party on one side and a particularly active aid provider on the other, should be viewed from this perspective. Together with its coalition partners, the kingdom claims to have disbursed over US$18 billion to Yemen in different forms of support since 2015 (Karasik and Depretto, 2019). This regional dimension of the conflict further complicates the roadmap for peace. Despite the conflict being referred to as a local manifestation of the transnational "Shi'ite Crescent" (RAND, 2010), the on-going peace negotiations have not involved the regional players, who are conspicuous by their absence. This raises serious questions regarding the success of the negotiations in building lasting peace and prosperity in Yemen.

Conclusion

The complex interplay of political, economic and regional factors has made Yemen's civil war a knot difficult to untangle. The conflict has taken on a logic and momentum of its own, transcending the initial regime or Houthi motives. The conflict became increasingly confessional and tribal, due to regional demography, rhetoric and alliance-making on both sides. The presence of numerous armed factions makes any political settlement difficult. Other than direct military and security operations, effective interventions will require eliminating the primary political, economic and social drivers of violence. While the prospects for the success of the negotiations remain uncertain, the efforts at negotiations to achieve a political breakthrough through the impasse need to continue, while involving the regional players. Any solution will have to entail the devolution of greater political power to the disenchanted and impoverished governorates. By providing partial internal autonomy to the ethnic and religious groups, the origin of the longer-term inter-group violence can be alleviated. To ensure that violence does not return to this fragile region, holistic policies need to be implemented with the financial help of the international community, starting with the reconstruction of Yemen's physical and health infrastructure.

A robust economy that provides opportunities to Yemen's youth needs to be put in place. At the current growth rate, the population is expected to grow from 22 million to 50 million by 2035. The resulting 'youth bulge' will further aggravate the problem of youth unemployment, putting severe stress on the social services and natural resources. Yemen will have to work on developing job opportunities to constructively employ its population. Areas like tourism should be explored as this incentivises maintenance of law and order and stability. Diversification of Yemen's economy becomes even more critical and necessary given that in the absence of new discoveries of oil, at current extraction rates, crude oil reserves are expected to be exhausted in the next 10 to 12 years. With oil representing about one-third of Yemen's GDP, almost three quarters of government revenues and 90 per cent of exports, failure to diversify its economy might see Yemen become a victim of political violence yet again. While there is potential in natural gas to generate revenues in the future, failure to develop and diversify will keep Yemen vulnerable. Yemen needs to work on improving its performance on the gender inequality front. Women's empowerment (their education and participation in the labour force) is associated with a decline in fertility rates, as well as an inclusive workforce and a more vibrant society.

Pumping in foreign aid will not suffice, Somalia being the poster child of aid done wrong. Donors need to work out mechanisms to ensure that aid creates the scaffolding for a stable economy and inclusive society. Income-generating and development activities targeting education, health, fishery, water, hygiene, and sanitation should be prioritised. Agriculture should be another focus area. Yemen's harsh climatic conditions involving low rainfall, combined with rapid urbanisation and population growth, have resulted in excessive pressure on natural water supplies. It has been estimated that in major population centres like the capital Sana'a, the aquifers that supply them may be fully depleted in 20 years. With climate change endangering right to life and threatening to undermine the rule of law, the UN has warned of a 'climate apartheid' where the rich pay to escape heat and hunger, while the poor see their rights to life, food, water and housing being compromised (Carrington, 2019). The combined wrath of economic and ecological stress has the potential to destabilise Yemen again. It is, therefore, pertinent that economic growth in agriculture is prioritised by upgrading farming skills—providing farmers with new skills and technologies to survive the current conflict and climate change. Initiatives wherein support was given to 1,782 farmers and these farmers, in turn, provided short-term and long-term job opportunities for 22,000 people should be replicated. In another project, 500 midwives and nurses were re-employed to provide life-saving health services for more than 110,000 people in the fight against cholera (Kretschmer, 2019).

Since the war began with discontent over political and institutional arrangements, a long-term solution to the problem of recurring conflict cannot be found without critically understanding and addressing the problems of Yemen's institutions. Institutions are not only the object of violent contention but also shape the opportunities and capacities for using violence. Hence, addressing the question of the nature of institutions is vital. If institutions allow inclusiveness and peaceful collective action, not only do they limit the opportunities for using violence, they are also less likely to be the object of contention. If war is indeed politics by other means, it makes sense to think of violence and democratic competition as strategic substitutes. It is for the Yemeni people and their representatives to decide the political arrangement they want for themselves, but these concerns should be factored in if a durable peace is to be achieved and maintained.

References

Ahmed, Nafeez (2016), "Saudi War for Yemen Oil Pipeline is Empowering al-Qaeda, IS", *Middle East Eye*, 10 February, https://www.middleeasteye.net/big-story/saudi-war-yemen-oil-pipeline-empowering-al-qaeda. Accessed on 8 July 2019.

Al-Jazeera (2015) "Yemen's Houthis form Own Government in Sanaa", 7 February, https://www.aljazeera.com/news/middleeast/2015/02/yemen-houthi-rebels-announce-presidential-council-150206122736448.html. Accessed on 8 July 2019.

Al-Jazeera (2018a), "Saudi Arabia, UAE, Launch Attack on Yemen's Port City of Hudaida", 13 June, https://www.aljazeera.com/news/2018/06/saudi-uae-launch-attack-yemen-port-city-hudaida-180613054921062.html. Accessed on 8 July 2019.

Al-Jazeera (2018b), "Yemen's War: Clashes Continue in Hodeidah Ahead of Ceasefire", 17 December, https://www.aljazeera.com/news/2018/12/yemen-war-clashes-continue-hodeidah-ceasefire-181217092041049.html. Last accessed on 8 July 2019.

Al-Bab (1934), "Treaty of Taif", 20 May, https://al-bab.com/treaty-taif-1934. Accessed on 8 July 2019.

Ansari, Ali & Aarabi, Kasra (2019), "Ideology and Iran's Revolution: How 1979 Changed the World", Tony Blair Institute for Global Change, 11 February, https://institute.global/insight/co-existence/ideology-and-irans-revolution-how-1979-changed-world. Accessed on 8 July 2019.

Bahgat, Karim; Kendra Dupuy; Scott Gates; Håvard Mokleiv Nygård; Siri Aas Rustad; Håvard Strand; Henrik Urdal; Gudrun Østby; Gray Barrett; & Solveig Hillesund (2017), "Inequality and Armed Conflict: Evidence and Data", Peace Research Institute Oslo Publication, 12 April, https://www.prio.org/utility/DownloadFile.ashx?id=954&type=publicationfile. Accessed on 8 July 2019.

BBC News (2018), "Yemen Separatists Capture Most of Aden, Residents Say", 30 January, https://www.bbc.com/news/world-middle-east-42877851. Accessed on 8 July 2019.

Bewley, Dakota (2019), "Economic Warfare: Iran-Saudi Proxy Conflict in Yemen", NATO Association Of Canada, 15 January, http://natoassociation.ca/economic-warfare-iran-saudi-proxy-conflict-in-yemen/. Accessed on 8 July 2019.

Borger, Julian (2018), "UN Agrees Yemen Ceasefire Resolution After Fraught Talks and US Veto Threat" *The Guardian*, 21 December, https://www.theguardian.com/world/2018/dec/21/un-yemen-ceasfire-stockholm-resolution-us. Accessed on 8 July 2019.

Boucek, Christopher (2010), "War in Saada: From Local Insurrection to National Challenge", *Yemen: On the Brink, Carnegie Paper Series,* April, https://carnegieendowment.org/files/war_in_saada.pdf. Accessed on 8 July 2019.

Carrington, Damian (2019), "Climate Apartheid': UN Expert Says Human Rights May not Survive", *The Guardian,* 25 June, https://www.theguardian.com/environment/2019/jun/25/climate-apartheid-united-nations-expert-says-human-rights-may-not-survive-crisis. Accessed on 8 July 2019.

Dunbar, C (1992), "The Unification of Yemen: Process, Politics, and Prospects", *Middle East Journal*, 46(3), 456-476, http://www.jstor.org/stable/4328466. Accessed on 8 July 2019.

Dunning, T (2011), "Fighting and Voting: Violent Conflict and Electoral Politics", *Journal of Conflict Resolution*, 55(3): 327–339.

Eldar, Ofer (2008), "Vote-Trading in International Institutions", *The European Journal of International Law*, Vol. 19 No. 1, http://ejil.org/pdfs/19/1/179.pdf. Accessed on 8 July 2019.

Fearon, J., & Laitin, D (2003), "Ethnicity, Insurgency, and Civil War", *American Political Science Review*, 97(1): 75-90.

Fore, Henrietta (2019), 'Violent Deaths of Five Children in Hudaydah a Harsh Reminder that War Rages on After Yemen Pledging Conference", *UNICEF,* 2 March, https://www.unicef.org/press-releases/violent-deaths-five-children-hudaydah-harsh-reminder-war-rages-after-yemen-pledging. Accessed on 8 July 2019.

Gros, A. Gard-Murray, A.S. & Bar-Yam, Y (2012), "Conflict in Yemen: From Ethnic Fighting to Food Riots", New England Complex Systems Institute, 24 July, arXiv:1207.5778, https://static1.squarespace.com/static/5b68a4e4a2772c2a206180a1/t/5bf5b9ed2b6a28025bd29ce1/1542830574398/Yemen_Conflict.pdf. Accessed on 8 July 2019.

Håvard Hegre, Tanja Ellingsen, Scott Gates, & Nils Petter Gleditsch (2001), "Toward a Democratic Civil Peace? Democracy, Political Change, and Civil War, 1816-1992", *The American Political Science Review*, 95(1): 33-48, http://www.jstor.org/stable/3117627. Accessed on 8 July 2019.

Horowitz, Donald L (1985), *Ethnic Groups in Conflict* (University of California Press); International Monetary Fund, 1999, "Republic of Yemen: Enhanced Structural Adjustment Facility Medium-Term Economic and Financial Policy Framework Paper 1999-2001", 5 March, https://www.imf.org/external/np/pfp/1999/yemen/. Accessed on 8 July 2019.

IRIN (2014), "Yemen Fuel Subsidy Cut Drives Poorest Deeper into Poverty", *The Guardian,* 26 August, https://www.theguardian.com/global-development/2014/aug/26/yemen-fuel-subsidy-cut-drives-poorest-poverty. Accessed on 8 July 2019.

Karasik, T. & Depretto, J.S. (2019), "Bombs, Then Food: Saudi Arabia's Humanitarian Strategy in Yemen", *Fair Observer,* 20 June, https://www.fairobserver.com/region/middle_east_north_africa/saudi-war-aid-yemen-middle-east-security-news-12351/. Accessed on 8 July 2019.

Katz, Mark N. (1992), "Yemeni Unity and Saudi Security", *Middle East Policy,* 1:1, http://ebot.gmu.edu/bitstream/handle/1920/3118/yemeni%20unity%20and%20saudi%20security.pdf?sequence=1&isAllowed=y. Last accessed on 8 July, 2019; Rapeir, Robert (2019). "How Much Oil Does Saudi Arabia Really Have?", in *Forbes,* 14 February, https://www.forbes.com/sites/rrapier/2019/02/14/how-much-oil-does-saudi-arabia-have/#24f00fbf7b33. Accessed on 8 July 2019.

Kretschmer, B.N. (2019), "Building Peace and a Peace-driven Economy for Yemen," *Nobel Women's Initiative,* 18 April, https://nobelwomensinitiative.org/building-peace-and-a-peace-driven-economy-for-yemen/. Last accessed on 8 July 2019.

Laub, Zachary (2015), "Yemen in Crisis", in *Backgrounder: Yemen's Civil War, the Houthis, and the Saudi Intervention-Council on Foreign Relations,* 29 April, https://www.files.ethz.ch/isn/190632/Backgrounder_%20Yemen's%20Ci...pdf. Accessed on 8 July 2019.

Lauria, Joe & Coker, Margaret (2015), "Former U.N. Envoy Says Yemen Political Deal was Close Before Saudi Airstrikes Began", *The Wall Street Journal,* 26 April, https://www.wsj.com/articles/former-u-n-envoy-says-yemen-political-deal-was-close-before-saudi-airstrikes-began-1430081791. Accessed on 8 July 2019.

Magdy, Samy (2019), "Database Says 91,600 Killed in Yemen Fighting Since 2015", *AP News*, 20 June, https://www.apnews.com/b28a2bdb1b01413689e05a7204e6ea90. Accessed on 8 July 2019.

Mohammad Pournik & Khalid Abu-Ismail (2013), "The ADCR 2011: Poverty Dymanics in Yemen as a Representative Arab LDC", *UNDP Report*, 2013, https://www.undp.org/content/dam/rbas/doc/poverty/BG_13_Poverty%20in%20Yemen.pdf. Accessed on 8 July 2019.

Munassar, Omar (2019), "Yemen's Stockholm Agreement: One Step Forward, One Step Back?", *LSE Middle East Centre Blog,* 15 April, https://blogs.lse.ac.uk/mec/2019/04/15/yemens-stockholm-agreement-one-step-forward-one-step-back/. Accessed on 8 July 2019.

Paul, C., Clarke, C., Grill, B., & Dunigan, M. (2013), "Yemen, 1962–1970: Case Outcome: COIN Loss", *Paths to Victory: Detailed Insurgency Case Studies* (pp. 250-264), RAND Corporation, http://www.jstor.org/stable/10.7249/j.ctt5hhsjk.32. Accessed on 8 July 2019.

Rabinovich, Itamar (2019), "How Iran's Regional Ambitions have Developed Since 1979", Brookings, 24 January, https://www.brookings.edu/blog/order-from-chaos/2019/01/24/how-irans-regional-ambitions-have-developed-since-1979/. Accessed on 8 July 2019.

RAND (2010), "Regime and Periphery in Northern Yemen: The Huthi Phenomenon", https://apps.dtic.mil/dtic/tr/fulltext/u2/a520460.pdf. Accessed on 8 July 2019.

Schmitz, Charles (2012), "Crisis in the Yemeni Economy: A Troubled Transition to Post-Hydrocarbon Growth", *Middle East Institute,* 13 January, https://www.mei.edu/publications/crisis-yemeni-economy-troubled-transition-post-hydrocarbon-growth. Accessed on 8 July 2019.

Stewart, Frances, Holdstock, Douglas, Jarquin, Antonio (2002), "Root Causes of Violent Conflict in Developing Countries-Commentary: Conflict—from Causes to Prevention?", *BMJ*, 324: 342.

Stewart, Frances (2000), "Crisis Prevention: Tackling Horizontal Inequalities", *Oxford Development Studies*, 28:3: 245-262,

The Economist (2017), "How Yemen Became the Most Wretched Place on Earth", 30 November, https://www.economist.com/briefing/2017/11/30/how-yemen-became-the-most-wretched-place-on-earth. Accessed on 8 July 2019.

The World Bank (2018a), "Yemen's Economic Outlook-October 2018", October, https://www.worldbank.org/en/country/yemen/publication/economic-outlook-october-2018. Accessed on 8 July 2019.

The World Bank (2018b), "GDP Data", https://data.worldbank.org/indicator/NY.GDP.PCAP.PP.CD?locations=YE. Last accessed on 8 July 2019.

The World Bank (2019), "Country Overview: Yemen", https://www.worldbank.org/en/country/yemen/overview. Accessed on 8 July 2019.

TRT World (2019), "Stockholm Agreement on Yemen's West Coast: What You Need to Know", 14 May, https://www.whitehouse.gov/briefings-statements/remarks-president-trump-joint-comprehensive-plan-action/. Accessed on 8 July 2019.

UN News (2018), "Yemen: Tackling the World's Largest Humanitarian Crisis", 24 September, https://news.un.org/en/story/2018/09/1020232. Accessed on 8 July 2019.

UN Office for the Coordination of Humanitarian Affairs (2017), "Ensuring Yemen's Lifeline: The Criticality of All Yemeni Ports (as of 13 Nov 2017)", Relief Web, 13 November, https://reliefweb.int/map/yemen/ensuring-yemen-s-lifeline-criticality-all-yemeni-ports-13-nov-2017-enar. Accessed on 8 July 2019.

UNDP (2018), "Human Development Indices and Indicators: 2018 Statistical Update", http://hdr.undp.org/sites/all/themes/hdr_theme/country-notes/YEM.pdf. Accessed on 8 July 2019.

UNDP (2019), "Human Development Index", http://hdr.undp.org/en/countries/profiles/YEM. Accessed on 8 July 2019.

UNICEF (2019), "Humanitarian Action for Children 2019 – Yemen", 29 January, https://m.reliefweb.int/report/2970689. Accessed on 8 July 2019.

United Nations (2000), "International Border Treaty between the Republic of Yemen and the Kingdom of Saudi Arabia", 12 June, https://www.un.org/Depts/los/LEGISLATIONANDTREATIES/PDFFILES/TREATIES/YEM-SAU2000IBT.PDF. Accessed on 8 July 2019.

United Nations Security Council Report (2018), "The Situation in the Middle East", 23 October, https://www.securitycouncilreport.org/atf/cf/%7b65BFCF9B-6D27-4E9C-8CD3-CF6E4FF96FF9%7d/s_pv_8379.pdf. Accessed on 8 July 2019.

United Nations Security Council Resolution *(UNSCR)* (1990), Resolution 678 of 29 November 1990, http://unscr.com/en/resolutions/doc/678. Accessed on 8 July 2019.

United Nations Security Council (2018a), "Stockholm Agreement", Annex to Letter dated 20 December 2018 from the Secretary-General addressed to the President of the Security Council, 20 December, https://undocs.org/en/S/2018/1134. Accessed on 8 July 2019.

United Nations Security Council (2018b), "The Situation in the Middle East", Report on 8379th meeting of UNSC, No. S/PV.8379, October 23, https://www.securitycouncilreport.org/atf/cf/%7b65BFCF9B-6D27-4E9C-8CD3-CF6E4FF96FF9%7d/s_pv_8379.pdf. Accessed on 8 July 2019.

Lyons, Kate (2017), "Yemen's Cholera Outbreak Now the Worst in History as Millionth Case Looms", *The Guardian*, 12 October, https://www.theguardian.com/global-development/2017/oct/12/yemen-cholera-outbreak-worst-in-history-1-million-cases-by-end-of-year. Accessed on 8 July 2019.

Vreeland, J. R. (2008), "The Effect of Political Regime on Civil War: Unpacking Anocracy", *Journal of Conflict Resolution*, 52(3): 401–425.

Whitaker, Brian (2015), "Yemen and Saudi Arabia: A Tangled Relationship", in Al-bab.com, https://al-bab.com/yemen-and-saudi-arabia-tangled-relationship. Accessed on 8 July 2019.

Winter, Lucas (2011), "Conflict in Yemen: Simple People, Complicated Circumstances", *Middle East Policy,* Vol XVIII, Issue 1, Spring, https://doi.org/10.1111/j.1475-4967.2011.00476.x. Accessed on 8 July 2019.

World Bank (2012), "Facing the Hard Facts in Yemen", 26 September, https://www.worldbank.org/en/news/feature/2012/09/26/yemen-talking-points. Accessed on 8 July 2019.

World Health Organisation (2019), "Outbreak Update - Cholera in Yemen", 5 May 2019, 12 May, http://www.emro.who.int/pandemic-epidemic-diseases/cholera/outbreak-update-cholera-in-yemen-12-may-2019.html. Accessed on 8 July 2019.

Index